DISCUSSION-BASED ONLINE TEACHING TO ENHANCE STUDENT LEARNING

DISCUSSION-BASED ONLINE TEACHING TO ENHANCE STUDENT LEARNING

Theory, Practice, and Assessment

Tisha Bender

SECOND EDITION

Sty/us

STERLING, VIRGINIA

COPYRIGHT © 2012 BY
STYLUS PUBLISHING, LLC.

Published by Stylus Publishing, LLC.
22883 Quicksilver Drive
Sterling, Virginia 20166

Library of Congress Cataloging-in-Publication Data
Bender, Tisha, 1953–
    Discussion-based online teaching to enhance student
learning : theory, practice, and assessment / Tisha Bender.
        p. cm.
    Includes bibliographical references and index.
    ISBN 978-1-57922-746-3 (cloth : alk. paper)
    ISBN 978-1-57922-747-0 (pbk. : alk. paper)
    ISBN 978-1-57922-699-2 (library networkable e-edition)
    ISBN 978-1-57922-700-5 (consumer e-edition)
    1. Internet in higher education—Social aspects.
2. Education, Higher—Computer-assisted instruction—
Social aspects.   I. Title.
LB1044.87.B43   2012
378.1'7344678—dc23   2011049304

13-digit ISBN: 978-1-57922-746-3 (cloth)
13-digit ISBN: 978-1-57922-747-0 (paper)
13-digit ISBN: 978-1-57922-699-2 (library networkable
e-edition)
13-digit ISBN: 978-1-57922-700-5 (consumer e-edition)

Printed in the United States of America

All first editions printed on acid-free paper
that meets the American National Standards Institute
Z39-48 Standard.

Bulk Purchases

Quantity discounts are available for
use in workshops and for staff
development.
Call 1-800-232-0223

Second Edition, 2012

To Thelma and Charles Loodmer

CONTENTS

vii

ACKNOWLEDGMENTS

I said in the first edition of this book that writing a book was like producing a play as it involved the coordination of many actors and technicians, all of whom made a vital and significant contribution. And now, to carry this analogy one step further, I would like to say that writing a second edition is akin to Act II, with the curtain sweeping up to reveal many of the same people in the cast, and some new ones as well. And, as before, although some play larger parts than others, all are equally important to the harmony of the final production, and so I thank them all most warmly and sincerely.

At Rutgers, my warmest thanks go to Dr. Rudy Bell for his enthusiastic conversations with me about online education; to Dr. Kurt Spellmeyer for his willingness for me to establish hybrid writing courses in the Rutgers Writing Program; to Chris Scherer, who believes in me and has given me wonderful opportunities; to Jeris Cassel, who is unfailingly helpful and knows how to find any book or article throughout the Rutgers library system; and to Dr. Peter Sorrell, who is himself so adept at teaching with technology in innovative and engaging ways. I would also like to thank my friend and colleague, Dr. Letizia Schmid, for all the inspiring conversations about teaching in general and about writing. And special thanks are in order, too, to all my students at Rutgers who have taken a hybrid class with me, and have responded about their experience in such thoughtful ways. Their level of metacognition about this new way of learning has been astounding.

My sincere thanks also go to Chunyan Xu, at Jilin University, China, whom I would otherwise be missing terribly if it were not for the fact that we can teach together across the seas and the continents because of the opportunities that online teaching offers us.

I would also like to thank my editor and publisher, John von Knorring, for his clearheaded, exciting, and challenging suggestions, and for his civility and promptness in responding to me at all times; and to McKinley Gillespie, production assistant at Stylus, for all the patience and encouragement.

Finally, I would like to sincerely thank my friends and family. Special thanks to Dr. Gerda Lederer for being such a great role model; to Dr. Lori

Rosenberg, who is a character of unfailing patience and kindness and who helps in immeasurable ways; and to Bev Brown for her benevolence, understanding, and terrific sense of fun. I also give my heartfelt thanks to my parents, Thelma and Charles Loodmer, who were my first teachers and fine teachers in their own right, and who established in me the love of teaching; and to Billy, Nigel, Joanna, Chris, and baby Leon for their encouragement and their humor. And most of all, my deepest and most profound thanks go to Charlie for his technical wizardry that surpasses all others; to Jonathan and Meng, who, despite the distance, are interested, involved, and encouraging; and to Jeremy for his interest, intelligence, and kindness. And, of course, this acknowledgment cannot be complete without also thanking Wilkie for not stepping on the keyboard of my laptop when inspiration strikes, and to J. S. Bach for the beautiful cello suites that accompany me while I work.

Since writing the first edition of this book in 2003, there have been enormous technological developments, most notably from 2004 onward, with the advent of Web 2.0, a second generation of the Web. Some feel that this new use of the Web came about in response to the bursting of the dot-com bubble in 2001 (O'Reilly, 2005). Essentially, however, as was observed by Marshall McLuhan 30 years before the Internet was invented, each new medium first enhances communication, obsolesces the previous medium, retrieves something of value, and then, when it is pushed to its limits, flips into some new iteration (WNYC, 2011). (McLuhan, who would have celebrated his 100th birthday on July 21, 2011, foresaw a networked world that he termed a *global village*.) This could well offer a plausible explanation of the development of Web 2.0; people at first marveled at all the Internet could offer, but then became frustrated that they had to return to the computer and could not have the Internet with them at all times. And so evolved the iPhone, the Blackberry, the Android, and the iPad, which each allow us to connect with the Internet immediately and when we are on the go.

But what exactly is Web 2.0? Essentially Web pages are no longer static, but incorporate Web *apps* to provide an infrastructure in which users can dynamically participate in such uses as Gmail, Google Maps, and social networking sites such as Facebook, blogs, wikis, Flickr, Twitter, podcasts, and more. In addition, computers have decreased in size from requiring a desktop to accommodate a fairly space-consuming monitor, to flat-screen desktops, to laptops, and now to smartphones and iPads. Carlson (2011) tells us that a report put out by Goldman Sachs in January 2011 claimed that Facebook, which originated in 2004, had over 600 million monthly active users worldwide. And by June of 2010, Twitter, which had been launched in 2006, had 190 million users tweeting 65 million times a day (Schonfeld, 2010). Gmail was available to the public in a beta version in 2007, and was upgraded from beta status in July 2009. As of November 2010, it had 193.3 million monthly users (BBC News Technology, 2010). As MacManus (2005) says, Web 2.0 is social, and "it's mixing the global with the local," thus producing the term *glocal*. It permits new ways of searching the Web, as well as providing a platform for anyone to create Web applications. It means that we have easy access to vast amounts of information through many forms of media, as well as the means to disseminate it worldwide. Messages range from trivial and intimate to crowd reporting on events of global significance such as popular uprisings in the Middle East and Northern Africa as occurred in February 2011, to reports of forest fires, blizzards, or flooding.

As Lanier (2010) states, the invention of the World Wide Web has been amazing, and people have flocked to it voluntarily, without any type of coercion, advertising, or threat if they stayed away. And, as David Crystal (2008), the British linguist, says about texting:

> In a logical world, text messaging should not have survived. Imagine a pitch to a potential investor. "I have this great idea. A new way of person-to-person communication, using your phone. The users won't have a familiar keyboard. Their fingers will have trouble finding the keys. They will be able to send messages, but with no more than 160 characters at a time. The writing on the screens will be very small and difficult to read, especially if you have a visual handicap. The messages will arrive at any time, interrupting your daily routine or your sleep. Oh, and every now and again you won't be able to send or receive anything because your battery will run out. Please invest in it." What would you have done? (pp. 173–174)

Crystal's statement could well be applied to many other Web apps used on a smartphone.

So what has been the draw of these various digital technologies? I think Anderson (2009) explains this well when he quotes the psychologist B.F. Skinner: "The most irresistible reward schedule is not, counter-intuitively, the one in which we are rewarded constantly, but something called 'variable ratio schedule' in which rewards arrive at random" (p. 5). By applying this to the Internet, we see that one of the reasons that the Internet is so compelling is that rewards are intermittent, such as a gratifying e-mail, or an inspirational online discovery, which makes us keep returning in the hope of finding more treasures.

And the hope for more is the very essence of these new digital technologies. But not necessarily for all of us, nor necessarily in the same way, as it seems very dependent on age. Rosen (2011) makes interesting distinctions between the characteristics of the different generations, starting with the Traditional Generation born between 1925 and 1946, who have an abiding respect for authority. After them come the Baby Boomers, born between 1946 and 1964, who are typically idealistic and hold education and consumer goods in high regard. From 1965 and 1979 is Generation X, as defined by Douglas Coupland (1991), the *X* signifying that they are not easily categorized.

The group that is of most concern in this book, however, are those who were born in the 1990s. Their birth coincided with the creation of the World Wide Web on March 13th, 1989, by Tim Berners-Lee, though it was not until Christmas Day of 1990 that the first successful communication between a Web browser and a server through the Internet occurred. It is the members of this generation born in the 1990s who are now undergraduates and constitute the heaviest users of Web apps. Rosen claims that even though the group born between the 1980s and the present have been called *Generation Y* or the *Millennials,* he thinks it much more reflective of their nature to either use Don Tapscott's term, the *Net Generation,* or his own, which is the *iGeneration.* It is indeed a clever pun, as the *i* refers both to various digital technologies such as the iPhone or iTunes, but also to the very individualized activities that these promote. Perhaps, too, a further pun on the use of *i* could be construed as the narcissistic tendencies of this young generation who were taught, according to Twenge (2006), to have a very heightened self-esteem. She even refers to them as *Generation Me,* although admittedly her sample was taken only from the privileged population, instead of poor inner-city racial minorities.

However categorized, Rosen says members of the iGeneration are "defined by their technology and media use, their love of electronic communication, and their need to multitask" (2011, p. 11), and it seems that smartphones have lessened the digital divide from when connection depended on computer ownership. Thus it can be inferred that the difference between generations is not so much ideological as it is neurological because this generation uses a different balance of senses to work with the current technology than was the case for the earlier TV-watching generation (WNYC, 2011). Pensky (2001) is of the same opinion, saying that this generation, which he calls *digital natives,* are native speakers of the digital language of the computer, the Internet, and video games. They enjoy, he says, fast information, multitasking, graphics in preference to text, and being networked, and many show a strong preference for games over serious work. And they are used to hypertext, downloaded music, cell phones, instant messaging, and finding information on the Internet. And Richtel (2010a) points out that different personality types are attracted to different types of technology, and the use of these various technologies seems to further amplify those personality traits. For example, highly sociable personalities tend to use Facebook a lot and also are heavy texters, whereas those who are less social might play video games. And the procrastinators might watch videos and surf the Web.

Rosen tells an amusing anecdote that many of us can probably relate to in which he was at a family reunion where there were quite a few 10- to 18-year-olds. Someone asked a question about a particular movie and within seconds each of these young people whipped out a smartphone, looked up the question, and came up with the answer. And none of them considered themselves exceptional for having such prowess and research capabilities. Rosen goes on to tell more stories, right down to when he saw a 3-year-old in a restaurant, who, when given her mother's smartphone to keep her amused while waiting for her food to arrive, immediately downloaded a game and started playing it. Gone, it seems, are the days when restaurants offered crayons and a paper placemat with a maze to color in. Gone, too, are the days of the clunky brightly colored toy phones, because what child would want those when she can perhaps get the real thing? As Rosen says,

> everything technological [are] not "tools" at all—they simply *are.* Just as we don't think about the existence of air, [young people] don't question the existence of technology and media. They expect technology to be there, and they expect it to do whatever they want it to do. Their WWW doesn't stand for *World Wide Web;* it stands for *Whatever, Whenever, Wherever.* (2011, p. 1)

The principal of a school in the Bronx was quoted as saying on the PBS Frontline documentary *Digital Nation* (2010) that "technology is like oxygen." When one of my hybrid writing students heard that remark, she commented, "As pathetic as it may be, it is certainly true for some of us." Are technology and air therefore interchangeable? Is technology a life support?

Rosen (2011), together with colleagues at the George Marshall Cognition Laboratory, conducted an anonymous online survey of about 3,000 people, asking them questions about how many hours per day they were online, using a computer offline, sending and receiving e-mail, using instant messaging or chat, talking on the phone, texting, listening to music, playing video games, and watching television. The findings showed that Baby Boomers tend to prefer face-to-face conversations or speaking on the phone, and that many also use e-mail; Generation Xers tend to like cell phones, e-mail, and instant messaging; and the iGeneration favored social networks such as Facebook, instant messaging, Skype, and texting. In fact, many children and teens spent nearly all the time they were awake engrossed in some form of technology or media, and frequently were connected to more than one device at the same time.

Rosen quoted the Nielsen company, which surveys a significant number of adolescents every three months, and their results were remarkable; the typical teenager sends and receives almost 3,340 texts a month, as compared with 191 phone calls (Nielsen, 2010). The difference between the number of text messages and the number of phone calls is even more amazing because, as the Nielsen report pointed out, only two years earlier adolescents had sent and received approximately the same number of texts as phone calls. As Rosen says, "To members of the iGeneration, a phone is not a phone. It is a portable computer that they use to tweet, surf the web, and of course, text, text, text" (2011, p. 12).

A Kaiser Family Foundation study undertaken in January 2010, which sampled 2,000 8- to 18-year-olds across the United States, asked 700 of them to keep a week-long diary recording their media use every half hour. This study found results similar to the Nielsen survey, especially when they compared their 2010 study with an equivalent survey carried out five years earlier. Most noteworthy of all was that, because multitasking has increased, this age group is spending vastly more time on different forms of media, including playing video games, looking at Web sites, listening to music, watching TV shows and movies, texting, and so on. Indeed, it was found that in general this age group is devoting at least two and a quarter hours more to media content exposure than was the case five years ago. It is possible that more children and adolescents have a TV in their bedroom, but more significant is the increase in cell phone ownership from 39% in 2005 to 66% in 2010. And more and more of these cell phones are smartphones. This means that, whereas about five years ago a multitasking child or adolescent might have been surfing the Web while listening to music or watching TV, now the consumption of the media applications is "on the go," from their cell phone or iPhone, which they constantly carry around with them (Rideout, Foehr, and Roberts, 2010). As Carr says, the Internet now provides a "moveable feast as computers shrink to the size of an iPhone or Blackberry" (2008, p. 4).

Many in this age group even go to sleep with their cell phone or laptop nestled next to them on their pillow! But what are the specific ways in which cell phones are used? According to the Kaiser Family Foundation, over half an hour a day is spent speaking, whereas almost 50 minutes is spent playing games, watching movies or TV shows, and a full hour and a half for those in seventh through twelfth grade is spent text messaging, which corresponds with the results of Rosen's study. TV is still the dominant form of media entertainment, with this age group spending about four and a half hours a day watching TV (which is up more than half an hour from five years ago), but the significant difference is that, whereas 59% watch a TV show on a TV set at the time it is broadcast, 41% watch TV shows from a mobile device at a time other than when it was broadcast. And there is, of course, increased consumption of online media, such as YouTube and Facebook, to about an hour and a half a day, which is a half-hour increase from five years ago (Rideout, Foehr, and Roberts, 2010).

As a mother of three sons born during and since 1982, and as a university professor working with undergraduates, I find that the results of the online habits of the iGeneration, although amazing, are not in themselves surprising. In fact, my youngest son, born in 1990, learned to write his name on the keyboard of a computer before he could write it by hand. As for students, I was teaching a hybrid expository writing course at Rutgers in the fall semester of 2010, and asked my students to comment on their own use of the new digital technologies. One student very honestly exclaimed in her online response, "In terms of multitasking I find myself now, listening to television in the background while I have five tabs open on different pages of the internet—including Facebook of course! Teenagers these days have grown up with such a vast amount of technology that we take it for granted." This level of multitasking, therefore, seems to be the norm. Another student agreed, saying, "I believe that all people in our age groups (regardless of which university we attend) claim that we're experts at multitasking."

My students also seemed to be aware of the rapid proliferation of new technologies. As one said, "Although I have memories of the dreadful dial-up Internet connection, there is not a time that I remember NOT ever having Internet. This limitless communication is wondrous and shows just how far we have technologically advanced." And speaking of technological advancement, another student, who is 19 years old, remarked after watching the PBS Frontline documentary *Digital Nation* (2010), "I couldn't help but wonder where our world is headed because I actually felt old while watching it. I had seen these children in grades two and three were using PCs and laptops almost as effectively as I can!" This student was reinforcing the observation Rosen made about the 3-year-old in the restaurant downloading and then playing a new game on her mother's smartphone.

What happens, though, when there is such a marked generational difference in lifestyle between parents and children, teachers and students? If, as

Rosen said, the typical Baby Boomer speaks on a cell phone and sends e-mails, but the typical member of the iGeneration does so much more than that in terms of digital technologies, can we truly communicate and understand each other? And Pensky (2001), having coined the term *digital natives* for this age group, refers to the rest of us as *digital immigrants* with all the accompanying problems of accent and assimilation, as we will always have a foot in the door to the past. So the question comes down to whether the digital natives should learn in the old traditional ways, or whether the digital immigrants should open themselves up to teaching in new ways by employing the digital media? And because this digital technology seems to be an integral part of socioeconomic progress and development, shouldn't the immigrants learn how to adapt so as to be happy, and isn't this generally true for all immigrants? Bemoaning a generation gap is not uncommon, but is this gap entirely more significant than at any other time in recent history?

And most importantly, what are the implications for discussion-based online education? When I wrote the first edition of this book, online learning was, relatively speaking, in its infancy. I had pondered at that time using the term *distance learning* in the title, but refrained for fear that the juxtaposition of "distance" and "learning" was an oxymoron and would therefore sound too bewildering. Now much of the way that the iGeneration communicates is at a distance, so learning via the Internet has come into its own. However, there have been, as shown previously, many recent additions to digital technology in the form of a variety of Web apps with resultant changes in communication behavior, and possibly in the manner of learning itself. Although the bulk of what I wrote in the first edition remains true, I feel now the need to explore the impact that multitasking of the new Web apps has on our brains and our style of knowledge acquisition. This I have done in a new chapter called "Paradigm Lost" (Chapter 4). In addition, because many of these Web apps are familiar to most undergraduates, I speak throughout the new edition about how to skillfully co-opt these into our online classrooms in such a way as to still achieve desired learning outcomes, while remembering all along that any form of digital media must be used judiciously, with the decision to use it being always pedagogically driven.

INTRODUCTION

The reasonable man adapts himself to
the world: the unreasonable one persists
in trying to adapt the world to himself.
Therefore all progress depends on
the unreasonable man.

—Shaw, B., 1983,

Man and Superman
(*The Revolutionist Handbook*)

easonable or not, those of us who embark on online teaching do so
because we want to do something that is educationally progressive,
is innovative and beneficial, and adds an extra dimension to the
courses taught on campus. The rapid diffusion of computer acquisition and
Internet access is well known, and online education is snowballing. How
quickly we take what is innovative, and heap each new paradigm shift onto
our grateful laps. But without careful deliberation and intentional focus on
the needs to understand pedagogy as it unfurls online, we run the risk of
producing a cohort of students who pass through the educational process
missing out on true opportunities for inspirational and meaningful learning,
and for whom the online class might amount to little more than knowing
where to click within a labyrinth of links. The specific purpose of this book
is to switch emphasis from the technical issues of online teaching to the
human implications of teaching and learning by communicating through
the Internet. It aims to investigate the thinking behind the technology, why
we use it, and how we can make it effective for our needs. Online pedagogy
is in its infancy. In the campus class, we generally know what works well,
such as the importance of speaking sufficiently loudly, writing clearly on the
board, being dynamic, maintaining eye contact with students, and inviting

students to take an active role in discussion. But what works well online? It is the discovery of the most effective online teaching methods that is the focus of this book.

Discussion-based online education is primarily text based. It is also asynchronous in nature, meaning that all online participants can log on and participate in discussions at a time convenient to them. This can present new intellectual challenges, but it can also make education accessible in innovative and exciting ways. Online discussion can reach beyond the temporal and spatial constraints of the campus class, and as a result can often add a richer and deeper perspective as students respond when they are informed and inspired.

Many reasons account for the growing popularity of online classes. Faculty and students appreciate and benefit from the convenience and flexibility of online education, and enjoy not having to spend the time or money traveling to class. Administrators are glad that online education alleviates any shortage of classroom space, which is an important concern as the population continues to grow, and there is increasing popularity in continuing education and lifelong learning. Many educators also feel that learning how to learn in an online course is becoming a necessity, and will equip students with a skill they will continue to need throughout their lives.

There are two alternative ways in which the Internet is used in online teaching. One is *the fully online class*, in which the students and instructor do not see each other face to face. This literally opens up global possibilities for learning, and students from across the country, as well as around the world, might log in to study in these classes. Students from New York, London, Mexico City, a traveling dance company, or a boat moored off the Florida coast, for example, can communicate with each other, with the instructor, and with the guest lecturer from India by a simple flick of the switch. Besides being tremendously exciting, it can also be very enriching for students to learn from others from different cultures, and it can help to break down cultural barriers.

The other way in which the Internet is used in teaching is when a class that meets on campus has an additional Web component; this type of class is called a *hybrid*. Some educators consider the hybrid to be the best of both worlds, as it facilitates the learning process and enhances both student–student and faculty–student communication. It provides the convenience and flexibility of the asynchronous online method of learning, with the real time face-to-face contact. We are all familiar with the situation of being immersed in a terrific discussion in the campus class, and then having to stop as it is the end of the scheduled class time. Rather than having to wait for the next campus class, by which time the idea might have lost some of its force, the discussion can continue online. In this way, the hybrid class can be thought of as "pushing back the classroom walls." As well as continuing discussions after class, the online environment can be used for preparation of materials for the next campus class as in, for example, holding an initial online discussion about a new reading before discussing it more fully on campus. This has the added advantage that it can assist in identifying any areas of difficulty.

Another advantage of the hybrid class is that different learning styles and methods can be accommodated. For example, some students might be shy or reluctant to speak in front of a group on campus, yet open up more freely in front of their computer screens, and the reverse might be true for other students. Some students do not learn well from lectures, and many students actually discover their own voice for the first time when working online. Furthermore, providing the means of communicating information through a variety of media and environments might help students to be able to engage in more class activities than if it was solely one type of environmental forum. As Dennis Pearl, a professor of statistics at Ohio State says, "You can make the best roast beef that you can, but a vegetarian is not going to have a good meal. I think the best model is to provide a really good buffet" (quoted in Young, 2002a).

A third advantage is that the different phases of learning can occur in different environments, which has important implications on instructional design. Kolb's (1984) Learning Cycle suggests that there is a continuous cycle of four processes when learning takes place: experience, reflection, conceptualization, and planning. The campus class might be the most suitable environment for gaining an experience (such as watching a film, seeing an exhibit, or hearing a reading) and possibly might also be the best place for planning, whereas sandwiched in between, the online class, due to its asynchronous environment, might be the most appropriate forum for reflection and conceptualization.

Yet another reason for choosing a hybrid rather than a fully online class might relate to the age of the student population. If students are mostly of typical undergraduate age, a hybrid might be better than an online class, as it provides opportunities for seeing each other and intervening, if necessary. In fact, in addition to the campus class time, and the option of office hours, I recommend that you hold mandatory individual conferences with students at least twice or three times per semester. Having the opportunity of meeting each student face-to-face—being immediately available to explain a difficult concept or answer questions and being able to ascertain from body language, facial expressions, and tone of voice if the student comprehends can sometimes be more powerful and effective than writing comments on papers or online, and it supplements very well the learning activities that take place online.

It should be pointed out that all the remarks made in this book address online teaching in general, whether the class is fully online or a hybrid, and that the book will consist of three parts:

- Theory: an application of learning theories to online discussion-based courses
- Practice: suggestions and techniques, illustrated by real examples, for stimulating and managing online discussion effectively, and for improving online teaching practices
- Assessment: methods for assessing the efficacy of discussion-based online courses

PART ONE

THEORETICAL IMPLICATIONS: BUILDING A BODY OF ONLINE PEDAGOGY

This section is devoted to building a substantial body of online pedagogy. Much exists in the literature about pedagogy of campus teaching, but to date more needs to be discovered about the theory of teaching students who are remote from us, and with whom we communicate via online discussions. In an effort to better understand online pedagogy, the following topics will be investigated.

- The distance factor
- Optimal roles of the online teacher
- Rethinking learning theory as applied to online learning
- Paradigm Lost

THE DISTANCE FACTOR

Now, here, you see, it takes all the running you
can do, to keep in the same place. If you want
to get somewhere else, you must run at least
twice as fast as that!

—Lewis Carroll, (1871), 1997
Through the Looking Glass

Can the Mind Exist Independently from the Body?

S tudents generally like to have a sense of belonging. When they attend
a class on campus, they become familiar both with the room in which
the class is held and with the regularity of attendance of the inhabi-
tants in that room. There is, in other words, a sense of predictability in
terms of environment. Feeling included in a group is an important factor for
encouraging the true potential for learning to take place. But is it possible
for a class that does not occupy spatial coordinates to still generate a feeling
of *place*? Given that students in an online class are working remotely, often
some distance from each other, does the association of "distance" and
"learning" constitute an oxymoron? After all, education is surely about the
meeting of minds, not their separation.

Dreyfus (as cited by Arnone, 2001) criticizes the possibility of learning
without physical presence, as is done via the Internet in online courses. His
book, *On the Internet,* covers the "hype" of hyperlinks (as he does not think
it leads to intelligent information retrieval), asks just how far distance learning is from education, talks of how a "telepresence" is necessarily disembodied and therefore inadequate, and explains how what he sees as the
anonymity of virtual online discussions leads to loss of meaning. He says that
early philosophers such as Plato, and later the French philosopher Descartes,
believed in the philosophy of dualism; namely, that the mind is self-sufficient

and in fact better off without the body as it can transcend time and space. He disputes this view, however, instead preferring to think as Kierkegaard and other existentialists did, that the body plays a crucial role in the learning process, as real immersion in any situation—which, in itself involves taking risks—can only occur through the physical body. However, I believe that within education, risk is generally experienced more by the emotions than by the physical body, and as such there is as much risk taking in the online class as there is in the traditional class on campus. Students in either setting risk being wrong, risk feeling embarrassed in front of the group, and risk not working at the same pace as others. Maybe the feeling is experienced and perceived differently, but it is still there.

When we participate in an online class, where are our bodies? Our physical bodies are positioned in front of our computers, but our virtual bodies can be anywhere imagined. We indeed use this split between the physical and virtual body when we talk on the telephone. I would disagree with Dreyfus that this split makes us anonymous because in the online class our responses are always posted with our names attached. But the fact that we have no physical presence, Dreyfus argues, means that any learning that occurs can only be intellectual, not pragmatic. In other words, it is more on an abstract plane than involving a grasping and mastery of particular skills. He thinks that true learning can only take place from physically being somewhere and doing a particular activity, and it is only under these conditions that information becomes relevant and people come to meaningfully understand reality. But if this is true, how can anyone learn anything from a book, newspaper, television, radio, a letter, or e-mail? Is not the expression of the content more important than the medium through which it is expressed?

Differentiating between Space and Place

Gertrude Stein, when looking about in Los Angeles, said, "There's no 'here,' here," and I think her words can be aptly applied to the online class. Perhaps, however, any confusion about the online class can be clarified by differentiating between the concepts of *space* and *place*.

Robinson defines space as "an abstract container determined by distance, direction and time" (2000, p. 112). In addition, she says that place exists within space as a localized region. Place, as in a class, should be like a magnet, which holds together the instructor with a community of students and their ideas, knowledge, thoughts, and memories. In short, *place* is defined as anything that is mutually shared within, and has a boundary for containment purposes (Robinson, 2000, p. 112).

But what of cyberspace? Because it is virtual, Robinson argues that it is "the world of imaginary tools, that produce art, poetry, literature." But, pragmatically speaking, place within cyberspace is created and defined by the computer program, and its strictures of authorized access and passwords, which ensure that only those intended to belong to this place actually do so.

Because the online class is potentially interactive, this will involve the element of time as well as space. Robinson questions whether the words of her response are present for the students when they appear, or only when they are read. Is she, as instructor, imagined as present in her class only when her responses are posted? But, by analogy, do students in the campus class that meets at discrete intervals only think of the instructor as present when the class actually meets? I believe that the main objective in either teaching environment is for the subject matter to be so inspirational, exciting, and challenging that students think about it beyond the time in class, whether on campus or online. In the online class, Robinson states, time becomes space because all responses, although posted temporally, must be laid out spatially across the two-dimensional computer screen.

Distinguishing between Physical Distance and Transactional Distance

In an effort to further understand the impact on teaching and learning of students and the instructor working remotely from each other, I want to focus on one element within Robinson's definition of space, and that is the word *distance*. *Webster's New World Dictionary* (1990) offers the following definitions.

1. Being separated in space or time; remoteness
2. An interval between two points in space or time
3. A remoteness in behavior; reserve
4. A faraway place

I believe that computers with Internet access can give us potential ways of meeting, if not physically, then at least in the exchange of knowledge and ideas. In other words, it is not physical distance that is our concern, but the relational distance between teacher and student.

In Webster's third definition of distance, we see something about remote relationships, but we as teachers certainly do not want to have a psychological remoteness between students and ourselves.

Michael G. Moore (1984), contemplating the meaning of distance in education, states: "There is now a distance between learner and teacher which is not merely geographic, but educational and psychological as well. It is a distance in the relationship of the two partners in the educational enterprise. It is a 'transactional distance.'" How can this transactional distance between teacher and student be understood? Saba and Shearer (1994) suggest that this can be thought of as the relationship between the requisite structure for the teacher and the degree by which students take the initiative in their own learning. In other words, transactional distance is the extent to which the teacher manages to successfully engage the students in their learning. If students are disengaged and not stimulated into being active learners, there can be a vast transactional distance, whether the students are under the teacher's nose or on the other side of the city. But if a teacher, whether online or on campus, can establish meaningful educational opportunities, with the right degree of challenge and relevance, and can give students a feeling of responsibility for their own learning and a commitment to this process, then the transactional gap shrinks and no one feels remote from each other or from the source of learning.

Some critics of online education believe that it is deficient as it lacks physical presence along with the information of body language and tone of voice associated with it. But have we considered the large lecture on campus, in which the instructor might be unable to see clearly to the back of the lecture hall, let alone correctly read body language?

Perhaps under these circumstances, very little besides obvious shuffling and student whisperings is even noticed. A reader's comment on Dreyfus's book, found on amazon.com, states: "I took one of Dreyfus's classes at Berkeley as an undergraduate and I never got to talk to him, there was no face-to-face learning." He went on to say how he had felt like a "disembodied presence" as an undergraduate, and how much more meaningful were interactive online classes that he had subsequently taken.

On a similar note, in a somewhat tongue-in-cheek comment, Bromell (2002) claimed, "It's obvious, isn't it, that a pre-packaged distance-learning course that gives you a limited field of options to 'click' is more tailored to your needs than a trained teacher standing in the room with you, a person who can misread your expression and ineptly judge whether he or she is effectively communicating?"

I strongly believe that when students demonstrate commitment, it is to learning, knowledge, and the pursuit of new ideas; it is not commitment to a particular physical classroom, however lovely it may be.

Therefore, I think that commitment to learning can take place without a physical setting, and certainly the online class can be effective as a virtual place to disseminate, collect, and exchange knowledge and ideas. In this way, then, it can be appreciated that physical distance and transactional distance are different measures, and whether a class is taught online or on campus, or a mixture of both, it seems that the goal is to minimize the transactional distance, thereby establishing a comfort level and ensuring ready access to fulfill all educational aspirations.

How the Social Dimension Impacts on Transactional Distance

Wegerif (1998) speaks of an important social dimension within online classes that will have a direct impact on transactional distance. In a fascinating study based on interviews with 21 students enrolled in an interactive online course at the Open University, Wegerif discovered that the degree of students' success or failure was closely related to whether each student felt like an insider or an outsider. Learning was therefore seen as a social process, as the degree of learning depends on whether there is a feeling of belonging to a community of practice.

One student remarked that what she had gained the most from the course was the collaboration with others, in which she learned an enormous amount from her peers and felt that great friendships blossomed between her and some of her online colleagues. Conversely, another student who had dropped the course before its end said she did not feel that collaboration could work well online because unless she was prepared to log into the class every day, the conversations would continue without her, leaving her behind the pace and thus feeling overwhelmed.

This process, concludes Wegerif, is a social experience, as it is the difference between the student who crossed over a threshold into the position of fully participating in the midst of all discussions, and the one who did not, but who was left on the outside uncomfortably looking in. The student who felt immersed in this online activity was highly motivated, and could not wait to log back on to see what else was being said. The student who felt like an outsider experienced online learning as cold and remote.

An important study published by the National Research Council (2001), entitled *Knowing What Students Know: The Science and Design of Educational Assessment,* takes a similar view in stating that learning takes place in a social context. Collaboration is vital to learning so that students understand questions, develop arguments, and share meaning and conclusions among a community of learners.

Knowledge, the National Research Council states, is not incorporeal or disembodied, but is developed through working with others. Although the study focused on grade-school children, their views are applicable to online learning as well because even though working remotely, by interacting in online discussions, students establish an online community of learners, and through their exchange of written ideas their thinking becomes apparent to the instructor.

How did students in the online class studied by Wegerif cross the threshold? It seems it was a matter of confidence for some. For example, one student said that she initially felt like a novice hiding in the corner, and said very little until there was a particular group exercise, and since no one was contributing anything, she dared herself to offer her ideas. She received a very positive response, and from then on, felt she was able to fully participate.

Many other factors also affected whether students felt they had insider or outsider status. Access to the Internet, for example, had a big impact, as those who only had a computer at work or in a library and not at home were more limited, as were students who had significantly high charges for Internet use. Additionally, some students found it easier to write online than others, and for some it was quite frightening, especially if they felt unsure about a particular topic. Without a doubt, the medium itself had an impact on communication. One female student who worked in the so-called real world in a male-dominated environment where she was fairly quiet found that online she could respond more frequently as she had a chance to think things through and not be interrupted when she was ready to express herself. On the other hand, student postings of excessive length created disincentives for discussion, especially for students who did not log in frequently.

As Wegerif concludes, "Forming a sense of community, where people feel they will be treated sympathetically by their fellows, seems to be a necessary first step for collaborative learning. Without a feeling of community people are on their own, likely to be anxious, defensive and unwilling to take the risks involved in learning." Moving from the feeling of being an outsider to being an insider was central to achieving a positive learning experience.

These conclusions are validated by Diane Grodney (2001), a colleague who teaches hybrid classes at New York University. She stated,

> I would frequently walk into my house, go to the computer and see if anyone was home. I shared this experience [with my class] as part of our ending process, and others said they strongly identified with the sense that we shared a home, a community or as one student put it, "an educational holding environment" (à la Winnicott). Another student referred, earlier on, to the class as a transitional object which he/she was able to carry throughout the week. I believe these references speak to the sense of the personal psychological space that can be created online.

One factor that Wegerif does not address, but which seems crucial in attempting to decrease the transactional distance, is the behavior of the instructor, who, after all, sets the tone for the whole class. I believe that it will be beneficial for the instructor to personalize the educational approach as it will provide an important step toward compensating for any feeling of coldness or remoteness that messages on a computer screen might otherwise entail. This can be hard, not only because of class size, but also because of the diversity of students. Nevertheless, it is important to try.

The next chapter explores in more depth the optimal role of the online teacher.

2

THE OPTIMAL ROLE OF THE ONLINE TEACHER

Passive acceptance of the teacher's wisdom is easy to most boys and girls. It involves no effort of independent thought, and seems rational because the teacher knows more than his pupils; it is moreover the way to win the favour of the teacher unless he is a very exceptional man. Yet the habit of passive acceptance is a disastrous one later in life. It causes man to seek and to accept a leader, and to accept as a leader whoever is established in that position.

—Bertrand Russell

Who Do We Teach?

There is a much greater diversity within the student body than even a decade ago. It has been thought that typical college teaching methods were tailored to deliver content to White, middle-class males, as they had traditionally been the dominant group. This group of individuals was thought in general to exhibit autonomous, competitive behavior, with an emphasis on achievement (Anderson and Adams, 1992). If this is indeed the case, then it calls for a need to diversify teaching methods, so as to pay attention to other learning styles.

Before exploring these ideas further, I would like to pause to question whether the assumptions of the White, male student learning style apply online. My experience, and the experience of many of my colleagues, is that, whereas White, middle-class male students might have the most to say in the campus class, and might even interrupt a female or minority student, such a thing is not possible online. (For a fuller discussion on the issues of gender and racial differences, see "How Do We Speak Online?" in Chapter 7.) There can be no interruptions because the class that exists in cyberspace is equally available to all class participants at all times, nor is the online instructor able to favor specific students by looking primarily in their direction. Furthermore, traditional teaching methods that were designed to be most suited to the White, middle-class male emphasized delivery of information in lengthy lectures; but online, there is the need for shorter, snappier mini-lectures, opening out into interactive discussion.

The Importance of Personalizing Education

We discussed in the previous chapter about how an effective online teacher should try to personalize the educational approach so as to minimize the transactional distance. Certainly those instructors who are more attentive to individual students are more effective. Anderson and Adams (1992) mention that some students are "field-dependent learners," meaning that they are almost as concerned about the personality and style of the instructor as the course material that is being delivered.

Factors possibly considered important in the instructor's style include being supportive and encouraging, giving ample feedback, being a good role model, being appropriately informal, and eliciting discussion. I firmly believe that these features can be perceived accurately online.

There are many different ways in which an instructor can be attentive to students, and this depends on the role an instructor might take. McKeachie (1978) identifies six teaching roles for the campus teacher, all of which can be applied to online teaching. These roles can be used for different purposes and at different times in the semester. For example, the teacher can be seen as the following:

- A *facilitator* who enhances student learning by encouraging active participation in discussion and by helping the student to see education as meaningful and relevant. The instructor should resist having a condescending attitude toward the students, as if handing down information from a "celestial throne" (p. 253), but should be able to empathize with them and see the situation as they see it, by carefully listening to and learning from them.
- An *expert* who communicates expertise through lectures and discussions, and is able to stimulate students without overwhelming them.

- A *formal authority* who helps students by establishing boundaries such as acceptable conduct and dates of submission of materials.
- A *socializing agent* who has contacts within the larger academic community, and as such can be helpful to students in providing such things as letters of recommendation and links to research and publication sources.
- An *ego ideal* who is charismatic and shows commitment and enthusiasm not only to the subject matter but also to the students themselves.
- A *person* who demonstrates compassion and understanding of student needs.

Good teaching, I believe, is about modification and adjustment in relation to the perceived needs of each individual student in the class at any time throughout the semester. McKeachie states: "Teaching should be a two-way process in which both students and teachers learn from one another; as long as teaching conditions facilitate two-way interaction, the good sense of teachers and students can be substantially relied upon" (1978, p. 255). This means that the online teacher should be attentive to each student in the class, in an attempt to bring out the best in each of them. Now, bringing out the best in each student does not necessarily imply giving each of them loads of attention, or even the same type of attention, as some might do better with more responsibility for individual work. Just as a parent does not treat each child identically, but reacts to the needs and personality traits of each, so too should the instructor do this with each student. It is all a question, therefore, of getting to know one's students.

Student Characteristics

McKeachie (1978) looks at various student characteristics, including independence and responsibility, authoritarianism, anxiety, intelligence, motivation, introversion–extroversion, gender, and cognitive style. Following are implications of these in terms of online teaching.

- *Independence and responsibility:* If insecure, a student will want more of a teacher's authoritative presence, whereas an independent student will want the teaching to be more permissive. I think the degree of independence can also be related to the learning activity. For example, in an online class of mine, I thought the students were articulate, highly motivated, and independent, as the discussion forums were positively explosive with their numerous responses. However, when I introduced a new activity of role-playing (see "Other Forms of Group Work" in Chapter 8) they became largely dumbfounded and in need of much direction and nurturing.

- *Authoritarianism*: Authoritarian students prefer a high degree of control, and listening to lectures. However, I feel that a hierarchical structure of this sort would not work well online, as lengthy online lectures by an overly authoritative online instructor might dissipate some of the energy of interactive online discussion.
- *Anxiety*. Because anxiety can be increased by uncertainty, it follows that anxious students do best in a highly structured environment. Anxiety can arise at different times in the semester, depending on the materials studied and the learning activities, so the online teacher must be encouraging, supportive, and prompt at supplying guidance.

I would like to mention at this point that the questions of independence and responsibility, authoritarianism, and anxiety are interrelated, especially over the decision that the teacher might make as to whether the class should be competitive or cooperative. If the teacher opts for collaboration, which works best in an online class within an online discussion, or could be continued through online collaborative projects and role-playing, this might also imply delegating more responsibility to the students themselves, which can cause anxiety for some. This might be because of the departure from an authoritarian, spoon-fed class, into one in which students are encouraged to think creatively.

As Kathleen Hull (2002), a colleague and instructor of a hybrid class at New York University, said, "Getting young people to think on their own and solve problems is inefficient, time consuming, and sometimes uncomfortable." But this, Hull concludes, provides the potential for a powerful learning experience for the students, and one that they are more likely to retain. I believe, too, if discomfort of this sort does arise, it is best for the online instructor not to supply the answers, but to be nurturing, encouraging, and available to student questions. It is in this way that online education is personalized and humanized. An interesting study conducted by the Higher Education Research Institute at the University of California–Los Angeles in late 2002, which interviewed 32,840 full-time faculty in 358 colleges, found a significant increase (over findings in the base year of 1989) in faculty interest in students' well-being, and a commitment to helping students both academically and personally (Wilson, 2002).

Although this study focused on campus teachers, the same sort of commitment is feasible for online teachers as well. The collaborative work could be balanced with independent work in which the student works alone offline by reading, researching, and writing papers. Together, independent and collaborative work can lead to greater learning and the development of critical-thinking skills.

- *Intelligence*: In the past, educators believed that a single intelligence test could measure whether a student was more or less intelligent. The thinking on this subject then changed, and scholars such as Howard Gardner (2000) put forward the view that students have diverse styles of learning and strengths in different areas. He believed that there are multiple intelligences, so that, for example, some students might be visual learners; others intake information better if they hear it, or if they act it, or use their logical powers of reasoning. In fact, Gardner identified seven categories of intelligence, namely, linguistic-verbal, logical-mathematical, visual-spatial, bodily-kinesthetic, musical-rhythmic, interpersonal, and intrapersonal. He then added existential, spiritual, and naturalistic (Gardner, 2000). More recent thinking, however, disputes the claims to multiple intelligence, and there is some controversy surrounding this view. Opinions are various, but some center on there being insufficient empirical evidence, and others that such factors as gender, culture, and generation are not sufficiently taken into consideration. In addition, a case can definitely be made that learning styles change when education takes place online. Generally, the online environment fosters increased participation, collaboration, and interactive learning. And, within this, I still feel it is necessary to see students as individual learners who bring different backgrounds, skills, and misconceptions to class with them, and that it is our mission as teachers to try to offer a variety of teaching styles and activities so that we can reach each student. Good teaching, then, should be cognizant of and tailored to the diversity of learners. How this can be carried out online is the subject of much of this book.
- *Motivation*: To be a successful online learner, devoid of the peer pressure of the campus class, demands a high degree of self-reliance.
- *Introverts and extroverts:* McKeachie (1978) found that extroverts learn better when studying with another extrovert than when studying alone, and when performing original research. Introverts, in contrast, do better when directly fed information. Furthermore, extroverts care

less for feedback than do introverts. It would be the subject of much fascinating research as to whether traits of introversion or extroversion are altered by communicating online as opposed to interacting face-to-face.

- *Gender*: McKeachie (1978) believed that female students were more concerned with achievement and were more willing to try to please the instructor than were their male counterparts.

- *Cognitive style*: If a student is new to a subject area, or is predisposed to learning facts rather than application, greater personal contact with the instructor is preferable. This, however, depends on the type of interaction, the personalities of those involved, and the subject matter. I also would like to suggest that environment makes a significant difference, and if students do not see their instructor, as in the online class, they might feel that they need more frequent online contact than if they were on campus, irrespective of learning style. This might be especially true for students who are new to online learning.

The next chapter looks in more depth at the question of concept formation in an online class.

3

RETHINKING LEARNING THEORY WITHIN THE ONLINE CLASS

Some time ago, on a journey across the Atlantic,
I reflected that the spoonful of mashed potato I
was about to put in my mouth was actually traveling faster than a rifle bullet.

—Edward de Bono, 1986,
De Bono's Thinking Course

Hierarchy of Thoughts and Acquisition of Knowledge

The other day, a student in my online class wrote, "What do thoughts look like online? I mean, I know when someone is thinking when I see them, but online I only see the finished product of those thoughts." What a fascinating question! It points to how, in traditional, face-to-face education, so much emphasis is on the spoken word and on sensory cues that provide further information. But the advent of online learning speaks to a legitimate need to develop new teaching and learning paradigms, and to rethink learning theory within the online environment (Boettcher, 1999). This chapter explores the impact that the primarily text-based environment of the online class has on a student's ability to learn.

John Dewey, in his 1910 essay "What Is Thought?" wrote of four levels of thought. First are the random, fleeting thoughts of which we are not particularly aware. For example, "I just heard a dog bark." The second level of thought is restricted to that which is not perceived by any of the five senses, so is more properly understood as thinking about something. The third level of thought is belief based, but these beliefs are unquestioned as they seem reasonably probable. The fourth level of thought is more reflective. These thoughts center on important consequences of particular beliefs, so it is important to provide evidence as to whether the initial belief is true. This implies that there is a level of doubt and uncertainty, which in turn stimulates an investigation. This fourth level of thought is therefore conscious and voluntary.

Assuming the reflective thinker is up to the challenge, what is the process of gaining knowledge? Dewey ([1910] 1991) likens reflective thinking to a traveler being at a fork in the road, in other words, where there is ambiguity and a dilemma. The thinker, like the traveler, has to search for some facts and evidence to provide direction. Thus, thoughts cannot exist in isolation from the real world.

Berge and Muilenburg (2000) also believe in a hierarchy of types of thoughts, culminating in reflective or "constructivist" thinking, which is constructing knowledge from personal experience. In addition, they identify different types of thought leading to this stage, including critical thinking, which involves concept formation; higher-level thinking, which is creative problem solving; and distributive thinking, which is shared thinking among the group. When there is collaboration and a sharing of personal experience among all class members, these shared multiple perspectives can lead to socially constructed meaning (Berge and Muilenburg, 2000; National Research Council, 2001; Wegerif, 1998).

Benjamin Bloom's Taxonomy

There is a definite need to enhance reflective thinking well beyond the simple acquisition of facts to be memorized, and to delegate more responsibility to students for their own learning. Benjamin Bloom proposes six developmental levels pertaining to the acquisition of knowledge and of intellectual analysis and skills (Cameson, Delpierre, and Masters, 2002). These are as follows:

- *Knowledge*: The lowest level of learning in the cognitive domain. It implies pure recall of memorized information.
- *Comprehension*: The second level of learning, and the first level of understanding. It could involve, for example, having the ability to translate words into graphics, interpreting the meaning of certain facts, or making predictions for the future. These can be achieved through discussion, either online or face to face.

- *Application*: The ability to meaningfully apply what has been learned to new situations. It involves a more sophisticated level of understanding than basic comprehension. Examples include solving mathematical problems, constructing charts, or applying theories to particular situations, such as in essays or role-playing.
- *Analysis*: Comprehension of the organizational principle of the material, so that it can be meaningfully broken down to its component parts, and the relationship between the parts can be understood. This is an even higher form of understanding than comprehension or application, as it involves understanding not only the content as a whole but also the constituent parts involved in its structure. Examples include understanding the structure of a creative piece of work such as writing, music, or art; identifying fallacies in assumptions; and distinguishing between facts and inferences.
- *Synthesis*: A higher level of understanding that refers to the ability to put what had been considered as disparate parts together to form a coherent whole. This might involve developing a new system of classification of facts or putting forward a research proposal. This is a creative process that endeavors to formulate a new structure for classification purposes; write a poem, story, or speech; or propose a scientific experiment.
- *Evaluation*: The highest area in the hierarchy of cognitive learning. It assumes all other areas and introduces value judgments based on defined criteria. The criteria can be internal, judging the organization of the work, or external, such as consideration of relevance; examples include judging the consistency of a piece of written work, the value of a work of art, or whether the conclusion of an experiment is supported by the data.

Paying Attention

If learning is based on experience, it would imply that a key ingredient in learning is the ability and motivation to pay close attention (Fardouly, 2001; Levine, 2002). There can, of course, be various external stimuli that either increase or distract from potentially learning a new subject. If a subject seems relevant, meaningful, and exciting, then a student is likely to pay closer attention, although there is a diversity of learning styles, interest, and rate of comprehension. Students differ with respect to how they think, perceive, organize, remember, and solve problems. They differ also in their degree of interpersonal skills and level of independence, and whether they prefer active experimentation, reflection, or abstract concepts (Liu and Ginther, 1999). Ability to comprehend the language of the communication is another factor that influences learning, so that if it is not a native language or if the student has learning disabilities, this might interfere with attention span. Levine (2002) identifies the following three categories that affect how we pay attention.

- *Mental energy control:* The body's ability to know when to concentrate and exert mental effort, and alternatively when to shut down at appropriate times, so as to rest or sleep.
- *Intake and processing:* The mind's ability to be selective, to know how to sort through a vast amount of data and choose what is relevant. It concerns establishing priorities and affects the ability to take good notes and develop good study habits.
- *Depth of information processing:* The mind's ability to incorporate information. The expression "In one ear and out the other" represents a shallow incorporation of information that is quickly forgotten. Some people, Levine says, naturally tend to see the broad picture, but nothing in much depth; and the reverse is true for others.

The Role of Long-Term Memory and Prior Knowledge

Developments in the field of cognitive science reveal that not only do conditions for optimal learning take place when a student is actively involved within a social context, but also that long-term memory plays a crucial role in one's ability to reason effectively about current information and problems. Short-term memory (also called *working memory*) is limited, so therefore it is best in learning situations for a student to evoke knowledge from long-term memory.

As stated by the National Research Council (2001), it is of crucial importance to understand long-term memory to see what students know; how they know it; and how they use that knowledge to answer questions, solve problems, and learn new information. It also helps to understand why certain situations seem relevant or meaningful to a student, and how a student organizes new information into manageable bundles or folders, termed *schema*. These schema imply that a student is sorting information into patterns that can be easily recognized, provide accessible storage for new information by making associations with something already known rather than being an isolated fact in a vacuum (Levine, 2002), and allow rapid retrieval of knowledge. It is through this storage of well-organized facts within long-term memory that a student can develop expertise in a subject area.

Prior learning, therefore, is of great importance and might assist students in learning new information. No one is a blank slate. When a student receives new information, he or she reconciles it with what is already known in the long-term memory. This might lead to reevaluating or revisiting existing understanding, and the prior knowledge will help in judging the accuracy of the new information received (National Research Council, 2001). If the new information is judged to be accurate, it will be incorporated and thus knowledge in this area will be expanded.

Prior knowledge might unfortunately also cause some stickiness to old, incorrect ideas and unconscious resistance to change. For example, Ehrmann (1995, p. 23) describes the film, *A Private Universe*, in which, during the commencement ceremony in Harvard Yard in the late 1980s, 22 graduating students, faculty, and alumni were asked why it is warmer in summer than winter, and why the moon has a different shape each night. Only two of those questioned provided the right answer, despite the fact that they should have been repeatedly given this information while in school. Ninth graders in a nearby school of good quality were then asked the same questions, and gave the same erroneous answers as did those at Harvard. They were then taught about these scientific phenomena and asked the same questions again, yet clung to their preconceived notions despite having been taught the correct scientific explanations. It would seem, therefore, that during class time, the teacher asked canned questions and the students gave canned answers, while all along their preexisting theories remained invisible to the teacher and therefore unchallenged. This implies that even if teachers teach the right materials, it still might not impact on true learning, if the teacher remains unaware of the way students think. Enabling processes whereby student thinking becomes more visible to the teacher is of crucial importance, and is studied in more depth in Chapter 10, which assesses the efficacy of online education.

Self-Regulating and Reinforcing Long-Term Memory

Because learning, therefore, seems so dependent on memory of what has already been learned, how do we ensure that we retain our memories accurately and do not become forgetful? The National Research Council states that if a student thinks about his or her thinking process, which is termed *metacognition,* this process of deliberation not only helps in self-regulation, understanding, and self-correction, but also assists in reinforcing long-term memory.

Levine (2002) also mentions that memory might be improved by transforming the information into a different representation. For example, if some information is given in words, then it could be transformed into a picture, or conversely a picture could be transformed into words. Furthermore, he states, memory will be influenced by time. If, for example, we learn one subject in one class, and quickly move on to the next class of a totally different subject, then it is possible that some information from the first class will be erased by the second.

When the acquisition of knowledge is brought about by directly experiencing the external environment, then the learner is thought to be active, as opposed to being a passive recipient of spoon-fed information. Fardouly (2001) breaks this process down into four steps: thinking about a new explanation, experimenting with it, experiencing what is occurring, and reflecting upon the process. Learning, Fardouly states, is an emotional process, but the right balance must be struck. Some excitement, encouragement, and challenge can be motivating, whereas too much anxiety over a course can severely limit the potential for learning.

Application of Learning Theories to the Online Environment

How can we apply these various theories of learning and knowledge acquisition to the online environment? Bruce (1998) poses the following questions:

- How does learning through technology serve in the development of experience?
- Is learning through the computer a substitute for other modes of learning?
- Is learning through technology in the same relation as a map is to its territory? If so, does this imply that it is not a real experience but a feeble abstraction?
- Conversely, can learning through technology give access to that which was previously inaccessible?
- Does learning through technology change knowledge?
- What is gained and what is lost as we move into the information age?

In an attempt to answer Bruce's questions, I first do not believe that technology is a substitute for other modes of learning, but that it forms a supplement to learning in the case of the hybrid class, or that it aims to produce a legitimate alternative in the case of the class held entirely online. However, quite how learning through technology serves in the development of experience is a question needing deep exploration. I think it is important to point out, though, that the computer is no more an experience than is the chalk an instructor might use to write on the board of the campus class. The computer is purely a tool of communication, in the discussion of experiences as related to education, and not the experience itself. In this way, I do not see technology in education as analogous to a map and its landscape as it is interactive and dynamic as opposed to being flat and static, and so I do not think in any way that it provides a "feeble abstraction."

Can Technology Give Access to Previously Inaccessible Information?

Bruce (1998) asks whether learning through technology can give access to information that was previously inaccessible, and I believe this can be so in certain circumstances. Technology, for example, can be invaluable in a course on meteorology, in which data could be retrieved on the Web of almost up-to-the-minute changes in temperature and wind conditions in any particular location around the world. On a different scale, an electronic simulation can show precisely in a matter of minutes how a flower grows, whereas in nature we might miss some steps in our passing observations (Turkle, 1995). But do we experience the flower the same way? No, I would argue that we do not; for we cannot bring all our senses to the flower, to feel its silky petals or drink in its fragrance. On the other hand, we might learn more about the growth of a flower through technology than firsthand observation, and as such, technology might well give access to that which was previously inaccessible. Perhaps if a Web site is of high quality, it might be of great immediacy and excitement, as sometimes technology enables us to experience things in a way that is larger than life. Thus, I would think that technology does change knowledge, but quite what is gained and what is lost is still to be determined and cannot be generalized.

Electronic simulations are but a small part of discussion-based online learning, in which the technology provides a medium for the exchange of thoughts as well as the growth and development of knowledge. As such, the technology can all but disappear, as the focus shifts away from it, to the challenge of a good discussion in which the technology is merely the conduit. This permits Dewey's fourth level of thought, the reflective level, to occur.

Learning How to Use the Technology

By no means does the technology become immediately invisible. Any newcomer to an online class must first learn how to use the software. As with learning any new cognitive skill, initial use of the technology needed to access the online class will require effort, and will depend on the limitations of the short-term (working) memory (National Research Council, 2001). At first, the new online student or instructor will be very conscious of using the technology, and will have to talk his or her way through each step. It is only with continued use and positive feedback (meaning that the online user can access every part of the class immediately as desired) that familiarity with the technology will ensue, implying that both the skill and competence needed to obtain desired ends have moved into long-term memory. This will make the operation of the technology much more "fluent and automatic" (National Research Council, 2001, p. 85) because it no longer depends on the conscious monitoring of short-term memory used in the early days of the course. This freeing up of attention from the technology permits the online user to focus on the course content, which after all, is the goal of the course.

Translating Concepts from the Real World to the Virtual World

The question remains as to how concepts, once formed through reflections about experience in the real world, are actually communicated in the virtual world of cyberspace? Do so-called relational learners (Anderson and Adams, 1992), who find relevance in the real world, place sufficient credence in the virtual world, the world of Web links and interesting and relevant online sites? Furthermore, in the campus class, we talk and listen; but online, the primary mode of communication is text based. When the online student reads the words of a lecture or discussion, that student co-constructs the meaning in a process that involves changing these symbols that appear on the screen into something meaningful by interpreting them in the light of individual experience. This is why, when any two people read the same material, they interpret it in different ways.

This highlights the tremendous importance of the written word in conveying meaning in the online class. Reading and writing, as opposed to speaking and listening, will no doubt have an impact on the way in which learning occurs, and the student who is a good text-based communicator will be at an advantage. Additional factors that will impact learning in the online class include the constant availability of every aspect of the course at any particular point in time because there is an archive of all written discussion, and the asynchronous nature of the communications, which allows more time for reflection.

Impact of Constant Information Availability and Asynchronicity on Mental Energy Control

This constant availability of information in the online class is in marked contrast to the campus class, in which once the session is over it is over, and is no longer available except through memory or notes taken. This continued availability of information online, combined with the asynchronicity of the environment, will impact greatly on what Levine (2002) has termed "mental energy control" (to know when to be alert and when to "shut down"), as it can allow for everyone to log on and participate when they are feeling inspired, and their concentration level is high and efficient. Conversely, it can be argued that the online class never goes away throughout the semester—there is no closing the door and imposing a limit, a boundary—so that there might be an artificial inducement for faculty and students alike to get sucked in, to always feel the need to be there, even if they are beyond their normal limits of full concentration.

Added to this is the temptation for many students nowadays to multitask, and whether this increases efficiency and achievement, or whether the "mental energy control" is challenged, is a subject of much debate. This issue is more fully explored in the following chapter, "Paradigm Lost."

Impact of Constant Information Availability and Asynchronicity on Intake and Processing

Levine (2002) talks about the need for the student to be selective, establish priorities, and develop good study habits. But what happens in the online class, during which there is no need to take notes on a lecture, as all the information is available on the screen, all mini-lectures and discussions fully documented? What impact do so many words have on learning? I would like to speculate that it most certainly eradicates the need for memorization, but I think it absolutely challenges the need to be selective. Information can grow rapidly in the online class, and students will need to be shown which topics are of greatest significance, if they cannot determine this on their own.

It would be helpful to students, in terms of knowing how to be selective and properly establish priorities, if the course being taught is specific about its goals and objectives. In this way, students can gain a clear idea as to where they are going, and how topics are relevant within the larger context of the class (see Chapter 10). It has been found that chances for successful learning are greater when students are clear about the course goals and objectives because then they know what is expected of them.

The pacing of the course, even an online asynchronous course, is important, too, so that it is not so fast as to lose people, nor is it so slow that it makes some students frustrated (Fardouly, 2001). Furthermore, in a face-to-face class, students can often tell from the instructor's tone of voice which points are most important. Perhaps the best way to add emphasis in the online setting is either for the teacher to rephrase the information in a new way so as to help different styles of learners, or to write the most important remarks in bold or colored text.

Impact of Constant Information Availability and Asynchronicity on the Depth of Processing of That Information and on Attention Spans

The question remains as to how deeply information is being processed (Levine, 2002). Does information presented primarily in written form make some people aware of details that they would normally overlook in a face-to-face context? I believe students have a great potential to absorb more information in the online setting because they can take their time, work when they are at their best, and reread especially if they missed information through lack of concentration the first time.

We might be learning at what Dewey labeled level-four reflective thoughts, but random level-one thoughts pop in and out of our minds, uncalled for and distracting: "I'm hungry," "Her hair looks nice today," "This evening I will iron my dress for the concert." One advantage of the online class over the campus class is that, if this occurs and we lose our concentration, the words are still in front of us on the screen, whereas on campus they would have evaporated into the air and become lost. Attention is more likely to be retained by a clear online course design and layout, with easy-to-find, meaningful sequences that have an inherent logic, and by short, succinct mini-lectures and discussion responses, rather than excessively long texts.

Tangentially related to this is that some claim we are teaching undergraduates who have grown up with short, snappy vignettes on *Sesame Street*; and that even in the popular culture, we hear truncated symphonies on the radio and read novels with shorter chapters and shorter total length (although there is a renaissance of public interest in lengthy novels such as *Lord of the Rings* by J. R. R. Tolkien, the *Harry Potter* series by J. K. Rowling, and other epics). I believe that this is a reflection of social and cultural change, in which both children and adults often lead busy, overscheduled lives, possibly resulting in shortened attention spans. Also, the dominant influence of television and computer screens might encourage students to become visual learners, and point to the benefit of including graphics in the online classes. What is interesting to speculate upon, however, is the impact of seeing written text. Although the text is not a graphic, it is seen rather than heard. Quite possibly this has appeal to visual learners, by helping them to see the information rather than hear it, especially for students who have a photographic memory and can usually remember where certain words appear on the screen. Perhaps, contrary to the popular belief about the visual deprivation of the online class due to the lack of usual cues of the traditional classroom, there is for some people a different and incredibly effective visual component of seeing the written word.

Debate continues about how the Web has impacted our concentration span. An article by the *BBC Sci/Tech News* titled "Turning into Digital Goldfish" (2002) claims that most people click so rapidly through different Web sites, pausing only as much as nine seconds before clicking on to the next, that they have the attention span of a goldfish. This behavior indicates a feeling that the best is yet to come, that there is something just beyond reach that is ready to be discovered.

This points to the need to design and facilitate an online class in such a way as to grab a student's attention, and retain it. Nik Halton's comment on the *BBC Sci/Tech News* interactive Web site is of particular interest: "I don't think the web is lowering concentration spans, just changing the nature of concentration used. With the ability to multi-task, looking at many sites at the same time, web users need to be able to hold parallel strands of narrative simultaneously, not just one. In this regard, it is no worse for concentration spans than a book or theatrical production which runs several plot lines concurrently." If this is indeed true, it has important implications for the online class, in which it might be possible to hold two discussion forums simultaneously, as well as other class activities such as visiting a relevant Web site or holding a group discussion in preparation for a presentation. (See Chapter 4 for a fuller look at the implications of multitasking.)

Information is likely to be more deeply processed and comprehension will be helped if, as in the traditional classroom, the most important information is repeated in different ways to accommodate different learning styles, not so that it feels boring and redundant, but so that it can be explored from different angles and truly comprehended. Boettcher (1999), for example, cites Stephen Hawking's book, *A Brief History of Time*, in which one reviewer commented that he knew what all the words actually meant individually, but in aggregate, he could not follow the text at all. Thus this reviewer could only see the symbols (words) representing the concept, yet had no access to the concept itself.

To avoid an equivalent lack of comprehension about material taught in the online class, it might be necessary to not only give alternative written explanations, but to also perhaps insert graphics or a sound or video clip where possible. A variety of learning activities also stimulates learning and helps to keep students attentive.

In the case of the hybrid class, students can log on to their computer after the campus class to watch, read, or hear parts of the class again, which may be useful to them if, in an effort to write it all down, they missed certain portions of the information. Despite the fact that some people worried that this online availability would encourage students to skip class on campus, the rate of absenteeism was no higher in hybrid classes than any other class on campus (Cabell, 1999). Some teachers of hybrid classes, however, prefer for the online component not to merely duplicate the campus class, but to enhance it by offering something more, and I most definitely agree with this view. For instance, the same information taught on campus could be presented in a different way, or have an entirely different learning activity associated with it. Examples include allowing for discussions that took place in the campus class to be continued online, or the online environment could be used to prepare for a debate or role-playing that could take place on campus. (See Chapter 8, "Innovative Online Teaching Techniques.") These kinds of reinforcement, I think, assist both in attention and retention.

Impact of Constant Information Availability and Asynchronicity on Memory

Memory is the first building block of learning. We talked earlier of the advantages of constructing knowledge and establishing meaning by associating new information with existing concepts stored in long-term memory. It is important to bear in mind that short-term memory can be affected by time, and as Levine (2002) points out, a new piece of information can erase a previously known fact, if it succeeds it too quickly. In fact, Levine is concerned that in the act of moving from one class immediately to another on campus, some information from the previous class might be blotted out.

This points to an argument in favor of the online class, in which each participant can become absorbed and work hopefully without interruptions, and have sufficient time for the information to be fully comprehended. If this is so, it is more likely to stay in the mind for much longer. Furthermore, whereas the campus class meetings are at discrete intervals throughout the weeks, necessitating starting each new class by reviewing what had been covered in the previous class, the steady flow of information through online discussion, I think, assists learners in terms of holding their attention and helping them to retain this information.

The Significance of Active Learning on Knowledge Acquisition

For a thorough acquisition of knowledge, it is vital to have discussion about topics learned, which can be conducted effectively online, whether the class is a hybrid or is conducted entirely in cyberspace. Frequent feedback is helpful in letting students know how they are doing and in maintaining their motivation. The feedback must be encouraging so that it stresses the positive aspects of the student's achievement before mentioning suggestions for improvement, as this reinforcement further increases motivation. Positive feedback is especially important online, where tone of voice and facial expression are absent, so that critical words can come across sounding more harsh than intended (see Part Two).

In this way, the online teacher is concerned with personalizing education and thus is responsive to each individual student. Knowledge, Boettcher (1999) states, has the most chance of flourishing in an environment that is rich, supportive, encouraging, and enthusiastic. Students can pool their knowledge and learn new concepts, and feel safe admitting if they are confused. Admission of confusion is often a ripe launching point, if a new explanation is given, for the student to hopefully experience the wonderful feeling of pure insight and clarity, as the new concept makes sense and becomes meaningful.

The Importance of Awareness of Student Needs and Differing Abilities

In a fully online class, it is only through online discussion that the instructor can come to know the students, and know how they think. Online discussion might shed light on difficulties faced by a student for whom English is not the first language, or even on students with learning disabilities. Dyslexia, for example, could make the online class a perplexing place, and problems with written expression might inhibit the student from fully participating.

Not knowing this about the student might lead the instructor to erroneously conclude that the student is not paying attention or is being lax about conforming to the minimum participation requirement. Becoming acquainted with one's students through online discussion might also inform the instructor that students are from different disciplinary backgrounds or that they have varying skills and interests.

It is in your students' interest, as much as is feasible, to be attentive to their particular needs. If you decide to adapt your class to match the array of cognitive styles among your students, you could do so either by varying your teaching style, enhancing your instructional materials, or both (Liu and Ginther, 1999). If you vary your teaching style, it is probably a good idea in any case, even before knowing the strengths and weaknesses of your students, to aim to provide a mix of cooperative and individual learning, both of which can be done effectively online. Individual learning can include research papers or essays, whereas cooperative learning can embrace general discussion as well as group learning of varying kinds.

In terms of enhancing your instructional materials, on the other hand, this might simply mean that if you know about other courses students are taking or know their career goals, then you could provide examples or reinforcement, within the context of the material you are teaching, that are specific to their other interests and long-term goals. It might also mean providing more diagrams alongside the written lectures, if you are aware that you have some students who are visual learners. Nowadays there are many new Web applications that can be used to suit many of the learning styles mentioned by Howard Gardner (see "Student Characteristics: Intelligence" in Chapter 2). For example, for the visual learners, there are Mind Mapping programs such as bubbl.us, which can chart thoughts in a colorful format that can then be embedded in blogs or Web sites or sent as e-mails, and Thinkature, which allows for real-time collaboration on flow charts, diagrams, and even free-hand drawings. Also for the visual learners, videos and photos can be shared by programs such as Google's Picassa; the social networking site Flickr, which allows for posting photos and images to share with the class or to reinforce some notes taken; or Jing, which enables screenshots to be taken of the desktop and then e-mailed.

Similarly, for auditory learners, there are podcasts such as Moodle, which allows sharing of the podcast with the online class, and First Class, which is a collaborative podcast publishing feature. There are audio tools such as Audacity, which enable the user to listen to or edit sounds or music. Students who understand better when text is read out loud can use audio books produced by companies such as LibriVox and Project Gutenberg.

Kinesthetic learners, who do best when they interact with or touch objects, can even learn well online now too, as they can use programs such as Google Docs for taking notes and collaborating online with peers; Quia for creating one's own educational games or quizzes and sending them to others; and of course Facebook for interacting with others, chatting about assignments, posting links to Web sites and videos or photos, and much more. (See throughout the book many specific examples of ways in which Facebook can be used in online education.)

Factors That Work against Knowledge Acquisition and Feeling of Community

Many factors could either enhance knowledge acquisition through online discussion or act as a deterrent. It is crucial to personalize the teaching approach, give frequent and encouraging feedback, and establish a good sense of camaraderie in the online class (see Chapter 2). Some conditions, however, can work against the potential for the acquisition of knowledge and a feeling of community. This can also be true for the campus class. On campus, for example, we know that the potential to process information can be severely reduced if more than one person speaks at a time, or if a session lasts beyond a student's attention span.

What are the deterrents to knowledge acquired online? One is the feeling of being overwhelmed, brought on by an excessive number of online responses, lectures or responses that are too long to be easily digestible, or numerous responsibilities outside the class. This might lead to the situation in which some students might not read everything that is contributed to the discussion, as it might seem an excessive amount. Perhaps one can argue that they are being selective, but they might be leaving out the most pertinent points.

A second deterrent involves technical difficulties, without timely and helpful technical support. Students benefit if, at the start of the online class, they take an orientation to learn how to navigate around the class, submit assignments, download from the Web, and so on. During the class, however, the student who experiences technical difficulties can feel panic or frustration. Some technical difficulties might affect the whole class, such as the server going down or a frequent generation of error messages. In this case, the instructor can reassure the class by changing due dates of submissions and empathizing with the expressed frustrations. If an individual student experiences frustrations of being unable to access the class or post responses, then the student should inform the instructor. If the excuse is legitimate and not a cyberversion of "the dog ate my homework," then some latitude should be given.

The Impact of Nonlinear Learning

No study of online learning theory is complete without considering the impact of nonlinear learning. In the campus class, students are used to learning chronologically in a linear progression through time. In contrast, the online class might have the potential for nonlinear learning because it is an asynchronous environment and because of the layout of the discussion threads. There is a very real consequence of the way the discussion responses are displayed, and this varies with the different software programs. If the responses are laid out in a chronological fashion, I feel this would be more likely to lead to linear thought, as the discussion progresses along a linear time line. But many software programs have a threaded discussion, which means that messages are attached to the comments to which they are responding. This leads to a pattern in which responses are distributed thematically, not chronologically. Time, the great organizer, is now out of the equation, and we all have the possibility of dipping in and out of topics. This might be confusing to some, but liberating for others.

Online teaching might also lead to nonlinearity if hypertext is used. Hypertext fiction, for example, breaks free of the two-dimensional constraints of the printed page, and can lead off, by clicking on links, in many possible directions within a three-dimensional universe through a veritable cyberspatial labyrinth. The same applies to clicking on Web sites, whose links often lead to more Web sites, and then yet more. I think the question arises as to just how much clicking we should invite our students to do, before they become too disorientated, too dizzy, too remote from the place that is their online class.

The most interesting challenge about the existence of nonlinear learning in the online class is whether this is reflective of how our minds work and how our memory functions. Do we actually make mental leaps and start new threads within our thought processes when jolted by associations? Or, in our thinking, do we tunnel deeper and deeper along the same channel? Furthermore, just because technology makes nonlinear learning feasible, is it always desirable? Could it result in students each working independently, immersed in their own thought paths, and tackling questions and becoming excited by concepts at different rates and in different places from each other? If so, how can an instructor hold a cohesive class and encourage meaningful communication and the social construction of knowledge between and among all members of the class? Also, does it not depend on the subject matter being taught because are there not some disciplines in which knowledge and understanding has to be accumulated sequentially? Could a student, for example, understand gravitational theory without first having a good grasp on how to calculate equations? Is the acquisition of knowledge all about building on what one has known before in a strictly linear fashion?

In turn, however, is this steady, linear acquisition of learning and knowledge overemphasizing the need for familiarity and comfort? I wonder whether it might be true to say that one needs some discomfort, some agitation, some tension to be challenged, to be creative, to find new thought pathways. I am a great admirer of Edward de Bono, who talked about paradigms of knowledge. He believed in the importance of creative lateral, not linear, thinking; of leaping out of the deep, linear hole of one paradigm to start a new paradigm elsewhere; and of thinking about a problem in a fresh, innovative way.

My personal feeling is that it is important to have a blend between linear thinking and lateral leaps into a new area where a new strand of linear thought can begin. I believe that the online environment can provide scope for both linear and lateral thought, but this is an enormous task and a dual role for the online instructor. The online instructor should allow for freedom within learning to make concepts meaningful, realizing that this can often be brought about by nonlinear, associative means. The instructor also must be a great facilitator in pulling together disparate strands of conversations, expertly weaving the different threads of expressed thought to make a cohesive body of knowledge, which can move forward in a linear fashion until it naturally starts to branch out again. This, I believe, leads to meaningful learning, as well as richness and diversity of thought and discussion. More about the possible impacts of technology on our thinking and learning are discussed in the next chapter, "Paradigm Lost."

4

PARADIGM LOST

The mind is its own place, and in itself
Can make a heav'n of hell, a hell of heav'n.

—Milton, *Paradise Lost,* 1:254–255

The New Digital Media and Its Impact on Contemporary Education

We are all familiar now with what is becoming a fairly typical scene around a family dinner table in which, rather than speaking with each other, the adolescents are looking at their iPhones or Androids to send texts or use Facebook; the father is checking e-mails on his laptop or iPad; and the mother, having pulled the pizza from the microwave and distributed it on plastic plates, is speaking to someone on her cell phone.

Facebook and Twitter are social networking sites that are particularly popular. I devote specific attention to these sites to see how they can be integrated into discussion-based online education. Facebook is a social networking site originally designed for college students that now accepts anyone over the age of 13. Its users can create and customize their own profiles with information about themselves, including photos and videos. Each profile has a "timeline," with the option of strict privacy settings so as to limit access to friends only. Friends can post comments on each other's timelines, implying that those conversations are fairly public (visible to all the permitted "friends"). But Facebook also provides the option to post private messages, much as e-mails, if the participants wish to do so. Facebook also has the ability to add Web applications, such as news feeds and others, which are discussed later in this book.

Twitter is a program that only allows for 140 characters per message or "tweet," posted to the Web via a browser or cell phone in a streamlined feed, with the most recent tweet on top of the list. Although Thompson said in

37

2008 that Twitter seemed like "modern narcissism taken to a new, supermetabolic extreme—the ultimate expression of a generation of celebrity-addled youths who believe their every utterance is fascinating" (n.p.), he went on to say that despite the fact that each tweet deals with minutia, and when taken alone seems rather "insignificant and mundane," they do coalesce over time to create an understanding of the rhythm of people's lives. As Thompson concluded, the flow of multitudes of tweets was ultimately equivalent to "the thousands of dots making a pointillist painting" (n.p.). The constancy of these updates, he felt, was intriguing and addictive, giving rise to what is called "ambient awareness," which is the same as being physically close to someone and being peripherally aware of his or her every sigh, yawn, stretch, and smile. Having such constant awareness of another person almost gives one a telepathic sense of what that person is doing (Thompson, 2007). Thompson concluded that this is the social equivalent of proprioception (your body's ability to know where your limbs are), but in this context it is knowing where your friends are and what they are doing.

However, Turkle does not seem to value social media very highly, as seen in her application of the Shakespeare quotation that "'We are consumed by that which we are nourished by'" (*Digital Nation,* 2010). Is this indeed true in the case of the impact of these new technologies on social behavior? And more importantly in the context of this book, because teaching and learning are essentially based on communication, what impact might these changed societal styles of communicating with others have on contemporary education? Furthermore, what might be the potential behind employing some of these digital media for the purpose of teaching? Might they be able to meaningfully enhance education? Throughout this book we look at certain ways in which Facebook, Twitter, and other digital media can be used in education, and investigate whether these powerful means of communication can provide students with opportunities to gather, collect, assimilate, and construct a shared understanding.

One of my students in my hybrid expository writing class in the fall 2010 semester put it very well when she said,

> This hybrid course itself is a very obvious manifestation of the growing significance of technology in the academic world and the lives of students as a whole. We all had different reasons for choosing to take the hybrid course, whether because we're on the computer a lot anyway or it seemed novel or it just happened to fit into our schedule, but I don't think any of

us can say that we didn't mold to it pretty much immediately. As a generation, we're very comfortable with technology and the Internet; using them in our education seems natural.

I think my student represents very well the view of many undergraduates in terms of their comfort in using technology within their classes. But what are the consequences of using these new digital media on teaching and learning? This is explored by looking at the following criteria:

- Alteration of interpersonal relationships within online settings
- The influence of connectivity on one's frame of mind
- Changes in the style of reading and the pursuit of knowledge
- Whether digital media can change the way we think
- Changes in the style of writing and the expression of knowledge
- Multitasking
- The impact of video games

Alteration of Interpersonal Relationships within Online Settings

When we interact with others online, we all appear as names on a screen, implying that there is a flattening-out of rank among online participants. This is clearly fine when texting friends or interacting with them on Facebook. But what about the online interactions within an online class? Aboujaoude, a practicing psychiatrist of Internet-related disorders at Stanford, refers to

> the dissolution of offline hierarchical relationships . . . be they child-parent, student-teacher, patient-doctor, or layman-expert. Hailed by many as the "great equalizer," the Internet is a societal leveler the likes of which humankind has never seen before. . . . [H]owever, one can say that there has been a downside to this "Athens without slaves," as Rheingold called it. A lack of boundaries between groups online has led to situations that challenge the utopian version of democracy, as everybody feels equally informed and qualified. (2011, pp. 198–199)

This indeed could challenge the role of the teacher, who appears, like everyone else in the online class, as just another name on the screen.

This concern could be particularly pertinent for classes that incorporate Facebook as a learning tool because of the term *friend*. On Facebook, anyone who contacts another is a friend, but this is a questionable term to use for a teacher-student relationship. Runyon (2009) quotes Aristotle as saying that there are three types of friendship: one is grounded in *virtue,* implying wishing well for another and without the expectation of reciprocation; another is friendship based on *utility,* as in a business contact; and the third form of friendship is *pleasure,* usually involving enjoyment and possibly sex. Perhaps the teacher could be thought of as a friend from the virtue standpoint because the teacher imparts knowledge to students without expecting anything back, and the student could be thought of as a friend in terms of utility because the student gains useful information. But it seems to me best to discard the notion of friendship altogether; teachers are often in a reciprocal relationship with students, sometimes also learning from them, and also gaining in return the joy of seeing students learn and grow intellectually. In other words, then, teachers might expect some reward out of the teaching relationship (unless it can be argued that virtue is its own reward), so from that point of view it seems inaccurate to categorize this as a virtuous friendship. Thus if Facebook is used as an online teaching and learning tool, I think it is appropriate to change the terms from *friend* to *student* and *teacher* if possible.

To address the fear that the teacher's authority might crumble in the face of digital technology, perhaps a hybrid class might be better than a completely online class for undergraduates. Their campus visits serve as a reminder of who their teacher is and gives the teacher an opportunity to regain any respect for his or her knowledge and rank that might have been inadvertently ironed out when communicating online.

An alternative and equally credible interpretation, however, as I mention in Chapter 7, under the section "The Socratic Method: Establish a Circle of Learning," is that if students are less intimidated because of a lack of hierarchy online, this could encourage them to participate more fully in online discussions in an interactive and collaborative way than they might do in the campus class. Seen in this way, the online democratization of all participants, be they teachers or students, could be very beneficial indeed. Aboujaoude (2011) sees the Internet as a great disinhibiter, as people often participate much more when they feel invisible, a point that is mentioned in Chapter 7 of this book ("Aspects of Online Communication"). However, Aboujaoude sees this as a negative because he feels that the invisibility factor prompts people to adopt a personality other than their own: "Having an e-personality that seems freer and more resilient can offer a welcome break from the tensions and inhibitions of our real circumstances" (p. 23). But, he warns, this can come at a price: "The cost of feeling too powerful or having too much fun online is typically felt away from the screen, in the form of tension at home, as when new Facebook friends start taking too much time away from family . . . or distraction in the classroom, because the pace of our online activities has compromised our attention span" (p. 23).

I believe that Aboujaoude (2011) makes fascinating and verifiable points; however, I also feel that our overt behavior has always had a tendency to fluctuate according to contexts and situations, and not only the situation of communicating online. I behave differently, for example, when I open the door to the gas man who has come to read my meter than when I am teaching my class than when I am with particular friends. And as for online students, I do not think they will alter their personality in an online class just because they are online, as I think the context of the academic milieu takes precedence over the fact that learning takes place through the Internet. Also, when teaching a hybrid, I start the semester by conducting a particular exercise with the students so as to seamlessly join the campus class with its online component, so that students all become well acquainted and therefore comfortable communicating with each other (see "Getting to Know Each Other in a Hybrid" in Chapter 6). I strongly believe that the fact that students might feel "disinhibited" and therefore more responsive online is beneficial because, as we know, active participation is key to a good learning environment. As one of my hybrid students remarked, "I personally am more comfortable talking online because I tend to be a bit shy. . . . I feel as if . . . the Internet allows people to say things they might otherwise not have the courage to say in person." She, and the others in the class, participated fully and richly in all the discussion forums.

The Influence of Connectivity on One's Frame of Mind

Whether or not we believe social media makes members of the iGeneration happier, lonelier, more connected, or more powerful (and many different views are expressed later in this text), our main inquiry here is the impact that this changed frame of mind might have on receptivity to learning if education is conducted by some means of discussion-based online teaching. I think this goes beyond making a choice as to whether to employ various digital media just because they might be familiar to students, as instead we should be focusing on the very aspect of emotional outcome generated by their use. Learning is very much an affective process; generally, the happier and more excited a student is, the more that student will become engaged and consequently the better he or she will learn. Of course, we certainly cannot generalize about emotions with any accuracy, as these will all be individually based, but we can infer from broad trends, based on frequency of usage, that members of the iGeneration seem to enjoy the social media that surrounds them.

Returning to the family dinner scene described previously in which the family does not interact with those sharing the same physical space, one wonders whether this is much different from the "olden days" in which some families, rather than congregating around the dinner table, ate TV dinners while watching television. As Gopnik (2011) reminds us, in the 1970s many used to lament TV addiction. Even *The Simpsons* TV show always starts with an ironic image of the questionably happy family all sitting staring at the TV set in front of them. Perhaps, Gopnik suggests, the past evil of the TV "was not because of its essence but its omnipresence," and maybe the same can now be said about the Internet.

Essentially, however, the question comes down to whether, as a result of these new technologies, we are all now more in touch, more connected with more people than has ever been previously possible. One student in my class perceptively remarked, with reference to the PBS Frontline documentary *Digital Nation* (2010),

> All the children presented, even cross-culturally, seemed to be extremely involved in themselves and their technology . . . overall interaction with one another seemed to also be pretty much absent. The focus instead was student and computer, student and cell phone, student and gaming. Parent and child, friend and friend, sibling and sibling, even teacher and student seemed to be altered off our typical norm.

This remark, given by a student in the very generation of which we speak, indicates her own incredulity at seeing children and teenagers in contemporary society, as shown in the documentary, seemingly so connected to each other but in actuality quite isolated from the very people with whom they share a dining room table.

Yes, technology can instantly connect us with people and information all over the world, but are the connections with people true emotional attachments? Lanier thinks not, when he warns that "widespread practice of fragmentary, impersonal communication has demeaned interpersonal interaction" (2010, p. 4). Has the use of digital technology now become something of a Pandora's Box? Are adolescents afraid to disconnect not only because they might constantly wonder what they are missing, but also because they fear that others might be angry with them if they do not respond immediately? Many of us have perhaps questioned how it is possible, as Facebook enables, to have so many "friends." It might be argued that being able to connect electronically is beneficial for many people, especially those who are shy, as this digital technology might even provide the means of breaking down communication barriers. However, as Turkle says, this might only be creating the illusion of companionship without the true demands of genuine friendship. Perhaps, however, this might not matter to the iGeneration, who might harbor such a fear of being disconnected that they might even imagine a phantom ring of their cell phone (*Digital Nation,* 2010).

All this has led to what Powers terms "Digital Maximalism" (2010). He cites a teen in California who sends 300,000 text messages a month. Being so connected, Powers feels, makes us rely on others to tell us how to think, which leads to a struggle to reconcile the inner private self with the outer social self. Do we want a world, he asks, in which we are all staring at a screen all the time? Certainly he understands that the technology of a cell phone has more appeal than the technology of a vacuum cleaner, as the former has the excitement of interacting with others (and performing many other apps as well), but when these come so fast and so indiscriminately, do we have time to savor each message inwardly? Also, is the timing of the message sent or received always appropriate for the circumstance the person is currently inhabiting? After all, he says, many take their cell phones to bed with them, to a restaurant, on a walk, on vacation. And we perhaps have heard stories of people answering a call on their cell phone during a job interview.

When we are connected, there is a feeling of "compulsory, needy outwardness" (Powers, 2010, p. 47), a reassurance to the questions "Who needs me?" and "Who is writing to me?" This brings with it the exclusion of an inner self-reliance, a sustained inner thinking of a deeper nature. And here Powers quotes from the philosopher, Paul Tillich, who pointed out the difference between loneliness, which feels miserable, and solitude, which is the glory of being alone (Powers, 2010, p. 42). After all, as Powers points out, "Some information is like wine; it gets better if you let it rest a while" (p. 48). Turkle agrees with this point, saying that "loneliness is failed solitude" (*Digital Nation,* 2010) because there is intellectual and emotional value in being alone. Loneliness only sets in, she says, if we forget to use solitude to replenish our self-esteem. Thus she thinks that adolescents who feel they must be connected to prevent loneliness are taking an unhealthy psychological approach to their lives. As a student in my hybrid class realized, "People get addicted and hooked on their cell phones, computer games, TV, Internet, and become more isolated. In a sense, they are isolating themselves from society by using a tool that is seen as necessary to fit into society."

And do we need not only time, but also proximity, for meaningful connections? As long ago as 1979, AT&T ran the famous "Reach Out and Touch Someone" commercial (http://www.porticus.org/bell/bellsystem_ads-1.html) in an effort to encourage people to make more long-distance phone calls (this was before the days of cell phones), showing, among other situations, a clip of a man on a business trip calling his family. But even in those days, it struck me that a phone call, however nice, could not be a true substitute for being physically there, reading a story to a child and giving a cuddle before bedtime. How much more, then, is this the case now?

Connection and open communication are crucial to good education. But, as I say in Chapter 1 in the section "Distinguishing between Physical Distance and Transactional Distance," we do not necessarily need to be sitting physically close together to have meaningful discussions and for learning to take place. Online discussions can provide open and free opportunities for active participation for all students, as well as ample opportunities for them to collaborate. Therefore it seems that many social media applications, if wisely used, could be beneficial for educational purposes. And, as is shown throughout this book, there are many social media, such as Skype, that also permit participants to see each other and speak in "real time" over the Internet, which could be useful if a particular skill needs to be demonstrated. As Gopnik states when describing the thinking of those who are very supportive of the potential of the Internet (whom he calls the "Never Betters"), the Internet has enabled not so much a global village (which he sees as the result of TV), but a global *psyche* because we can all be keyed in to one place and benefit from the knowledge expounded by many brains.

Changes in the Style of Reading and the Pursuit of Knowledge

A behavioral change brought about by the new Web applications is the way in which many people read. Carr (2008), although acknowledging the benefits of the Web in terms of rapid access to information, says that we "take in information the way the Net distributes it: in a swiftly moving stream of particles" (p. 57). He says that the technique of deep reading has been replaced for many by a more rapid skimming and hopping from one online site to another, a type of "power browse," a term Carr quotes from a study by scholars at University College London. As Carr says of his own experience, "Once I was a scuba diver in the sea of words. Now I zip along the surface like a guy on a Jet Ski" (p. 57).

Carr quotes Wolf, a developmental psychologist, who agrees with this view, remarking, "[W]e are not only *what* we read. . . . We are *how* we read" (2007, p. 58). Here she is referring to how, when online, many of us quickly flip from one site to another. She thinks this deprives us of the time for sustained deep thinking, thus limiting our ability to analyze and make profound mental connections. So, even though the Internet gives us rapid access to huge amounts of information that we can share with others online, the deep linear and logical thinking that we had developed from reading books has been replaced with quick jumping around between sites. Aboujaoude (2011) reports on studies done on eye tracking of Internet users, which find that a typical online reader reads in an "F" shape, reading all the way along the first line of text, moving down and reading half way along a line of text further down, and then scrolling down to the end. He thinks that this shows that Internet readers "scan and forage," especially because of the competition between Web sites. Aboujaoude says, "Words: We have lost patience for their complexity . . . and do not think of them as something to capture and hold on to anymore" (p. 190).

In fact, Carr (2008) interestingly applies Frederick Winslow Taylor's stopwatch method of automated factory efficiency via the technique of the conveyor belt to the storage and retrieval of information on the Internet, with special reference to search engines. Carr states,

> And now . . . Taylor's ethic is beginning to govern the realm of the mind
> as well. The Internet is a machine designed for the efficient and automated
> collection, transmission, and manipulation of information, and its legions
> of programmers are intent on finding the "one best method"—the perfect
> algorithm—to carry out every mental movement of what we've come to
> describe as "knowledge work." (2008, p. 62)

However, Peter Norvig, Google Research Director, disagrees with the "Taylorism" analogy (Anderson and Rainie, 2010), saying that Taylor's factory conveyor belts shifted responsibility from the workers to the management, whereas Google gives full responsibility to the "knowledge workers" to be creative with the information that they discover online. I agree with Norvig, and feel that Carr has overgeneralized; certainly Carr's view of skimming meaninglessly over an abundance of facts and collecting little is true for some, but is certainly not true for many in education, who know more precisely what it is they are researching.

But there are definitely some students who, if using a search engine—which will probably be Google—to research some information, might not know how to determine the good, reliable information from information that is inaccurate. As Gardner says, "[I]f we consider the welter of information and misinformation available on any search engine, how can we possibly determine what is true, or even whether the *search* for the truth has become a fool's errand" (2011, p. 7)? He also warns of the danger of truth being determined by the consensus of a crowd rather than the judgment of an expert, as when he says,

> Or if we were to cede all judgments to the digital media—if we posited that the truth is nothing more than a majority vote on a webpage, or believed that the most recent edit of an online encyclopedia is more definitive than the accumulated judgments of experts—we would be relinquishing considered judgment to the whim of the crowd (or to the web-surfers with the most time on their hands). (p. 20)

Gardner is concerned by the ease of posting anything on the Internet, bereft as it could be of scholarly peer review or publishers' scrutiny. Bauerlein shares these concerns and cites studies of decreased academic achievement when teaching with technology. He says, "The ETS and EDUCAUSE results, purveyed by organizations that favor technology in the classrooms, belie the high-flying forecasts of digitally inspired dexterity and intelligence. Students can image and browse and post and play, but they can't judge the materials they process, at least not in the intellectual or professional terms of college classes" (2008, p. 115). Aboujaoude agrees, eloquently stating,

> [W]hat an appropriate word—*surfing*—to capture the horizontal process of gaining knowledge on the Web. . . . One glides, barely scratching the surface, atop mountains of information, with no easy way to sift the good from the bad, often finding amid the detritus whatever evidence one needs to confirm a preconceived opinion already made. . . . We trust the search engine to present information in the right hierarchy of importance and relevance . . . blinded to any motives Google might have for assigning its rankings. Independent sifting, like independent thinking, takes a backseat. (2011, p. 207)

Gardner does say, however, that at times he is optimistic about the "democratic nirvana" of the Web, but he asks if we can "survey widely, synthesize wisely, and converge on what has actually happened?" (2011, p. 31) and this is exactly where the role of the teacher as an expert in the discipline being taught is so crucial to students in helping them to differentiate among sources of information. (See "Guidelines for Students Doing Web Research" in Chapter 8.) The potential is there for gaining more and possibly even better information than in the predigital age, but, once more quoting Gardner, "any educator working with adolescents must think constantly about how best to use the digital media, and how, as it were, to reinvent the methods of establishing truth, so that they will be clear to the 'digital natives'" (p. 153). The Pew Internet and American Life Project (Anderson and Rainie, 2010) agrees, saying that of course if a person is lazy, he or she will only look at the first few Google hits and will be easily distracted, but an intelligent Internet user will be motivated to learn in exciting new ways. They say this has always been the case; clever people discover and read clever things, and the less intelligent are content with shoddy and superficial material, thus showing that it is not the digital revolution that is the culprit.

I agree with this assertion. And so, apparently, does Gopnik (2011) when he says that there have always been outcries when there have been technological revolutions, with many despairing cries that the world has become a fractured place. But he concludes by saying, "If all you have is a hammer . . . everything looks like a nail; and if you think the world is broken, every machine will look like the hammer that broke it" (p. 3). Less engaged students will display "satisficing" behavior, meaning they will be quickly satisfied with very few hits in a Google search, even if this does not reach the more rigorously discovered and pertinent information on a particular topic. Yes, it is true that it could be hard to distinguish between good information and information that is without value, but there has always been exposure to some misleading or inaccurate information in the media. What it takes is asking the right questions and being trained in online literacy. There could even be a new way of being thought "smart," which could imply an ability to retrieve quality information and know how to use it in a meaningful way.

This might imply that sound education might now be rethought in such a way as to decide that it is feasible to claim that students actually don't *need* to memorize information, as the Internet has become our digital memory. Problems could arise, however, if there are teachers who do not share this view. Forni (2008), for example, says teachers value *knowledge retention,* which forms the building blocks for knowledge formation, whereas students value *knowledge retrieval* of what exists online, which, by virtue of its online presence, does not need to be memorized. And because of this divergent view, students might feel bored and frustrated in class, and might not appreciate being graded according to the traditional standards of knowledge they have remembered. In my opinion, good teaching involves more than just knowledge retention, as it also involves all the higher levels of Bloom's taxonomy, including application, analysis, and evaluation. This can be gained by encouraging students to make connections with prior knowledge, and then question and think critically about the information learned or retrieved online. Perhaps it could be hypothesized that not having to memorize information could free the mind to do other things, such as analyze and synthesize information.

Can Digital Media Change the Way We Think?

There has long been discussion as to whether the medium through which a message is transmitted can change the nature of that message itself. In other words, does the *method* by which we receive information affect both our comprehension and retention of that knowledge? Marshall McLuhan thought it did; in 1964 he stated his now-famous adage, "[T]he medium is the message" (WNYC, 2011). McLuhan was convinced that the medium alters patterns of perception. Or is the means of transporting information— whether by phone, book, radio, television, or Internet—invisible, as the primary focus is on the *content* of that information and not the way by which it was received? McLuhan thought not; he stated that the content is just "a juicy piece of meat carried by the burglar to distract the watchdog of the mind" (as quoted by Carr, 2010).

Lanier (2010) seems to agree with McLuhan's thinking; he bemoans the fact that the digital revolution leads to a pack mentality, what he calls the "hive mind," thus decreasing the uniqueness of the individual human voice. He calls for a "new digital humanism" before we get completely locked into these new modes of electronic communication. Just as the building of railroads, he argues, locked us in to a mode of travel, so too might the Taylorism of software design, as mentioned previously, channel us permanently into a distinct and lasting mode of interaction. As to whether this locked-in state is good, Lanier says, "[T]he corresponding philosophies of how humans can express meaning have been so ingrained into the interlocked software designs of the Internet that we might never be able to fully get rid of them, or even remember that things could have been different" (p. 13). He feels that the Internet has gone sour, saying that "the idea that a collective consciousness emerges from all the users on the web, echo Marxist social determinism and Freud's calculus of perversion" (p. 18). He worries that the loss of individuality on the Web could lead to bad, moblike behavior, a sort of *Lord of the Flies* disordering of society, in which harmful views, which would normally dissipate, would gather momentum on the Web and become reinforced to the extreme. However, Lanier should perhaps be reminded that some people feared the printing of books because they could also be used to spread dangerous opinions, leading to such things as anti-Semitism and other types of religious warfare (Gopnik, 2011). But Lanier considers the online world as a pseudoworld in which participants encourage their Peter Pan fantasies of being an entitled child forever, without the responsibilities of becoming an adult, and in which emotional responses weigh more heavily than intellectual ones, thus encouraging subjectivity and the proliferation of trivia (Kakutani, 2010).

But why should the method by which we receive information alter the way we think about it? I think the answer to this can be provided by neuroscience, which stipulates that our brains have immense powers of "neuroplasticity": they can change according to need and circumstance. It used to be believed that the brain only changed during childhood, and that in adulthood the form and structure of the brain was fixed and concrete. However, experiments by Merzenich in the 1960s with adult monkeys' brains showed that adult brains do change. Merzenich severed the nerve endings in the monkeys' hands, which first caused the monkeys to think sensations were coming from the other hand, but after a few months, there was no more confusion (Carr, 2010). This suggested that the brain can indeed reprogram itself, as its cellular components are not rigidly fixed. As Carr says, "We become neurologically what we think" (p. 33). So now it is believed that the way we experience information that is being delivered in rapid abundance via the new digital technologies is impacting the brains especially of the young, giving them the ability to quickly shift from one task to another.

Wolf (2007) points out that reading is not an instinctive skill (unlike speaking), and this very act of learning how to read provides in fact great evidence for the fact that the brain can rearrange its circuits and pathways, and this in turn leads to preparing the foundation for being able to think in innovative ways beyond the text itself. According to Wolf, reading books results in an expansion of the cortical region of the brain, which facilitates an increase in inference, analysis, and critical evaluation. But now, with increased electronic delivery of information, it could well be that this digital revolution is impacting our ways of thinking in new ways. Wolf asks whether deep reflection and imaginative pondering might all seem a bit anachronistic to the young. Gopnik amusingly points out that the first *Harry Potter* book, which was published in 1997 one year before Google was created, described the studious Hermione frequently reading through books in the library stacks; Gopnik says this might prompt many young readers to ask why she is trying to find information that way. In fact, Carr says that just as cartographers changed how we understand spatial distributions and clocks changed how we understand temporal distributions, so now, it seems, has the Internet reprogrammed the brain and the consequent way we think. However, having access to libraries did not make us any more stupid, as Socrates had feared. Nor did having a calculator make us any more stupid than our grandparents; however, our adoption of calculators indicates how our brains have changed to make use of these devices (Anderson and Rainie, 2010). So, yes, our brains might have changed because of the Internet, but this does not necessarily mean they have changed for the worse.

Even so, Wolf questions the value of the "power browse," as she speaks about how "in music, in poetry, and in life, the rest, the pause, the slow movement are essential to comprehending the whole" (2007, p. 213). She says there are "delay neurons" that slow down neuronal transmission by a few milliseconds, but that are, nonetheless, essential for allowing us to comprehend order and sequence, and that give us the ability to anticipate. Will reading information online, therefore, lead to less critical thinking because thinking takes time? Wolf wonders, "Will the split-second immediacy of information gained from a search engine and the sheer volume of what is available derail the slower, more deliberative processes that deepen our understanding of complex concepts, of another's inner thought processes, and of our own consciousness" (p. 221)? Menzies (2005) is of a similar opinion. She interviewed the poet and educator, Solway, who, in reference to the "cybernetic milieu," stated, " 'It's the great video arcade of time. . . . Everything glittering in the moment. But the glitter is encapsulated in the immediate, in what Yeats called the 'glance.' Everything is a function of glances, as opposed to the gaze, which lingers. . . . [With the glance] we only perceive instantly and then forget as we move on to the next glance' " (Menzies, 2005, p. 189).

I have discussed in Chapter 3, in the section "Self-Regulating and Reinforcing Long-Term Memory," how Levine (2002) makes the point that we need time for memories to solidify and be retained; if students switch too quickly from one class to another, the new information gained in the second class could obliterate the information learned in the first class. Switching classes often takes 10 minutes or more. How much more true, then, might this be as we flick rapidly between Web sites!

As educators, we need to be aware that our students, brought up on the rapid scene changes of *Sesame Street* and now having the swift flow of online information, might think differently from the way we think, and so we need to adjust our teaching accordingly so as to capture their attention and engage them in sustained learning. It is by no means an impossible task; after all, it had been thought that the generation brought up on TV would not be able to learn from their print-bound teachers, but this turned out not to be the case (WNYC, 2010). Throughout this book I advocate the Socratic method of interactive learning as opposed to long lectures, and in addition I think there should be a variety of activities offering different ways in which to present the information and directly involve the students in their acquisition of knowledge. Many examples of these different learning activities are presented in Chapter 8, "Innovative Online Teaching Techniques."

Changes in the Style of Writing and the Expression of Knowledge

Writing, which is generally the end product of reading and thinking, therefore, has also been affected by the digital revolution. Furthermore, not only is writing affected by the way we read and think, but it is also influenced by the methods we use to write and in the writing habits we adopt. For example, Carr (2008) speaks about how Nietzsche, who was nearly blind from a horse-riding accent, learned how to touch-type on a typewriter (which had been invented only a few years earlier), and how his writing style changed and tightened as a result. Carr quotes Nietzsche as saying, "Our writing equipment takes part in the forming of our thoughts" (Carr, 2008, p. 60).

I can see this has been true for me. Before I started teaching online, I had been used to composing my thoughts on paper, so when I taught my first online class, I thought I would have to continue this habit. I did start that way, writing down with pen and paper the responses I wanted to offer to my students, and then laboriously typing these written comments into the response box of the online class. But it did not take me long to realize that this was much too time consuming, so I started, tentatively at first but then with added confidence, composing my original thoughts directly online. I found this beneficial because it took me longer to type than to write, which allowed time for me to have additional thoughts and make new realizations, all of which I could add to my typed online response, thus deepening and enriching its content. Students of online classes have told me that it is also true for them; typing a response rather than saying it out loud gives them more time to realize their thoughts, and this is further enabled by the asynchronicity of responding because they can take as long as they want to type in their response.

There is much concern that the way young people write is suffering, however, because of texting, but the linguist David Crystal does not agree. He says, "[T]here are indeed children who are weak at writing, poor spellers, and bad punctuators. There always have been. . . . They were there long before texting was invented" (2008, p. 156). Crystal quoted a British firm that lamented the problems " 'in obtaining junior clerks who can speak and write English clearly and correctly.' . . . That was in 1921" (p. 157). He thinks that young people who have difficulty reading and writing would in fact be less likely to want to use a technology in which these skills are needed. If they do participate, this additional exercise should in fact help them as it provides more opportunities for writing practice. In fact, Crystal goes on to say, "[C]hildren could not be good at texting if they had not already developed considerable literacy awareness" (p. 162) because he feels that they must know basic spellings and rules of grammar before knowing there are alternatives. As he says, "If you are aware that your texting behaviour is different, you must have already intuited that there is such a thing as a standard" (p. 162).

Crystal advises that teenagers should be taught when it is appropriate to text and when it is not, just as students are taught when it is appropriate to use poetic language or scientific jargon. In other words, he sees texting as just another form of language. One concern is that the short, succinct nature of texts makes those who frequently compose them less able to write longer academic papers. But the results on this are mixed. Some think just the opposite, as they believe texting could assist in more concise expression (pp. 167–168). Crystal concludes that "texting is one of the most innovative phenomena of modern times, and perhaps that is why it has generated such strong emotions. . . . Yet all the evidence suggests that belief in an impending linguistic disaster is a consequence of a mythology largely created by the media" (pp. 172–173). And he admits to a great fondness for texting, as "in texting we are seeing, in a small way, language in evolution" (p. 175).

In addition to the method of writing influencing the form and output of writing itself, there is also the factor of the perfect archive of online discussions. Many students have commented that this has been an immense help to them in writing their papers. I have definitely witnessed this. Sometimes, in contrast, in a class I have held on campus, we have had a phenomenal discussion, leading me to expect really rich papers from the students, only to be disappointed. I think the reason for this is that mostly students do not write notes when participating in face-to-face discussions, so perhaps a lot of material we had spoken about was forgotten. But this cannot happen online. Countering this, however, is the view of some teachers that students no longer devote sustained attention to writing their papers, as they become distracted each time a new text message or e-mail arrives. And it is to this relatively recent phenomenon of multitasking that we now turn our attention.

Multitasking

Turkle reminisces about the 1980s, in which students confessed to often doing homework with television and music playing, as well as some hand-held video games, and feels that this now "sound[s] almost pastoral" (2011, p. 162) in contrast to the multiplicity of tasks that most students currently attend to almost simultaneously. When interviewed in the documentary *Digital Nation* (2010), Turkle said that when students multitask, "everything is done a little worse." She understands that when studying becomes hard, there is a temptation to stop and check e-mail or send a few text messages, but she feels that this sort of break is not equivalent to having a walk or a cup of tea (my favorite). When walking or drinking tea, one is still thinking through the problem, even subconsciously, but when looking at an e-mail or text message this focus totally blows aside the original problem that was being considered.

Some Massachusetts Institute of Technology (MIT) professors report that students are no longer writing coherent papers; rather, they write in little bursts and snippets between texts or Facebook checks. They return to write the next paragraph, but by then their attention has been distracted, so that the next paragraph has no connection with the previous one. This is problematic as studying can be challenging, so it needs sustained attention, as does the process of writing a paper. As *Digital Nation* reported, despite MIT students saying that they felt very competent academically regardless of increased multitasking, the scores on their tests unfortunately indicate otherwise. Turkle says we should not be lured by things "exploding on the screen," or by a text message, and she insists that even though a computer is attractive because of its interactive potential, she thinks that one can interact a lot with a book. Otherwise, she remarks, "[W]e are taking human imagination out of our conversation about interactivity" (*Digital Nation,* 2010).

As Richtel (2010a) profoundly asks, what should students want: immediate gratification, or an investment in their future? He is also of the opinion that multitasking can lead to a decrease in the ability to pay attention. He backs up his assertion by referring to a study done by Eyal Ophir at Stanford, in which Ophir asked subjects to look quickly at a series of red and blue rectangles, some of which rotated and some of which did not, and then try to recall which were stationery and which moved. The multitaskers did worse on this test. Another study at Stanford by Clifford Nass, as mentioned on *Digital Nation,* was performed to see how quickly a subject could focus on a task while many other stimuli compete for attention. Student volunteers were shown odd and even numbers, along with much distracting information. Results showed that there was a significant decrease in ability to recall the numbers precisely because switching focus takes time. Results from both of these experiments therefore show the negative impact that multitasking has on short-term memory and analytical reasoning, which by extension shows the harmful consequences of stopping focused studying every time an e-mail or text message arrives.

Stone (as quoted by Anderson, 2009) said multitasking leads to "continuous partial attention" (Anderson, p. 3); she feels that every interruption causes a 25-minute loss in productivity. This can be accounted for, according to Anderson, through information derived from magnetic resonance imaging (MRI) scans, which show neurons, blood surges, and oxygen flows in the brain, and indicate that if multitasking occurs, the processing of the information leaves the hippocampus—the area of the brain responsible for the creation of memories—and moves to the striatum section of the brain, which is responsible for rote tasks. And it is precisely because of this that multitasking makes it hard to learn new things or remember them.

Also, as Powers points out, even if our *brain* is able to cope with multitasking, perhaps our *mind*—as defined by our consciousness and emotions—might not be able to cope. This view is certainly also held by Aboujaoude, who says that "mindless Web surfing, without forethought or plan, and without awareness of the passage of time or any real-life anchoring, is our era's very common version of the symptom of dissociation" (2011, p. 36). Aboujaoude defines *dissociation* as "a disruption of the normal integration of thoughts and behaviors into consciousness and memory, so that for a period of time certain information is not integrated, or 'associated,' with other information as it normally and logically would be" (p. 36). This is not to say that all dissociation is bad, as it can actually vary by degrees. Certainly the feeling of immersion in researching or writing, with the consequent loss of recognition of the passage of time, can be wonderfully rewarding and productive, as it is in this state that creativity and synthesis of ideas can occur. But this can be contrasted with the hours wasted by "mindless Web surfing," much akin to the rapid and empty switching of channels on the television.

I feel, however, that we should give at least some students more credit for being conscientious. In my own hybrid courses, some students have told me they were voluntarily making a conscious effort to limit their multitasking, as shown by the following comments:

- "On a personal level, I found it totally feasible; during high school I would spend countless hours on a computer, trying to avoid doing that history paper that was due the next morning. Via e-mail, Myspace, AIM, and among other distractions, I helped my procrastination grow to extreme lengths. Presently, [now that I am in college] in order to get work done, I have to avoid bringing my computer to places like the library; by doing so I'm left with no other alternative but to actually use my time wisely."
- "I decided two weeks ago to take myself off from Facebook, simply because I was spending more time catching [up] with my friends on Internet rather than face to face. For me, technology may save us time but for sure it is taking us away from the reality."
- "What I have changed, though, in the past year [now that I am in college] is that I have stopped checking my Facebook constantly. I actually only go on it like twice a week now. So overall I feel that you really just got to know when to limit yourself because technology is definitely the way to live now, but it also can take you on a path that you might just not be able to get out of."

Another student of mine, who was a member of the student government, was seriously considering suggesting the enforcement of No Facebook zones at certain strategic places around the campus, just as there are No Smoking areas to give students a much needed reprieve.

Interestingly, Anderson (2009) defends the benefits of some degree of distraction. Anderson quotes the economist, Herbert A. Simon, who wrote in the pre-Internet days of 1971, "A wealth of information creates a poverty of attention, and a need to allocate that attention efficiently among the overabundance of informational sources that might consume it" (p. 1). Anderson demonstrates that he is familiar with the fears that people have about information overload. He goes on to say that many feel that having the Internet as the hub of our work, play, and business is equivalent to a national diet of corn syrup that is making us obese. But he pushes these ideas aside with reassurances that there are benefits to be gained from the digital technologies. After all, he says, if we only focus excessively and exclusively on one thing, this could lead to being obsessive or compulsive, and ideally in life we need a balance between *attention,* which is derived from Latin and means "to stretch out or reach toward," and *distraction,* which is also from the Latin and means "a pulling apart." He states categorically, "Focus is a paradox—it has distraction built into it" (Anderson, 2009, p. 7).

And so, in answer to the argument that if Einstein were alive today he would never have discovered the theory of relativity because he would've been too distracted, he says that Einstein was brilliant precisely because he indulged in lateral thinking (as opposed to sharply focused thinking) by associating Newton's ideas about gravity with particle physics. In much the same way, Anderson hopes that the iGeneration, through the neuroplasticity of their brains that will enable them to cope efficiently with large amounts of information, will be able to synthesize this great amount of data and possibly come up with some innovative discoveries of their own. Henry Jenkins, quoted in *Digital Nation* (2010), shares this opinion, arguing that distraction is not new; we have felt overloaded by excessive amounts of information before and we have coped. He believes that we are better off as a society if we can embrace information with an open, inquisitive, and exploring mind.

This indeed could be plausible when we consider that our minds rarely stay focused on one thing for long. Those of us who meditate can see that this is true; even as we try to focus on one thought or mantra, generally a host of other thoughts come flooding in. This could be an evolutionary trait, as suggested by Gallager in her book *Rapt* (as referred to by Anderson, 2009, pp. 3–4) in which she mentions that even as we are focused on one task, we have an involuntary awareness of things going on around us, such as a sudden noise or smell or movement, and that peripheral awareness of these events serves to protect us from dangers or heightens the possibilities of reaping rewards, as in a tasty dinner. But, says Richtel (2010a), just as this awareness of what is happening on the periphery could have alerted our ancient ancestors to a prowling lion coming dangerously close, now it seems that many of us are alert to the chime of a newly arrived e-mail or text message, and this often distracts us from the task we have been focusing on. Gallager concludes that because we mostly cannot ignore distractions, we need to make a conscious choice as to what to focus on. Anderson quotes

William James as saying, "My experience is what I agree to attend to" (2009, p. 4). But even as we focus, we need to be aware of the complexity of stimuli swirling around us, and, as Anderson says, "The truly wise mind will harness, rather than abandon, the power of distraction" (p. 7). Anderson feels that one needs free, associative thinking to produce the spark for creativity.

I wonder, however, if Anderson would be wise to consider specifically the impact of different *kinds* of distractions. I agree that hopping around between Web sites with a defined mission to hunt out sources relating to a particular research topic could lead to a rich abundance of information that could, in turn, be synthesized in interesting ways and might lead to a new and exciting realization and advancement of knowledge. The problem might only manifest itself if someone switches rapidly from studying, to Facebook, to texts, and more.

David Meyer, interviewed by Anderson (2009, p. 3), reinforces this view by saying that each task we carry out involves different channels of the brain, and if we rapidly switch between tasks, there is a loss of information and inefficiency, which increases the likelihood of making mistakes. He says we can only multitask successfully if each task involves completely separate channels of the brain, such as listening to music while reading. But if two tasks involve the same channel, such as the visual channel as exemplified by driving and texting at the same time, it might prove impossible to do both successfully.

So, whereas multitasking between entirely different activities could impede concentration and hinder sustained engagement in studying, there would definitely be some activities that at the very least might offer a needed change in pace and some relaxation, and at best might further enhance the learning and discovery process.

Increase in the Playing of Video Games

We should also make brief note of the proliferation of video games. *Digital Nation* documents this, especially in South Korea, which refashioned itself around digital technology so that it could enhance its economic development. The documentary showed us how many young people in South Korea flock to Internet cafes that offer cheap access to the Internet for video games, possibly staying all night, often with little food or drink. There are genuine fears of addiction. Aboujaoude (2011) talks about the neurotransmitter dopamine, which is generally released during such pleasurable experiences as sex, eating, and use of addictive drugs. He also cites studies by a Harvard psychiatrist, Renshaw, which confirm that dopamine is also released during the playing of video games (pp. 38–39). Renshaw defines Internet addiction as occurring both when large amounts of time are wasted, and when this wasted time results in a significant loss in the real world, such as being unable to relate closely to a loved one or failing at school or work (p. 217).

Although there are undoubtedly possible problems with limitless playing of video games, Johnson (2006) is very favorably disposed toward them, as he believes that they are educational in that they make the player think and strategize. Video games are constructed in levels, and there is a reward at each level, which, when achieved, results in the release of dopamine. Johnson thinks working through simulated problems and then being rewarded if correct is beneficial, as it helps players to develop skills to solve a puzzle in a systematic way by using the scientific method of exploring, creating a hypothesis, gathering evidence, and then testing and rethinking the hypothesis. Their greatest asset, he says, is their complexity, which can often lead the player to feel frustrated or confused, and perhaps to continue working on a resolution to the game even when away from it. And it is precisely because of this level of difficulty that video games, Johnson feels, can be valuable as they can simulate complex things in the real world, such as building a city or flying a plane. However, the possible solutions are limited by the design of the game itself.

Pensky (2001) thinks an effective way to teach students of the digital age is to present information as a game. This is both a fun way to engage students, and it also encourages them to be active participants, learners, thinkers, and collaborators. Pensky uses the term *edutainment*. I admit I am not very fond of this term, but I do like the idea of games as a learning tool. I think games could appeal to today's students, as they have good graphic awareness and simulation could help them understand hard concepts. Games can also be collaborative and interactive, which are beneficial features. One example of a game of some value was mentioned by Wieder (2011a), who spoke of a game called BiblioBouts. This game was designed at the University of Michigan to assist students in learning how to develop their bibliographies in a fun way. Essentially this game uses a reward system to help students develop their research skills and be able to differentiate between good and bad sources. The game is competitive in that students all collect citations and then judge and are judged by their peers for relevance and credibility in a fun and motivating way. More research remains, however, to determine whether students who receive a high score in the game also end up with a higher grade on their paper. Games do not have to be "out of the box," but could be designed in class, as I discuss later in this book. (See Chapter 8, "Innovative Online Teaching Techniques," sections "Role-Playing" and "A Writing Game.")

A Look Back and a Speculative Look Ahead

Whether surfing through lots of information on the Web, using Web applications, or multitasking by trying to do many of these simultaneously, clearly we are only at the beginning of the analysis of the full impact of the digital revolution on contemporary education. Are mumblings of discontent typical any time there is a radical paradigm shift, or is this new paradigm rampant with inherent dangers? Should we worry, as does Wolf when she asks plaintively,

> Will the present generation become so accustomed to immediate access to on-screen information that the range of attentional, inferential, and reflective capacities in the present reading brain become less developed? . . . Are Socrates' concerns about unguided access to information more warranted today than they were in ancient Greece? (2007, p. 214)

To try to make sense of these questions, we first look back to trace how reading and writing evolved. And then, having traced the path of evolution forward to the present day, we speculate as to where we are heading in terms of the impact of the digital revolution on education.

We are now at the *convergence* of what have been considered the traditional ways of reading and writing, with the new online literacy. And perhaps it is precisely the point at which a new paradigm bumps up against a long-established paradigm that all the problems of adoption and adaptation, integration and assimilation arise. In other words, it might be the transition that is hard, rather than that the new paradigm is at fault. As Wolf says in reference to the cultural historian Walter Ong, "Two decades ago, Ong asserted that the real issue in human intellectual evolution is not the set of skills advanced by one cultural mode of communication versus another, but the transformative changes bestowed on humans steeped in both" (2007, p. 219). Although Ong was addressing the relationship between the spoken word and literacy, I believe the same could be true for us now. It might just be that it is harder for we Baby Boomers, straddling the new and old worlds, than for the iGeneration born into digital technologies. Perhaps with time questions of acceptance might well become less abrupt.

The Evolution of Reading and Writing, and Its Impact on Learning

This is not the first time that there has been a radical paradigm shift in modes of communication. As Wolf (2007) says, tracing the evolution of reading and writing offers a great lens on ourselves as a species, and the fact that we can read and write at all—in other words, that we can draw meaning from symbols on a page—is truly remarkable. As previously mentioned, reading, unlike speech, is not an instinctive skill; we have to teach our minds how to do it. In other words, every healthy baby naturally starts to speak at a certain young age, but all little children, however intelligent, have to be taught how to read and write. By about the age of six, Wolf tells us that children must connect perceptual, cognitive, and linguistic systems so as to be able to learn how to read, and this must be repeatedly practiced in order to train the brain so that reading becomes an automatic skill. And, she remarks, dyslexia is evidence that our brains are not naturally wired to read.

Before there was any alphabet, tokens were used in trading and exchanges of goods to try to keep track of the transactions. The first comprehensive writing systems have been discovered as having been done by the Sumerians dating from 4000 BC. They did what has been called *cuneiform* writing, which means "wedge shaped," as they wrote on clay tablets with a blunt reed called a *stylus.* Archeological discoveries have found Egyptians were writing their hieroglyphics from about 3300 BC. They used scrolls made from papyrus plants.

In about 360 BC in ancient Greece, Plato wrote *Phaedrus,* which was meant as a written dialogue between himself and his teacher, Socrates. However, as Carr tells us, *Phaedrus* greatly upset Socrates, as the latter was of the opinion that the only true way to explore knowledge was through spoken dialogue with a teacher. Writing things down, he feared, would give the young too much information, and they would not know how to think critically about it, thus resulting in a "false wisdom." Wolf also speaks of Socrates' concerns when she said he worried "about what might happen to knowledge if the young had unguided, uncritical access to information" (2007, p. 220). In addition, Socrates was concerned that writing things down would diminish the power of memory. Up until then, there had been an oral culture in which information was sung or chanted with lots of repetition, rhythm, and even clichés, so that people would be able to remember what was being said. Knowledge in those days was often embedded in poetry.

Despite Socrates' objections, writing spread, and gradually, after the birth of Christ, separate parchments were sewn together, especially for the making of early Bibles (Carr, 2010). However, early writing was hard to decipher, as there were no spaces between words, and punctuation was lacking, so in general many of these writings were actually read aloud to others. Punctuation and spacing between words originated in Britain in the Middle Ages, and helped to increase the number of people who could read silently. This was especially encouraged in universities and in libraries. All of this, of course, necessitated mass production of books, and this in fact occurred in 1445 with Johannes Gutenberg's invention of the printing press.

Gutenberg had metal-working skills and had worked with a press for wine making. He then, with the aid of a loan, designed a metal cast for letters and invented an oil-based ink that would adhere to the letters (Carr, 2010). He printed the first Bible, which was 1,200 pages in length. But, after printing 200 copies, he had unfortunately completely depleted his funds, and ceased operations. It was a personal tragedy for Gutenberg, but his invention made an enormous and lasting impact on human history. It coincided with the adoption of paper from China, which was much cheaper than the parchment previously used. Carr tells us that in the 50 years following the invention of the printing press, the number of books produced was equivalent to the number of books laboriously made by European scribes in the previous 1,000 years. And by the seventeenth century there were book presses throughout the world, increasing the number of available books and consequent number of readers. Because the number of books being printed was increasing, more and more people wanted to write, and this led to the advent of pencils and fountain pens. Broadsheets and newspapers also started to be printed so as to give people daily information.

And, because of the availability of so much reading material, reading changed from being restricted to and only appreciated by the few to being consumed by the majority. Two types of reading developed: the shallow reading of material such as road signs or product labels and the deep reading of whole books. This deep reading necessitated sustained concentration and a dissociation from one's immediate environment, as a result of a total immersion in a book. As Carr concludes, the advantages of deep reading include an increase in vocabulary and an ability to appreciate more abstract concepts, to become more contemplative and reflective, and to develop a better imagination (2010, p. 75). And Wolf (2007) thinks that when we read books, we see not only the consciousness of the writer, but our own consciousness as well. In other words, when we read books, we bring to the maze of symbols on the page not only a literal understanding of what each word means, but also an understanding of what it means in the context of the other words on the page. Our interpretation of this overall meaning is influenced by our own experiences and understandings. There is, then, what is termed a *co-construction of meaning,* a building up of the meaning between the author's original words and the reader's interpretation of those words.

All this takes time, and time was something we gained when we did not need to commit to memory all the information that had been passed on in the oral tradition. As Wolf concludes,

> Socrates never knew the secret at the heart of reading: the time it frees for the brain to have thoughts deeper than those that came before. . . . The mysterious, invisible gift of *time to think beyond* is the reading brain's greatest achievement; those built-in milliseconds form the basis of our ability to propel knowledge, to ponder virtue, and to articulate what was once inexpressible. (2007, p. 229)

All this is possible with the linear and deep thinking that reading books can give us.

But certainly this was not a universal opinion, as the concern about books that Socrates had still lingered among some people. Witness, for example, Edgar Allen Poe's statement in 1845 that "the enormous multiplication of books in every branch of knowledge is one of the greatest evils of this age, since it presents one of the most serious obstacles to the acquisition of correct knowledge by throwing in the reader's way piles of lumber in which he must painfully grope for the scraps of useful matter, peradventure interspersed" (cited in Carruth and Ehrlich, 1988, p. 35).

The first widespread adoption of electronic media—the radio, cinema, records, television—in the 1950s in no way competed with the book as none of these transmitted the written word. However, the development of the Web "replays, with the velocity of a time capsule film, the entire history of modern media" (Carr, 2010, p. 83). Text can exist online, thus replicating the printing press. Graphics, sound, and video can all exist online as well. And because material is online, it has the added advantage of being interactive, so that we are no longer passive listeners or viewers, but can actively participate in these varying forms of media. And we can incorporate them into our educational systems.

Some Current Applications of Digital Technologies in Education

There are many ways in which teaching with the new digital media can make possible that which has not hitherto been feasible. As a particular example, I team-taught an online course in the fall of 2011 at Rutgers with a friend and colleague, Chunyan Xu, from Jilin University in China, on the ethics of food production, distribution, and consumption. In this way, we enabled students from two distant continents to learn "side by side" and have the ability to be in constant conversation with each other. They learned more than the course content at face value, as in addition they came to understand and appreciate each others' culture in the context of food ethics in a way that could not have been done before electronic communication. We became acquainted at the start of the semester by introducing ourselves to each other asynchronously in what we termed the Virtual Student Lounge, and thereafter we held our online discussions in the discussion forums. Although we had hoped to use Skype so as to hold some face-to-face synchronous conversations with each other, especially when students were conducting oral presentations of their research findings, we had to abandon this idea because of the 13-hour time difference between the two universities. Instead we filmed students as they conducted their oral presentations, and then we posted these films online. In addition, students were required to create posters so as to graphically display their research findings. Some students at both universities made digital posters, which they posted online for all to see; for those who made a conventional poster, we took photos and posted these online.

Online team-taught international courses have also been taught by Dr. Lederer at New School University, with her colleague, Dr. Lichtblau in Austria (see Chapter 8, section "Intriguing Uses of the Team Teaching Concept"). There is also a fascinating example of two grade schools across the world from each other—the American School of Bombay in India and a school in Australia—that connect online with each other, enabling students to work collaboratively about global as well as local issues, using Skype and video-conferencing ("Teachers' Views," 2010).

Besides the new digital media being used to transcend the constraints of space, it can also be used to transcend the constraints of time, as was done in a fascinating way in the History department at Rutgers University by Dr. Rudy Bell, who runs two parallel courses, one online and one face-to-face, called "History and the News." This course looks at significant global news exactly as it breaks, and can therefore only be done in this up-to-the-minute way via the new technologies. As soon as a newsworthy event occurs, such as the Japanese tsunami or the Middle East uprisings, Dr. Bell interviews a local expert, often by Skype, and then creates a video of the interview, which he posts online. Dr. Bell's mantra for his course is "online and on time." Students watch the online video, read related materials, and then hold discussions (face-to-face or online) with teaching assistants (TAs) in small groups. The TAs who have taught both live and online confess to preferring the online discussions as it gives them time to look up information about, for example, the history of Japan or Egypt, which is not possible in the campus class.

Speculations on the Future Value of the New Digital Media in Education

Throughout this chapter I have quoted not only those enthusiastic about the potential of new technologies, but also those who are very skeptical indeed about the way forward using the new digital media in education. I agree that digital media, if used badly or used just for fun, would not help true teaching and learning to ensue. But even though this is conjectural, I would like to put forward a few speculative ideas as to how I think the digital revolution could have very positive impacts on student learning, beyond the fact that using technology in the classrooms might well provide good preparation for the media-laden work world when students join the job market.

In the first place, it is not new to agonize about the demise of academic standards. It seems that this fear crops up frequently. We have only to read from Bloom's book, *The Closing of the American Mind,* published in 1987, to see that his concerns sound like a distant echo of some of the fears we have now, although for radically different reasons. He states, for example,

> In short, there is no vision, nor is there a set of competing visions, of what an educated human being is. The question has disappeared, for to pose it would be a threat to the peace. There is . . . no tree of knowledge. Out of chaos emerges dispiritedness, because it is impossible to make a reasonable choice. Better to give up on a liberal education and get on with a specialty in which there is at least a prescribed curriculum and a prospective career. (p. 337)

So perhaps if these dire predictions about the lowering of intellectual standards and the "dumbing down" of America are true—and even this is controversial because some would certainly argue otherwise—then technology might well not be to blame. As we have seen, complaints about information overload are not new, and certainly did not originate with the Internet. And clearly there have always been some lazy, unmotivated students who are easily distracted, so it could just be that the nature of the distraction has changed from television to texting, and not that personalities have been detrimentally altered. As Crystal (2008) says, there have always been some students who struggle with their writing, and are poor spellers.

Digital technology is undoubtedly flourishing. Could we therefore rethink the situation? Instead of fearing that students are darting unthinkingly between Web sites and Web apps, pulling our knowledge and education into a virtual black hole, could we instead postulate that we could well be returning to *the culture of knowledge through dialogue* that Socrates preferred before there were books? Could we say, then, that the wheel has come full circle, in that forces for learning and knowledge acquisition are again enabled through giving participants equal access to discussion? And perhaps, better still, could we propose that our potential for dialogue now is actually superior to that which existed in ancient Greece, because now it can be online, as opposed to taking discussions down to the marketplace where its flow could have been impeded by excluding some who were present as they were shouted down by someone else, or because others were disadvantaged by being behind a mythical pillar and therefore not strategically located so as to have a voice? Are we correct in claiming that online discussion is more truly democratic, offering the possibility of full involvement by all present?

In some ways, might it not even be possible to say that what we have now, through online text-based discussion, is actually the perfect blend between speaking and reading? The very feature of reading through written online discussion responses in an asynchronous framework, which form the basis of a discussion-based online class, permits all online participants to have the time to engage their delay neurons to give them the opportunity to reflect deeply and to meaningfully synthesize complex issues. So indeed we have regained the time that Wolf (2007) feared so much that we had lost, and which she lamented meant that we left ourselves no opportunity to think beyond that which we had read. Not so at all! The marriage between a return to discussion as a form of learning, and the opportunities of asynchronicity when reading and responding that the Internet provides, could be very rich and rewarding indeed. Herein lies the potential beauty of the online class, as a case can certainly be made that online discussion blends the best aspects of discussion with the best aspects of reading. Furthermore, all this can be enhanced by some of the new digital media, which help us to become better acquainted and to see and talk to each other in real time on occasion, and which allow us to constructively enjoy the process.

So, in short, has the paradigm that we recognize as traditional learning been lost? No, not yet. And not completely. But there is definitely an intrusion by the new and enticing digital technologies. What we therefore need to impart to teachers who teach the students of the iGeneration is that we can't just throw technology at them and tell them to go ahead and use it without a well-defined rationale. And we can't allow ourselves or our students to be lured by technologies that beckon us seemingly only because of the possibility of a new friendship. No, we need to carefully construct a new pedagogy, an adaptation of the old methods, so as to meaningfully engage students through digital technologies. We need to train teachers as to how to do this. And this is exactly the mission of this book. It is to the practical applications of technology's impact on teaching and learning that we now turn in Part Two.

PART TWO

PRACTICAL APPLICATIONS

This section offers practical applications of the various learning theories discussed in Part One to online teaching so as to achieve inspirational results. Topics covered in this section include:

- Course design
- Starting to teach the online class
- Aspects of online communication
- Innovative online teaching techniques

5

COURSE DESIGN

Simplicity and repose are the qualities that measure the true value of any work of art. "Think simple" as my old master used to say—meaning reduce the whole of its parts into the simplest terms, getting back to first principles.

—Frank Lloyd Wright, 1932

As we have seen in Part One, it is both possible and indeed essential to establish a feeling of place in an online class, despite the fact that it does not occupy physical space. If a student feels lonely or remote from the learning process, chances are that the potential for meaningful and inspirational education will be reduced. This chapter discusses ways in which a robust online course can be designed so as to enhance a feeling of a community of learners. The energy of the online course occurs on the discussion boards, and a thorough look at varying aspects of online communication is given in Chapter 7. Let us first look at optimal ways in which to construct the basics of an online course shell, before the students arrive, as the layout has a big impact on the involvement of the students and on the potential for discussion and deep learning to occur.

Customizing the Class

Biographical Statement and Syllabus

Before your class begins, you should fill out some biographical and contact information about yourself. It is also advisable to post your syllabus online. Even if your class is a hybrid, it is beneficial for you to have your syllabus reside online, so that no student can claim to have lost it. Your syllabus should contain information on your course description, course goals and objectives, readings, learning activities, grading policy, schedule, and expectations. It is important that you specify how frequently students are expected to log on to your class, and participate in discussions and activities. It is not enough to only stipulate how often students should log on because they have no presence unless they participate. Also inform students that they should spread their time in your online class throughout the week, rather than, for example, only logging on four times each Friday. One online instructor tells her students, whether online or on campus, a story entitled, "The Three Bricklayers," as a device whereby to inform them of her expectation of them. The story goes as follows:

> Once there were three bricklayers.
> Each one of them was asked what they were doing.
> The first man answered gruffly,
> "I'm laying bricks."
> The second man replied,
> "I'm putting up a wall."
> But the third man said enthusiastically and with pride,
> "I'm building a cathedral."
>
> —Author Unknown

This story, found online at www.wow4u.com/3bricks/, she believes helps students to identify the importance of attitude and how having a good attitude can lead to a more successful outcome. It helps students to see the importance of keeping an eye on the bigger picture so that, rather than just doing the minimum and regarding it as an effort and a task, they can focus their energy and become more motivated. This is the difference between students simply logging on and those actively seeking to broaden their education.

Posting an Introductory Lecture

Having completed the syllabus, you should also post a first introductory lecture. But avoid making your lecture too long; break it up into smaller parts and then give opportunities for discussion before moving on to the next lecture. Some instructors like to create all their lectures before the class begins, and make the later lectures unavailable to students until the appropriate time in the semester. Others like to create lectures as they proceed through the course. Either way works well, but what I recommend is not to have all the lectures of the entire course available to the student at the start of the semester, as online classes should not be self-paced. If they were self-paced, it could rapidly become hectic, and also there would be less scope for interaction. Instead, the lecture material should unfold throughout the semester so as to best replicate what occurs in the campus class and to steadily and meaningfully progress through the course material.

Posting a First Discussion Forum

It is extremely beneficial to create a first discussion forum, which I like to call "The Virtual Lounge," specifically for all class participants to post personal introductions and to start to become acquainted. This reduces the chance of students feeling like they are sending out responses to the great unknown. Another advantage of this informal discussion forum is that it gives new online students some practice and experience with online discussions before needing to respond to specific, formal course content. I recommend that students should be invited to return to "The Virtual Lounge" throughout the semester so as to maintain a feeling of camaraderie. Indeed, I have found that students use this area exactly like a lounge. Online discussions are studied in more depth in Chapter 7.

Setting up Twitter Accounts and Google Docs

Some teachers like to use Twitter as a supplement to their classes to facilitate online discussion. One teacher who uses Twitter in his teaching is Peter Sorrell, an assistant director of the Rutgers Writing Program, and professor in the French department. Although, as Sorrell (2010) said, many undergraduates are unfamiliar with Twitter because they are more likely to use Facebook (a slightly older age group uses Twitter), he still feels it is a useful skill for them to acquire and might ultimately be of use to them in the business world. For now it has several advantages to their learning, as will be shown in the following chapters.

If a teacher uses Twitter, he or she needs to give students explicit instructions as to how to set up an account. Sorrell says he spends the first class of the semester with his students in a computer lab doing just this. And if some students already have an account, they should each make a new one specifically for the class, so that only class-related messages are sent, and there are no "intrusions" from friends. As Parry (2008) says, students should bring their cell phones to this first class, as once they have registered their Twitter account on the computer, they can then attach this service to their cell phone. Additionally, the Twitter account should be linked to the main online software program, so that it can be accessed from there. Although Sorrell said he was worried about spending the whole of the first class setting up Twitter, it was well worth it as the class could then be involved in a multitude of activities as described later in this book, all of which can contribute to the learning process. (See Chapter 6, "Starting to Teach the Online Class," section "Students Interview and Introduce Each Other"; Chapter 7, "Aspects of Online Conversation," section "Clearly Define Your Expectations for Discussion-Frequency of Participation"; and also in Chapter 7, section "Suggestions for Overcoming Lack of Participation-Using Social Media such as Twitter, Facebook, Blogs, or Skype to Stimulate Online Discussion"; as well as Chapter 8, "Innovative Online Teaching Techniques," section "A Writing Game" and section "Student Presentations of their Discovered Web Sites.")

Sample (2010) says tweets could be considered as "low-stakes writing," used either for an "adventurous claim" or for a "half-baked idea." And because they are limited by their tiny size, if a student has more that he or she would like to say, or has a paper to be reviewed by peers (see Chapter 8, "Innovative Online Teaching Techniques," section on "Student Portfolios"), then Google Docs could be used because students can share these documents online. Similarly important class material, such as the syllabus, could be put on Google Docs. Students can easily set up Google Docs if they already have an e-mail account on Google, and if they don't, they can then establish one. In this way, if later in the semester a student wants to submit a paper, he or she can simply send a tweet with the URL to the paper residing on Google Docs. Alternatively the discussion forums of the online class itself can be a place for students to post papers.

Posting an Announcement

You should also post an announcement, the area for which is positioned on the first screen that students will read when they log in to your class. The announcement area is a sort of in-between place, a virtual spot whose primary function is to point the way to other places; in fact, I like to think of it as equivalent to C.S. Lewis's "Wood Between the Worlds" in his marvelous story, *The Magician's Nephew*. As in Lewis's tale, it should be a friendly and welcoming place, as many new students might be feeling apprehensive in the same way that they felt on their first day of school. As well as greeting your students, your announcement could inform them as to how to navigate around your online class so that they can visit all its virtual rooms, such as your biographical statement, the syllabus, the lecture area, and the discussion forums (see Figure 5.1: Example of an Online Announcement).

Signposts

> You must walk. It is a long journey, through a country that is sometimes pleasant and sometimes dark and terrible. . . . "The road to the City of Emeralds is paved with yellow brick," said the Witch, "so you cannot miss it."
>
> —Excerpt from *The Wonderful Wizard of Oz*, by L. Frank Baum

Because the announcement area therefore can serve as a directional board, let us look more specifically at the question of creating clear signposts within your online class. This is of the utmost importance, as the goal is to make the technology as transparent and seamless as possible. In this way, students do not expend all their energy on wondering where to click to achieve a desired end, but can focus on the course content itself. After all, online

FIGURE 5.1
Example of an Online Announcement

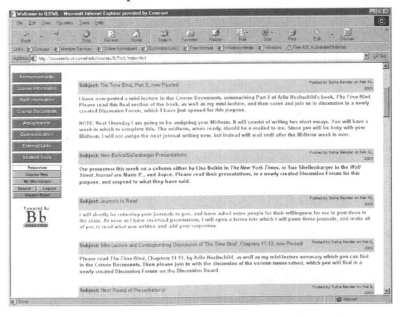

classes are just an alternative method of delivery and communication of information, and to me the fascination does not lie in the technology that takes us there, but in the course material itself. It seems to me to be directly analogous to driving a car; we learn to operate it, but for most of us, the emphasis is not on how the car works, but on the fact that it takes us to our destination.

Imagine you have arrived at a new college campus for an important function such as an interview or because you have been invited as a guest lecturer. Consequently you need to find your way, possibly with some urgency, to the right department. Maybe you will ask some people who you see strolling around the campus to direct you to the correct building, or maybe you will search for signposts. In either case, you might feel somewhat stressed, and would be grateful for as many clear directions as possible.

Now translate this into the cyberspatial campus. Imagine how students feel as they not only find their way to your course, but also try to navigate around the various virtual rooms you have established within your class. They also experience a feeling of urgency and possibly a little anxiety, just as you might when visiting an unfamiliar campus, as they want to quickly see what your class entails and what they need to do. In fact, the need for clear directions and signposts might be magnified in the cyberspatial campus because in this virtual world, form does not reflect function, as is generally the case in the real world.

So how best do you provide signposts in your online class? First, I advise that if you have chosen fancy names for any of the virtual rooms in your class, make sure you have explained your terms so that no students will feel lost or confused. It might also be helpful to provide information as to how to return home to the announcement area.

I recommend using the announcement area not only at the start of the semester to help students navigate around your online class, but also throughout the duration of the course to give ongoing information. For example, it can be used for keeping students informed about due dates for readings and assignments, pertinent course-related news on the media, relevant museum exhibits, and so on. Try to make each new announcement a different color from the last so that they are eye-catching and thus more apt to be read. Some online programs, such as Sakai, give the option of not only posting the announcement in the announcement area of your online class, but also of simultaneously generating an e-mail with the same information. This is a nice advantage, but if you do have this option, tell students to check their e-mail account (which is usually the university e-mail address) to which this is sent, or else to have their university e-mail automatically forwarded to the e-mail account they check with more frequency. If, on the other hand, yours is a software program in which each new announcement replaces the previous one, then it is important to keep each announcement up long enough to ensure that students, working asynchronously, will all have a chance to see it.

The question then arises as to how often you must repeat information. A colleague of mine emphasized the importance of redundancy in an online course, as she believed in posting the same information in many areas of the course. Another school of thought, however, is to resist redundancy on the grounds that it might insult the intelligence of students and therefore lead them to skip over these kinds of postings; and once a skipper, maybe always a skipper, tripping and skipping over other, more salient information. In fact, you want the students to read everything, every word you post, and certainly all the responses of their classmates.

In certain circumstances, however, I do think repetition might be a good and necessary idea. With an assignment, for example, you might want to give the directions, such as length, due date, and method of submission, both in the assignment itself and in the announcement area. You might also want to repeat information in the announcement area that is contained in your syllabus, or remind students to revisit the syllabus (which some students might otherwise look at only once at the start of the semester). If you receive an e-mail from a student asking where to go in the course for a particular function, or when to expect certain events such as midterms or finals, you might want to answer this as a general announcement in class because chances are that if this student lost her or his sense of direction, others might well have felt the same way.

Also, while on the topic of signposting, I think it enormously important to carefully streamline information of particular types and not allow confusing overflows. Again, this helps students to know where to find or post different types of information. For example, on the discussion board of your class, you should clearly construct each discussion forum so that students understand at a glance the topic of each one. An online class that has a discussion board containing a dull list of topics, labeled "Discussion 1," "Discussion 2," and so on, might confuse students and certainly will not spark their interest in the same way as a representative or catchy title to the discussion topic would do.

Even with careful directions, however, errors might occur from time to time. I have occasionally had a student post a response in the wrong forum.

In terms of the interruption to the flow of conversation, I was immediately reminded of being once deeply immersed in a complicated recipe in a cookbook for which I had no great fondness, and being up to my elbows in flour, only to be told to now turn to page 152. In cases of posting to the wrong forum, it might be best for you to paste it in to the correct forum and delete it from its original position before confusion mounts. It is also a good idea to send an e-mail to the author of that response, saying what you have done and why it was necessary.

Arrangement of Lecture Material

What is the optimal way of dividing up your lecture material so that it is logical, crisp and clear in format, and most readily comprehended by students? I would like to suggest that the course objectives should seem feasible and relevant, and that the course is well sequenced to allow logical progression from easier to more difficult concepts and tasks. If a jump is made too rapidly to difficult tasks or concepts, students might feel alienated, lack self-confidence, and might perhaps drop the course.

As the students progress along the spectrum from simpler to harder tasks, you as the instructor might need to reinforce concepts that serve as building blocks to knowledge. Reinforcement does not necessarily mean repetition, but could be done through a different activity, as in this way you might reach different types of learners (Vella, 1997). I suggest one of the following four alternatives to divide up your lecture material.

- *Thematic divisions:* You organize your material according to theme or topic. For example, in my "Ethics and the Family" course, I have thematic divisions such as the effect on family when one member commits a crime, when there is divorce, and so on. This format might work well for many courses in the humanities, social sciences, education, and health-related fields.
- *Chronological divisions:* If you are teaching a literature course, you could, for example, divide your lectures by literature published in different time periods. This type of structure works well for a course in any discipline that has as its basis an historical emphasis.
- *Divided by different books studied:* An alternative structure for a literature course is to divide according to the books to be read and analyzed. For example, in a course on D.H. Lawrence, you could open

separate lecture documents for *Sons and Lovers, The Rainbow, Women in Love,* and *Lady Chatterley's Lover.*

- *Divided by chapters in a book:* This format might be effective for any course that follows the basic structure of a textbook. If the textbook has a large number of chapters, it might be advantageous, if possible, to "bundle" a few chapters together in each lecture.

The Online Lecture Format

I recommend that the instructor post short, succinct, snappy lectures, more appropriately called "mini-lectures." By doing this, I am keeping Frank Lloyd Wright's words about the advantage of simplicity clearly in mind. If the lecture is too long (taking up more than a few screens), students might feel they could more easily be reading a book on a comfortable sofa, rather than sitting at a computer terminal. Excessively long lectures also lessen the opportunities for interactivity. If you feel your lecture is becoming too lengthy, divide it up into two or more mini-lectures of a more digestible size.

I also recommend that you create a corresponding discussion forum to accompany each mini-lecture, as this offers not only the opportunity for students to react to your mini-lecture, but also provides you with an opportunity to continue to give students information that might otherwise have been part of your lecture, but is now offered as a series of responses within the discussion. By this means, your information is unfolding in segments within an interactive framework.

Some professors are initially concerned about limiting the length of their lectures as they think the students might lose out on valuable information. I would say that this method does not dilute the information you are providing your students; it is instead repackaging it and parceling some out within discussion, to suit the online environment and promote interactivity (see Figure 5.2: Example of an Online Mini-Lecture).

Having now taken into explicit consideration the pertinent issues relating to course design, you are now ready to start teaching. And the factors surrounding starting to teach an online course are the focus of the next chapter.

FIGURE 5.2
Example of an Online Mini-Lecture

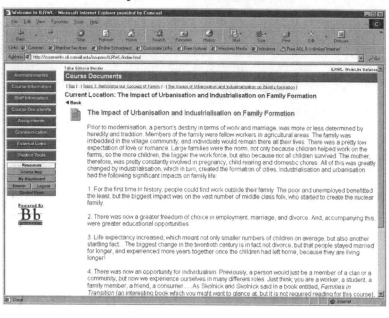

6

STARTING TO TEACH THE ONLINE CLASS

Teachers open the door; you enter by yourself.
—Chinese Proverb

I deally your institution will offer some sort of online orientation for new students before their course begins. They should be given their user ID and password in advance, and should be told the URL of your online course. The orientation should include a hands-on experience of the online environment so they become familiar with it or, if you are teaching a hybrid class, it would be advantageous if your institution has prepared a handout explaining the basics of navigating through your online course, and you could spend some time in your campus class going through this. It has been found that students who are given a basic orientation to the online environment do better than those who do not, as they can start to focus more quickly on the course content rather than on basic operations.

So the students should be ready for their online class, but what about you? Some new online instructors report feeling quite anxious before they start to teach; I heard one instructor say it felt like "navigating in the dark," and another say that she felt as though she "did not know where the chalk was." It is to varying forms of instructor anxiety, and methods to alleviate it, that we now turn our attention.

Anxiety

Campus teaching and online teaching involve different sets of worries. On campus there is the worry, especially before the first class, as to how to effectively grab each student's interest and sustain that over the allotted time slot, the worry about blanking out and looking stupid, the worry about how long it will take to remember every student's name, the worry about the suitability of the room and whether the arrangement of furniture is flexible, the worry that any and all equipment that might be needed for your class to run smoothly is present and in working order, maybe the worry about whether the new shoes you have bought will pinch your toes, the worry about the possibility of delays in the journey to class. Online you can be comforted about not having to worry about new shoes, delayed journeys, memorizing names, seating arrangements, or keeping everyone interested for a rigid time period, but it does not mean a total freedom from worries. Instead there is the worry about whether the technology will cooperate, the worry of making what might feel like an indelible error, the worry that your students might understand computers better than you do, the consequent worry that you might lose command of the class, and the worry about being insufficiently prepared. We have talked about preparing your course shell, and because you will have put a lot of thought and deliberation into your course design, it will have the potential of being a stimulating and fulfilling class.

Remember, anxiety is common when faced with any new enterprise, and a little nervousness about teaching is normal, is likely to be felt by others, and can actually be tapped to enhance good teaching, as long as it does not become overwhelming (Teaching and Educational Development Institute [TEDI], 2002). Some instructors let the students know that this is their first time teaching online, and they might even tell them they are a little anxious. This immediately helps, I believe, as the instructor is not so worried about trying to impress, and probably, as a result of letting students know, is likely to do a better job. Also, spending a few days in your "Virtual Lounge" before embarking on course content can make the students seem human as you become acquainted, rather than part of a long list of names on a screen. When teaching, as soon as I read responses from my students and enter into conversations with them, my nervousness subsides. By then we are involved together in the academic pursuit of the subject matter, and the excitement of the voyage has begun.

Means of Engagement

Ideally we should strive to involve our students to such an extent in the joy of learning that they become deeply immersed (Vella, 1997). We can tell this occurs online when their comments are frequent and involved, as well as being deep, thoughtful, insightful, and excited. This is the pitch that we as teachers enjoy.

However, even if students participate in an orientation, they still may not always enter your online class promptly. I had always expected that as soon as the virtual classroom door swung open at the start of the semester, my students would come pouring through, but this has not always been the case for all students, as there have been delays over acquiring passwords, technical difficulties, and any manner of cyberspatial excuses. Even though the online environment is an asynchronous one, we want to avoid having stragglers who pull the discussion in a backward direction by their late participation; and ideally we want everyone in the class to be involved in the same discussion at approximately the same time. The following sections provide suggestions as to how to engage students so that the online class is off to a sizzling start.

The Benefits of Contacting Each Student Individually at the Start of the Semester

It might be productive to assess individual student needs before the class begins, either by phone or in person (Vella, 1997). Generally in classes taught completely online, I have found that students have been gratified to receive a call, and it provides the additional benefit of making the teacher seem more of a real person to them. Students in hybrid classes might too be helped by this individual contact, as it can lead to better understanding as to why they should log on to the Web component of their class, and what they will gain in the process.

Designing an Informal First Discussion Topic

I think it is in both your and your students' interests to design a first discussion topic that is so enticing, so intriguing, and so marvelous that they really do not want to miss out on it. In other words, by providing a meaningful challenge from the start, you are giving students an opportunity for engagement.

We have talked about constructing a "Virtual Lounge," but what should be the initial topic of conversation? In what ways can you thaw the online "ice crystals" before the course content begins? The expression "Start as you mean to go on" generally echoes through my mind at the start of any class, as time and time again I see that a class that starts with a great deal of enthusiasm and energy generally maintains that dynamism, whereas a class with a few straggling and occasional remarks is often harder to spark.

Asking Students to Discuss Relevant Experiences in Their Personal Introductions

You might want to not only ask students to introduce themselves, but also to ask a few questions that are relevant to the context of your course and define its parameters. For example, if you are teaching a writing class, you might ask what students have already written; or in a literature course, you might ask what else they have read in this particular genre. You might choose to ask students to "free associate," and write anything that comes to mind as stimulated by a word or words in your course name (TEDI, 2002).

Completing a Sentence

Another idea is to start a sentence and ask students to complete it. For example, write, "I was riding the subway today, when I. . . ." Students generally love to see what others have written and enjoy interacting with each other immediately. Your sentence prompt could be about anything, but it might be helpful to tailor it, even subtly, to the subject matter of your course.

Students Interview and Introduce Each Other

Some instructors ask students to confess a secret that they have cherished, and the conversation can actually become quite amusing. Others ask students to interview each other, especially with questions related to the course topic, and then present an introduction about the interviewee.

Students could conduct these interviews by e-mail, or alternatively they could use Twitter. If they use Twitter they could become "Twitter Pals" in that they send short and frequent tweets to each other as a way of becoming acquainted. Another option is that they could meet each other on Facebook, which could also be an effective way of finding out about each other. The one thing to remind students of if they do use Facebook, however, is not to become so distracted by conversing with others on Facebook that they do not remember your class or the interview with their class peer.

Providing a Hook

One instructor, as an icebreaker, asked students to tell about the "weirdest gift" they had ever received. She later used this as an analogy to some aspect of their course content, which was on special education services. Other instructors, myself included, like to tell just a snippet of a personal anecdote, as this can provide a hook onto which students can tell related stories. Telling the latest adventures of the new and naughty tricks of my dog, Homer, for example, generally inspires others to relate a bit about their pets, too.

Visualization Techniques

Some instructors like to use visualization techniques, such as asking students to imagine they are sitting together in a comfortable classroom, preferably in a circle, which eradicates the feeling of hierarchy. Others paint a cozier picture, by telling students that this class will be run like a symposium, the true meaning of which is getting together and drinking with friends, while discussing topics of mutual interest. Hull (2002) conjured up to her online students at New York University the image of sitting with friends on the porch of an old country house during a delightful summer evening, sipping tea. I think these methods help prod the imagination into making up for any deficits in sensory stimuli of the online class.

Playing a Game

Another idea that I have seen used to good effect is to immediately involve students in playing a game. One such example is the game of the sinking ship, in which there is only one lifeboat left, with a capacity of twelve passengers, yet there are twenty passengers left on the ship. The instructor gives detailed descriptions of nineteen passengers by age, occupation, family status, income level, state of health, and so on, and with an added flourish, says the twentieth passenger is you! The challenge is to determine who should be allowed on the lifeboat. As you can imagine, a game of this nature immediately captures the imagination and appeals to the sense of excitement and adventure. The game could be used as an example of a concept taught later in the class, such as, by analogy, a corporate decision such as downsizing.

Asking Students What They Hope to Learn from the Course

Using the story "The Three Bricklayers" (see p. 70) as a way to exemplify different attitudes to learning, the instructor asks her students to name their own learning objectives, which is a great way of encouraging students to take responsibility. Although she does not mention it, it seems that from here the instructor and students could develop a learning contract, and if students want to learn more about areas that have not been included in the syllabus, then she could offer them individual research projects.

Asking Students to Write Short Descriptive Stories about Themselves

Jack A. Cummings, professor of Counseling and Educational Psychology at Indiana University, speaks of how he asked students to choose eight nouns that best describe themselves, and requested that each student write a short paragraph to elaborate on these nouns (Cummings, 1998). His own paragraph descriptions were so lovely that, if I had been a student in his class, I would have warmed up to him immediately. For example, one noun he used to describe himself was cyclist, and this is what he said:

> I have enjoyed riding bicycles since my parents bought a bike that was way too big for me when I was about five. I had to stand on an overturned bucket to even get on it. My feet only reached the pedals for about half a revolution. Now, riding through the hills of southern Indiana keeps me sane. My goal is to ride three to five times a week. On a good week, I sometimes get in three rides. The piles of paper in my office keep me chained to the desk.

Cummings recognized, in posting this information, that he was much more wordy than he would have been if he was meeting his students on campus, but online he did not have a time restraint, so he did not feel the need to summarize quite so much. He recognized a few other differences as well between online and face-to-face discussion.

For example, just as he could write his introduction in a leisurely fashion, so could everyone else, which was different, he said, from the campus setting in which, as student contributions are sequential, the ones asked last to contribute their introduction often have to rush before the end of the class session. Online, everyone can respond at virtually the same time, without taking up time from each other. Also, when students are asked to introduce themselves in a face-to-face classroom situation, many times they are so busy rehearsing what they are going to say, or so nervous about when it will be their turn, that they do not listen carefully to their classmates. Not so online!

Furthermore, Cummings points out, there is a permanent record of everyone's response, so if anyone wants to refresh his or her memory, he or she can simply click back to reread a student's comment. As a result of these fuller and more explicit introductions from the students, Cummings believes he became acquainted with each of the students much more quickly than in the campus class, in which it might take until midsemester to know just the more vocal students. I might add that it is also advantageous to the students as they too become familiar with each other quickly, and it eases their comfort level in participating in discussions of class content. Cummings illustrates a few student paragraph descriptions, my favorite of which is entitled "Ankle Twister":

> Ankle twister—Ever since I was a child, I have been falling on concrete, tripping on carpet, falling off my bike, and slipping on the ice. I am a very clumsy person by nature and I've sprained my ankle every year of my life. Attractive? . . . Many see this quality as simply irresistible

I have tried a similar technique of asking students to write short stories about themselves in my online classes, often to good effect. For example, in one online class on international children's literature, I asked students to complete the following sentence: "When I was young, I traveled to [you fill in the location] and the most outstanding part of my visit was when I. . . ." I then went ahead and composed my story first, as a way to illustrate to students the scope and possibilities of this exercise. I wrote:

> When I was young, I traveled to Lyons, France, to visit my French pen-pal, and the most outstanding part of my visit was when I was foolish enough to show off the few words of French that I knew to my pen-pal's mother, even though the words themselves were untrue.
> I brashly said, *"Je fais le regime!"* (I am on a diet) at which this remarkable French woman, robust and with a kitchen full of tempting ingredients, declared, *"Moi aussi!"* and that started my two weeks of terrific hunger. We would pass the boulanger, the windows full of baguettes and croissants, brioches and tempting and beautiful pastries, and my mouth would water. We would walk in the square, past the street market, and I'd have to be dragged from the counters with slabs of pâté, delicately thin sliced meats, frilly vegetables, and chocolate truffles. I would stare up at the grand, ornate stone buildings, thinking only of how the two *tranches de jambon* (slices of ham), which made up my entire dinner, made me feel hungrier still. But one fine day we had a visit into the country, to see my pen-pal's grandmother, and she put before me a steaming bowl full of soft, buttery, creamy pastina, and I will always remember how truly satisfying that tasted.

I received some wonderful student stories in return. One student from Texas visited Switzerland, and having never seen snow before, built her sister into a snowman. Another student traveled alone to the Philippines and shared this story:

> It was the beginning of hurricane season high up in the mountains and all I remember of the last half of our stay was sitting on the toilet in the bathroom wondering if porcelain could conduct electricity. My mother yelled at me for spending over $10.00 on a long-distance phone call just to ask her that.

In an online writing class, I started by asking students to complete the sentence, "Yesterday morning I received a letter from my close friend Julie, in Australia, and she said that whenever she thinks of me she thinks. . . ." I asked them to include within that letter at least three statements that best describe themselves. I again went first with my letter, and received some exceptionally witty responses back from students, which helped us to get to know each other and to positively look forward to reading future responses. Following are excerpts from the students' writings.

> In a conversation with friends, Julie said she spoke of me proudly and my ability to remain a vegan, even though I live with a chocolate lover and am tempted daily by one and all. She herself tries to give up meat, but those darn Australian steakhouses are so tantalizing!

> I received a letter from my friend Julie in Australia today and she said when she thinks of me she thinks about how heartily I laugh and how contagious my laugh is. She says she can still hear my outbursts of laughter through the living room walls when she lived next door to me.

> Quite a temper but a great judge of character, usually. I remember once we argued about the origins of cynicism all night. She proceeded to ramble something about how I was trying to be a cynic and even though I had an amazing "cynically-laced facade" she could see right through me. Apparently unbeknownst to myself I was an "idealist" in both thought and action. She was right.
> Julie was a trip. You know she was always saying the semi-right thing at the more than wrong time . . . hmmm . . . kind of glad she went back [to Australia].

Spending time at the start of the course to become familiar with the students, in any of the various ways mentioned, is crucial (a) to establishing an atmosphere of trust, enjoyment, and excitement; (b) to engaging them in future work throughout the semester; and (c) in being able to accurately assess their learning outcomes by the completion of the course.

Moving Beyond the Online Lounge: Getting to Know Your Students in a Hybrid

On one occasion while teaching the hybrid expository writing class at Rutgers, I wondered around the third week of the semester, whether when online, students felt that they were talking with each other or merely typing on a sterile computer in isolation. I think this is important to know, as I feel that to establish the feeling of class camaraderie that is so necessary for us to construct meaning together, we should know just who it is we are talking to. How else, after all, could a student become completely engaged in the online class? As one student remarked, "The discussion becomes more interesting once my classmates answer me; then I will imagine their faces and reaction when they read and were answering me."

Now, it just so happened that early in that semester, we read a piece by Oliver Sacks titled "The Mind's Eye: What the Blind See," which is about how some people, blinded later in life, retain a visual memory and imagination of how things looked. This seemed to me to provide a direct analogy to the online discussions that my students and I were conducting; we were also responding to each other while totally devoid of any visual stimuli of each other.

Given this analogy, and both as a way of understanding Sacks's piece as well as hoping to promote effective online communication, each time I now teach the hybrid expository writing course, I write this to my students:

> Well, we all see each other face to face on Wednesdays, but when we are online we need to resort to memory and imagination of what each of us looks like. Well, at least, I tend to do this. Do you? I'd love to know what you think about this! When you write your responses, do you imagine that you are talking to all of us and do you therefore see us, or do you just think you are typing a message in a box?

I have received an interesting range of responses, and most students by week three, in fact, admitted to feeling that they were only typing into a box when online. One responded by writing,

> I find myself laughing at these past posts because I also try to place a face with a name for the people in our class but find myself at a loss. I was also

thinking that I was the only one who felt this "awkwardness" but apparently I WAS WRONG! It's actually a depressing fact because you all seem brilliant and if only I knew who was who and could place a name with a face then I would understand the past thoughts and posts with a deeper meaning. In fact, the only thing I can remember clearly from our last class was how one of us locked his keys and belongings in his car.

What was particularly interesting about this response was that the student mentioned that he thought he was the only one who felt *awkward* about not knowing his classmates, and also he seemed to know intuitively that if he did know who was saying what, the dialogue would take on deeper significance.

Most of the other students also related that, despite being three weeks into the semester, their classmates were strangers to them. One remarked, "I absolutely love the analogy [between Sacks's article and] the online classroom! . . . Every time I log on, I try to match the names to the faces but so far I am horrible at doing such. Further along in the semester I know it will get easier; just like the blind have to get used to the lack of sight, so do I." At least she was showing some optimism, but I felt that it was not enough to wait and hope that with time this would be remedied. I wanted to accelerate the process. And another student responded by saying,

> I think I'm fairly good at memorizing faces; however, I'm not very good with names, so it becomes difficult associating names to the faces that I memorized. And to be honest, I do not recognize any names in this group, so I have no image of talking to them when I'm typing. Sometimes, I imagine others typing into their laptops or computers just as I am in some cozy spot alone. . . . we could be in the same room and not recognize each other typing into the same discussion.

And another succinctly concluded, "When I respond here I only see text appearing in a box. I don't feel like I am talking to my peers or imagine their faces. I don't hear other people's voices when I read their responses and I don't feel like I'm talking as I type. I see what I'm typing and nothing more." My despair grew as I read on. How could we all be such strangers to each other? The next student's response only further reinforced my concern. He wrote, "As I'm writing now, into this 'box,' I am not envisioning myself speaking with any one of you, or conjuring up anyone's face as I type. Although I know all of you will be reading this, I'm still not thinking of your faces as individuals or a group. Saying and thinking this seems quite odd, actually."

Yes, very odd indeed. In fact, not only odd but as one student said, scary: "When I type in this white boxy thingy, I imagine I'm talking to a white room empty of everything except a white chalk board and white desks. To think about that now, it's kind of scary to imagine, honestly, but I can't stop my mind from creating the random things it does." And another added that she feels she knows me but certainly not anyone else, as demonstrated by her remark:

> I'm pretty awful with facial recognition unless it's someone I live around, talk to frequently, something like that—I know what Dr. Bender looks like, mostly, in my mind because I'm watching her for most of the class. I don't know what most of the students look like, however, because I deal with them on a much more infrequent basis. I could probably stand on a bus next to one of you and not realize we have class together.

But I think the remark that clinched things for me more than any of the others was the following:

> Frankly speaking, I'm terrible at names. If I had to give some sort of parallel here between our Wednesday meetings and online discussion forum it would be Hull and his experience with losing sight. [Hull was a character Sacks had written about in his piece, who went into "deep blindness," not being able to ever recall visual memories at all, not even of his loved ones.] When I sit before the keyboard and go into [our online class] I immerse in deep blindness, I see names but I do not see any faces. When I'm in class, it is vice versa. Almost, as if I was taking two separate classes.

Two separate classes! That was a definite red flag for me, as my hope is for the online and campus classes to merge and intertwine seamlessly together, each enriching the other and giving the student plenty of opportunities for engagement. However, the students who confessed to having no visual memory of their classmates, although in the majority, did not represent all my students' views. For example, one interestingly tried to identify individuals not through images of what they looked like, but by how they write, as she explains: "I do not envision faces either when I am writing in these message boxes but I have gotten used to the style of writing certain people use and I've begun to associate people's name[s] with the way that they write." I liked this facility that the student had developed, and thought it was also true for me, but I could not help also finding an analogy with what Sacks had said about how some blind people cope for their lack of sight by developing their other senses such as sound. Whereas everything is obviously silent in the online class, this student's remark demonstrates how she could identify voices in the form of writing style.

And another seemed to follow a similar thought pattern, saying,

> When I post responses online I think that more so than actually talking to a person's actual figure in my mind that I am talking to their words and ideas. I think of people more along the lines of their words while online than the corresponding faces in class. Online, people are simply represented by the thoughts they've had that they've put into language, which is much different than someone talking in class, especially since the words here last and can be gone back to time and time again. So I feel like the online portion of the class is more idea based and language based than image based, for me at least.

This is definitely advantageous, and I very much liked the way this student was aware of focusing on ideas expressed by his classmates, and I also liked how the student noted the benefits of the archived online discussions.

But I still thought it would be beneficial if all students could also visualize each other as they spoke together online. And indeed a few of them said they were able to do this. For example, one student said, "I actually imagine myself sitting in my seat in class and actually talking to the class—of course this is not 100% accurate since I believe nothing can replicate the real experience (although Sacks does mention that that may not be the case!)." And some struggled and made a conscious effort, as with this student who said, "At this moment as I struggle to meet the 12pm deadline, I find it difficult to imagine my Expository Writing classmates in detail; however, if I close my eyes I can almost construct the classroom in my mind as the faces of the names I've known to associate with faces come to me in a hazy blur."

One, however, was much more certain, saying, "I ALWAYS imagine a person's face and put an image to their name whenever I converse with them (either through text messaging, on the phone, computer, etc.)." I thought it was interesting that this student mentioned texting, because I might have suspected that, because this is an activity that most students do frequently, they would have trained themselves to imagine the person with whom they were conversing. But only one student seemed to have this certainty.

So it was with this fear of the hybrid seeming "Almost, as if I was taking took two separate classes" as one student expressed previously, that I thought that I should swiftly take action to ensure that all the students, and not just those more visual learners, could visualize me and each other while we communicated together online. And what I did was, in the very next campus class, ask everyone to rearrange the furniture and sit in a circle. Second, I said that we should have another round of introductions, and that everyone should say one thing remarkable or surprising about himself or herself, and that all of us listening should then take a mental photo of each student while the introductions were taking place. I had amazing and memorable remarks from students by way of introduction, including one young woman who said she accidentally set her hair on fire twice, and one fellow from Canada who said he calls the letter *Z* "zed."

Once we returned online after that class, there was a noticeable change. "Needless to mention I'm now able to associate faces with names all thanks to today's circle-shaped class," one student wrote. Another amusingly remarked, "Okay, all! Now that I can 'see' you all mentally thanks to today's circle, I guess I'll get the ball rolling quickly in fear of dirty looks or directed anger next Wednesday—since now you can all place my name with my face as well!" Thereafter, it seemed that we started visualizing and knowing each other, and even more so as the weeks went by, and this really helped to establish a truly remarkable and beneficial class bond among us all.

So I would definitely recommend that you give hybrid students an exercise similar to the one I describe. You obviously do not need to read Sacks's piece about blind people (although it is a very fascinating piece, indeed), but try to discover early in the semester whether students feel they are talking to each other or just typing into a box on the computer. If the latter is the case, have another round of introductions in the next campus class. This is beneficial in terms of student engagement and learning for the remainder of the hybrid course. I make this recommendation because I have seen some hybrid classes in which bonding is not established, and as a consequence these generally exhibit much less student involvement and a scant amount of student participation in class discussions. And it is generally the case that if students participate less, the class becomes disappointing and learning is diminished.

Establishing the Right Tone

The TEDI (2002) article mentions the importance, if teaching on campus, of maintaining a confident demeanor as you stand before your students; that you have a clear, energetic tone of voice; and that you smile, maintain eye contact, and speak with enthusiasm. This establishes you in the students' minds as not only being an expert in your subject, but also being a good communicator of that information, and thus a good teacher.

With an enjoyment of and competence in writing, this same sort of enthusiasm can be conveyed online, not only through your choice of words, but also through your responsiveness to your students. Above all, it is important to convey to the students that your online class is a safe place in which all responses are welcomed and encouraged. Obviously feelings of safety and security (which help to promote collaborative learning) do not come all at once and cannot be there just because you tell the students it is a safe place. Instead you, as the instructor, need to instill it. You can do this by setting a warm, enthusiastic tone, and by replying to students, so that they are encouraged to check back to see if anyone responded to their comment. (For further discussion on safety in the online class, see the section in Chapter 7 called "How We Show We Are Listening and Caring Online.")

When students feel recognized and acknowledged by the instructor, which is usually their first priority, they can then start becoming familiar with each other, and it is in this way that trust gradually starts to build up. In addition, a warm, conversational tone can be combined effectively with a rigorous academic approach, in which there is challenge and discourse, leading to an extensive exploration of the subject matter. Remember that you want to be a good role model for your students at all times, and you want them to consider you approachable.

Whichever icebreaker activity you choose to do at the start of the semester, I recommend that you post the first response, as this not only provides the students with guidelines and a good model, but also helps to establish the tone that you would like your class to take. It is particularly important from the start of the semester to be encouraging and supportive. The tone of your conversation is important, as it can serve either to distance you from your students or bring you into a closer circle. I recommend that you adopt a conversational style, as this assists in overcoming feelings of coldness or remoteness that working online might otherwise bring. You want as much as possible to make the online class feel like an exciting forum, in which real people are speaking to each other about mutually fascinating ideas.

Students might never before have experienced asynchronous discussions within an academic framework, so you need to do what you can to help make them not only feel welcomed but also at their peak to do their best work. I particularly recommend that you log on frequently during the early days of the class, to acknowledge students by name when commenting on their responses, so that they know you have noticed them and they feel included in the group. It is wise, when commenting on students' initial responses, to ask another question so that the conversation continues.

It is frequently amazing to me how students unknowingly mimic the tone of the instructor. If you, as instructor, answer briefly and curtly, students will answer in kind. If you post long responses, chances are that the students' responses will be long. Often, instructors who post infrequently and have brief responses that do not address every student's comment do not encourage discussion.

An additional topic is how instructors prefer to be addressed by their students. Some instructors, in an effort to make for maximum conviviality and the decrease of hierarchy, ask students to call them by their first names, whereas others might prefer more formality. One observation I have made is that students generally treat faculty more informally in the online setting, but if this is not your preference, certainly let students know. It is also beneficial to ask students what they would like to be called. They may want to be called by their name posted on the screen, or they may have a nickname or other preference. I should mention, as an aside, that I came across one instructor who liked to call all his students by their last name, Mr. Smith, Ms. Jones, and so on. Certainly he gave to his class a most delightfully old-fashioned Oxford or Cambridge atmosphere, and one could almost imagine old dons gliding along wood-paneled corridors.

Having established ways in which to successfully engage students in the introductory stages of the online course, the concern now shifts to sustaining active participation on the part of all students, throughout the duration of the semester. The discussion forums are the life blood and center of energy of the online class, and we will turn to methods of stimulating online discussion in Chapter 7.

7

ASPECTS OF ONLINE
COMMUNICATION

Let me not to the marriage of true minds
Admit impediment.

—Shakespeare, Sonnet 116

How to Facilitate and Stimulate Online Discussion

We have discussed how students benefit from an online orientation to gain the technical information needed to navigate through their online class, and we have discussed including an icebreaker activity in the "Virtual Lounge" of your online class so as to help everyone become acquainted in the initial days of the semester. These, according to Gilly Salmon, are the first two steps in the learner's development, which she calls "Access and Motivation" and "Online Socialization," respectively (Salmon, 2000).

Having now gained familiarity with the technology, and having developed a general idea of the personality and interests of the instructor and classmates, the time is ripe for the learning of the course material to begin. This next step, which Salmon (2000) calls "Information Exchange," is the stage at which rigorous interactive discussion takes place, and it is to the techniques for promoting a good, in-depth discussion that this chapter turns attention. My basic premise is that learning is best achieved through dialogue. Dialogue comes from the word *dia,* meaning "between," and *logos,* meaning "word" (Vella, 1997). In this way, we can think of teaching and learning as being composed of and communicated by the words that flow between teacher and student, as well as student and student.

I believe that online teaching and learning has the potential to produce a true meeting of minds. This is because it is devoid of information that is extraneous in most courses, about factors such as age, race, possibly gender, and even such stereotypical distractions as clothing, hairstyle, accents of speech, and so on. Without those distractions, one can fully concentrate on the intellects, interests, and personalities of the participants. It is, in essence, a democratic system in which ideas and information are free to swirl in all directions. How can we fully realize this potential and establish the setting for a completely satisfying and rich online discussion? The following ideas suggest how this might be encouraged.

Clearly Define Your Expectations for Discussion

Frequency of Participation

Provide students with a clear idea as to how often they can expect you to be in the online class. Some instructors who operate better with structure like to be definitive about when they will log on, saying, for example, that they will be there every Monday, Wednesday, and Friday from 11:00 to 1:00. Others, making fuller use of the flexibility of the online environment, prefer to say that they will be logging on at least four times per week. Stipulating the approximate frequency of logging on to class without specifying time slots allows you, if you have an inspirational thought at 3 A.M. to grab it while it is still fresh and exciting, and enter it into your class. Similarly, you are not disappointing students if a sudden meeting comes up at the same time you told students you would be online.

Making explicit the frequency of your online participation in class helps students to anticipate when they will be hearing from you, and also will not give false impressions that just because the class is available 24/7, that you are, too. Try to be realistic about how frequently you can participate in your online class. One instructor told his class he would do so every day, and then, when on certain occasions he found this to be impossible, some students felt disappointed about not hearing from him.

Also, state at the beginning of the course how often you want your students to log on and participate. I emphasize that students should participate because just logging on is not sufficient. Unless you "hear" from your students in their responses, there is little you can know about them. If using Twitter, I advise that you should similarly specify at the start of the semester the frequency with which the students should tweet. Sample (2010) says this could be every day for a month, or once a week, depending on the learning objectives of the class. And it is a good idea if you, as the teacher, inform students as to how often you are likely to send tweets.

In a hybrid or traditional campus class, students could be encouraged to tweet *during* times in which their class meets on campus, creating what Sample calls a "digital back channel of conversation" (Sample, 2010). As Cohen observes, passing notes in class has probably occurred ever since there were classrooms, but this has now been elevated to a "digital art form" (2008). But instead of thinking of the note writer as the bad student who is "tuning out," he or she can be reconsidered as engaging in a metaconversation, an opportunity of creating a second layer to the discussion, disrupting perhaps the traditional method of teaching, but enabling shy students, nonnative speakers, or students in a very large lecture class to have a voice, and even allowing for them to bring in relevant Web links related to the topic of the class. In fact Young (2008) speaks of Professor Camptese, of Penn State University, who has two screens in his class, one for projecting his own slides, and one to project a dynamic Twitter stream from his students. Even though this could be thought of as distracting, Camptese encourages students to tweet frequently, as he feels this adds a rich, additional layer to the discussion. It also provides an opportunity for students to ask questions, and for the teacher to have immediate feedback as to whether the lecture information is comprehensible or needs to be restated or delivered again in a different way. Additionally, as Young (2008) notes, the immediacy of the messages can make the class feel more like a community. Furthermore, the Twitter stream could be a useful archive for later use.

Participation Counts Toward the Final Grade

You can make participation count significantly toward the final grade, but it should not only be a quantitative measure. After all, you cannot measure the success of a certain dish by the number of times the chef enters the kitchen. So the quality of response has to count as well. A student who logs on five times over two days only to say, "I agree with Miranda," for example, is obviously not contributing as much as another student who logs on only once during that time, but contributes a thoughtful, substantive, insightful response. Generally I have found that as the semester progresses, the class gathers a momentum of its own as certain topics heat up, and at these times some students participate several times a day!

If participation in discussion counts significantly toward the final grade, then it would be fair to let students know how they are doing at specific intervals throughout the semester, rather than leaving this a mystery until the end. Timing, however, is crucial. You do not want to grade the discussion of a particular topic until you are sure it is completed, as otherwise it will stifle further responses. If you let students know that you will be grading discussion topics, it might be a helpful incentive to motivate them to discuss the topic in a timely manner, rather than entering a discussion too late.

Style of Online Responses

Let students know that online discussion should have the feeling of a seminar. In one of the first online classes I taught in the early 1990s, I had a student with whom I had spoken on the phone at the beginning of the semester, and was immediately struck by how articulate, enthusiastic, and intelligent she sounded. Yet five days elapsed and there were no online responses from her. Surprised by this, I called her again. She explained her silence by saying that she thought she had to write something very formal in the online discussion, complete with an outline and footnotes. I told her the time for that sort of polish was in the written papers and exams. The online discussion, I informed her, was just that—an opportunity for bouncing intelligent, informative ideas off each other in a spontaneous stream of consciousness. Of course the hope is that student responses will not be full of grammatical and spelling mistakes, but I think it advisable that they feel that they are "talking" rather than composing an essay. Once I clarified my expectations both with her and the rest of the students, the class positively exploded with responses from everyone.

Discuss Rules for Civility

Blankespoor (1996) tells his students at the start of the semester that the class is like a "family" for a semester, and just as in a family, everyone should be "positive, sensitive, considerate, polite and tolerant." I inform my students that I love to thrash around in a thorough discussion of a topic from multiple perspectives, as I believe this is the stuff of good, balanced considerations. I welcome everyone's response, even if it runs counter to the prevailing ideology, as long as all responses can be substantiated.

Often the soundest learning is brought about through passionate argument, but this should be accompanied by mutual respect and toleration of differing viewpoints. Guidelines for this type of respectful debate are essential not only for the smooth functionality of the online class, but also because learning civil behavior is ultimately crucial for the students' survival in a pluralistic world, and for them to learn how to participate in rigorous challenges and exchange of ideas (Baldwin, 2000).

Once guidelines of civility are drawn up, it is important for faculty not to go into denial if rude or inappropriate behavior is occurring in the class, as this would imply that they are condoning this behavior. Furthermore, it would be a good idea for faculty to include a wide variety of teaching methods and learning activities, so that students with diverse skills and learning styles have a more equitable chance for full involvement. Instructors should learn student names (something that is easy to do online) and show an interest in each of them by responding frequently and thoughtfully to their comments.

There are various examples of student rudeness on campus, including lateness or leaving early, napping, reading a newspaper, speaking with each other rather than being attentive to the class, and possibly even threatening or actually physically attacking a professor over a grade (Schneider, 1998). Some students might even chat on their cell phones during classes or send text messages. Forni (2008) writes about incivility in the classroom and recommends that students should be told to give their undivided attention to whoever is speaking in the class. I find this an interesting point because in a class I taught, hardly any students had laptops and most never looked at their cell phones, but as soon as it was time for student presentations, out came all manner of technology, large or small, furtively under the desk or in plain view. I was horrified and felt it was so disrespectful of their classmates. I made an announcement pointing out that when it was their turn to present, they would not like it if everyone was texting or looking at Facebook, at which point all the "offenders" disconnected at once.

Although these circumstances can only occur in face-to-face situations, it does not mean that the online class is guaranteed to be free of expressions of incivility or lack of consideration. For example, a student who posts a very late response well after the class has moved on to a new topic is unfair and inconsiderate in expecting the collective class attention to be reverted to this previous topic.

Online students also can be impolite or disrespectful in their remarks to each other or to the professor. Perhaps students might behave in an uncivil manner because of the greater mix of diverse backgrounds, each with their own differing value system, or because the subject matter of the course seems esoteric (Baldwin, 2000). I believe that some students might feel unhappy in very large campus classes because of the remoteness from the professor and consequent feelings of anonymity. This certainly points to an advantage of adding a Web component to such a class, as the students could be split into smaller online groups and thus gain an increased means of communication and a better opportunity for becoming acquainted. This decrease in a sense of isolation through online discussion opportunities might reduce the likelihood of bad, attention-getting behavior from some disruptive students.

Should the instructor seek student opinions when making decisions that affect the class, or is it better for the instructor alone to make decisions (Anderson and Adams, 1992)? I advocate seeking student opinions, although of course I recognize that this might depend on the discipline of the course and the class size. As well as making explicit statements at the start of the semester about civility, involve students in drawing up a desired code of conduct, saying that everyone has a right to participate in its creation and that it is a living document that will evolve throughout the semester as situations change, as long as everyone is in agreement. I found that because students were directly and democratically involved in the creation of this code, and it was, therefore, a contract entered into together, they were more likely to keep to it. The only thing left to be decided upon, if you involve students in the creation of a code of conduct, is the system of enforcement. I found that students wanted to avoid "virtual finger-pointing" at each other when there was noncompliance, and preferred for me, as instructor, to take this role. Student opinion on this might vary, however, as some might want to take full responsibility not only for evolving the original contract but also for enforcement.

Whether you state your expectations on your syllabus before the start of the semester or have student involvement in drawing up a code of conduct, I advise that you explicitly state your views about whether you permit technology in your campus classroom. One of my colleagues designed a syllabus that banned cell phones during class time, but told me that it did not prevent a young male student's phone from ringing in class. When this happened, she apparently reached over to answer it herself. It turned out that it was the student's mother calling to remind him that it was her birthday, so my colleague told all the class to sing "Happy Birthday" to her, which embarrassed the student at the same time as teaching him to obey the rules, and hopefully pleased the mother that she had so many well-wishers. My sister, Gillian Stansfield, who teaches at a university in England and had threatened to throw the cell phone out of the window if she saw a student using one, had once confiscated a cell phone when a little text message popped up on its screen saying, "Please throw me out of the window!" She did not see the student who sent the message actually doing so, but she was too amused to also take his phone away.

Sherry Turkle (2011), who has been teaching at the Massachusetts Institute of Technology (MIT) for over 30 years, says MIT allows laptops into the class at the teacher's discretion. But Turkle says that when she stood at the back of the classroom, she saw many students clicking into Facebook or shopping for music during class time. Bauerlein quotes Oppenheimer as saying, after visiting a high school in Maryland that acquired lavish technology for the classroom, that when he walked round the room with the teacher he saw all the students conscientiously entering data into spreadsheets, but when he walked round the room by himself he "spie[d] the same students on the Dallas Cowboys Web site, joining a news exchange on favorite sodas, and checking out the Netscape headlines" (2008, p. 131). As for my own experience, a few years ago I was a consultant at the Teaching Excellence Center of a prestigious university, my job being to observe the teacher and give feedback on how effectively he or she taught the class. So as to be unobtrusive to students, and in this way not change the normal dynamics of the class, I would tend to sit in the back of the lecture hall, and I was somewhat dismayed by how many students were logging into sites on their laptops that had nothing to do with the topic of the class itself.

Turkle said that recently she decided to ban the use of laptops in her class, and remarked that some students were "annoyed, almost surly." She went on to say, however, "They were not in a position to defend their right to shop and download music in class, so they insisted that they liked taking notes on their computer" (2011, p. 163). One student asked her if doodling was permissible, and she said it was, as she thinks people often think of ideas while doodling. Essentially she wanted students off the Web so that they had time to think about how to think about a problem. I wonder if she did find that the students had learned to think about thinking about a problem, and if their grades improved as a reflection of this, but the following year she returned to allowing students to bring the laptop to class if they wanted to.

I have not restricted laptops in my campus classes, although I do sometimes wonder what the few students who bring them are doing behind their laptop lids. I allow cell phones, too, as I believe laptops and cell phones can be a great resource. Cell phones could be used in the class if you would like students to use Twitter for a "back channel of conversation" (Sample, 2010), as mentioned earlier in this chapter in the section "Clearly Define Your Expectations for Discussion." And cell phones, laptops, or even iPads could be useful if we stumble across something in discussion that we want to know more about, as students can simply and rapidly look it up and provide the information. Also, in one of my hybrid classes, I had had students prepare online for a debate that was carried out in the campus class, and I spontane-ously thought once in the classroom that it would add a good, dramatic touch if we had some appropriate music as an introduction to the debate itself. So one student took out his laptop, scrolled though YouTube videos, and came across some amusingly wonderful music, which he played to us, putting us in the mood for the debate to begin.

Some universities, such as Oklahoma State University and Illinois Insti-tute of Technology, gave students iPads at the start of the fall 2010 semester, as they wanted to detect if these would enhance learning, as well as decrease students' expenses on textbooks because some of the materials might be available online (Foresman, 2010). However, Wieder (2011b) feels that, despite iPads having many advantages—such as being fairly intuitive and easy to use, which makes the viewing of media very effective, as well as the fact that they are small and easily portable, have an extended battery life, and can foster collaboration between students who share their screens—they are still problematic for educational purposes. One disadvantage is their slow finger typing (as would also be true on a smartphone), and another issue is that it is not possible to mark up readings on the iPad. They do have one more distinctive advantage, however, and that is that it is not possible to multitask on an iPad because when reading an e-book the student cannot also have the e-mail window open simultaneously.

In general, I believe that bright students would resist using technology inappropriately during class time, as exemplified by one of my students who said,

> I do feel the need to note, though, that I've yet to bring my laptop to a class and I can't really see a need to. I don't want to allow myself to get distracted because I know that dividing my attention, trying to focus on two things at once, will lead to my diminished perception of one or the other, or possibly both. . . . I admit that technology is very important in my life, but I don't see a need for it, on an individual level, during classes.

However, this same student, after watching *Digital Nation,* remarked,

> As far as multitasking *with* technology and how it's affecting students' educations, I have to wonder how very different it is from multitasking *without* technology. There's a very obvious difference in appearance—teachers can very clearly see the presence of tech in their rooms—but is someone half-taking notes and half-checking Facebook any different, in practice, from someone half-taking notes and half-writing a handwritten

note to pass to a friend or half-daydreaming? I'm curious if the involvement of technology is really such a paradigm shift as the documentary implies or simply another outlet to feed a multitasking inclination that was already there.

I think the internal argument that was going on within this high-achieving student was an interesting one; it was almost as if she could justify technology-enabled distraction in the classrooms, but perhaps did not want it to apply to herself just yet. I find her hesitation fascinating as it implies that she could tell intuitively what many recent studies, as noted in Chapter 4, "Paradigm Lost," have recently shown; namely, that multitasking is in fact detrimental to learning, so it is not only classroom civility that is at stake, but also a diminished potential for individual academic achievement.

Employ the Socratic Method

Which is the better method in online teaching, lecturing to the students or employing the Socratic method? I would like to illustrate this debate by presenting a fictitious dialogue between two online professors. Although it is fictitious, it is the sort of dialogue I have heard, and maybe you have as well. Alternatively, maybe you have spoken some of these exact words yourself.

> SALLY: I'm setting up my online class and I'm definitely going to devote the first couple of days to personal introductions and shared anecdotes.
> BILL: I hate that "touchy-feely" sort of stuff. I want to let my students know that learning is serious, and we are getting right down to business. I suppose, throughout the semester, you encourage students to continue being "anecdotal."
> SALLY: Absolutely! I very much believe that students should relate their education to personal experiences, as that way it is more relevant and meaningful to them.
> BILL: I couldn't disagree more! What students want to pay all that money only to waste their time hearing trivial personal information from their classmates rather than instruction from their professor?

I think the subtext of this conversation is that no one can say with certainty which is the best approach to take. Most university instructors have not had teacher training, and what is more, they perform their teaching usually in the isolation of their own classroom or online course shell. When instructors talk with each other, it is more likely to be about the curriculum content than the method of communicating that content.

We teach in our own unique way. We have been conditioned, of course, by our own personal histories in general, and by profound teachers or mentors, by whom we were lucky enough to be taught, in particular. Both our upbringing and the influences on us as students will contribute toward our educational values and teaching techniques.

Furthermore, we are currently influenced not only by the institution in which we teach, but also by the students who occupy our classes. The greatest unknown and the current influential element each semester, therefore, is the student body. But, online, how else can we know who these students are, unless we hear from them? How can we know that our lectures have been read and understood unless we read our students' reactions to them? True, some software programs have tracking devices whereby we can see what a student has supposedly read, but unless a student responds to questions from the lecture, how can we be certain that the student did not merely log on to the lecture and then take the dog for a walk? My feeling about the tracking device is that it is actually more informative about what students have not read than what they supposedly have read.

I agree with Sally's viewpoint from the dialogue, namely, that students learn in a meaningful way when they are encouraged to actively and deliberately explore the links among education, prior knowledge, and personal experience, and respond accordingly. And I agree with Charles Kerns in his view that it is beneficial for students to exert control over their learning and have the possibility of reflection, assessment, and co-construction of knowledge (quoted by Young, 2002b).

Therefore, I do not advocate a purely lecture mode of instruction, in which the implicit assumption is that students, like newborn babies, are empty vessels in need of filling with knowledge. Instead, I think more can be gained online within a highly interactive environment.

Establish a Circle of Learning

It is quite amazing how relatively quickly some students begin to recognize each other's voice, as everyone's unique personality radiates through their response. For this to happen, however, students must be informed at the beginning of the semester that they should actively engage in online discussion. Rather than there being a hierarchical structure to discussions, encourage interactivity between students as well as from students to you. Students appreciate hearing from you frequently within the discussion forum, to know you are completely involved in the collaborative online conversations. Even though you, the instructor, are in the same circle of learning as the students, you still have the prerogative to guide the discussion, introduce new concepts, and steer things along, much as parents do within the family circle (Dewey, [1938] 1963).

Encourage Students to Be Active Learners

Encouragement of active participation from the students, as they contribute to the evolving dialogue, stimulates student learning. As Dewey ([1938] 1963) states, "I assume that amid all uncertainties there is one permanent frame of reference; namely the organic connection between education and personal experience." Similarly, Fisher says, "Education cannot take place without some degree of self-disclosure" (2001, p. 138). If information is seen as being meaningful and relevant, thus stimulating students to draw on their knowledge and experience, then true learning is taking place.

However, it is important to draw the right balance between a class that is too much of an "ivory tower" and one that slips into an excessive amount of personal, anecdotal discussions. The online environment can be alluring for some students, and with the protection of relative anonymity behind their computer screen, they can dip into more tales of intimacy than is common in the campus class (see "How We Show We Are Listening and Caring Online" later in the chapter).

Brookfield and Preskill (1999) believe that a personal narrative is acceptable, as long as it is accompanied by critical thinking, in which the student can perhaps understand his or her experience from a new perspective. In some skills-based classes, students might already be working in the field, and it could be beneficial to ask them to relate their experiences, and also to make comparisons between what they have learned in the classroom and what they are doing in practice. In such cases, it would be worthwhile to encourage students to interact with each other, and see if anyone has vastly similar or different experiences.

If students work too independently, then the class will take on the tone of a one-on-one type correspondence course and will lack the potentially exciting group dynamic. To encourage interactive discussion, the instructor should make every student feel recognized and included by responding quickly to comments and acknowledging students by name when referring to their contribution. As Blankespoor advises, "The key to reducing or eliminating bias about students is to take a personal interest in every student" (1996).

I do not think it is necessary for the instructor to answer each student individually, as if playing several games of ping-pong, one with each student; instead, it is more meaningful to respond to several students at a time, weaving together the similarities and differences in their responses and moving the analysis to a deeper and more profound level by asking new questions generated from the discussion. I think it also helps students enormously if your responses are positive in tone. Always try to draw on their strengths and build on them. If you disagree with them or feel that they have been incorrect, then correct them with tact, pointing out the positives in what they have said before giving suggestions for improvement, as online critiques can sound much harsher than perhaps intended because they are devoid of voice inflections and facial expressions.

We have talked about the advantages of students being active learners, but there is also a pragmatic reason as to why it is advantageous to read responses from students throughout the semester. For example, if two students both turn in a brilliant final paper, yet one participates actively throughout the semester while the other is mostly absent from discussion, how can you determine the authenticity of the second student's work or feel that this student is equally deserving of an A?

Are Personality Traits of Introversion and Extroversion Altered by Communicating Online?

I find it quite interesting to ponder whether certain behaviors, such as being naturally extroverted or introverted, are altered by communicating online rather than face to face. I wonder also about the consequent impact on the dynamics of the group as a whole. How many students are terrified by the seemingly indelible quality of their response, which, once submitted, is there for all to see? In other words, how many students are "cyber shy"?

I would argue that there are, in fact, many reasons why normally shy students in the campus class have greater opportunities for online participation. Many of the following constraints, which naturally exist in a face-to-face environment, are lifted.

Freedom from Spatial Constraints

In the campus class, we are sometimes restricted by the seating arrangement, especially in those classrooms that are oddly shaped or have built-in furniture; and often on campus, it is those students who occupy front-row seats who participate the most. Many instructors, often unconsciously, are positively prejudiced toward the best students, which raises the interesting question as to whom do we teach? Blankespoor states, "Most of us like to interact with those who are doing well in our class" (1996). It is gratifying and exciting, so it might well be the case that our eyes look more frequently to our brightest students, as it is from them that we receive the most encouragement and are likely to receive the best answers to our questions. We might, therefore, be allowing our favorites to dominate the discussion.

We should not ignore a whole section of our class—possibly the very students who need us the most or who have something to contribute but shy away instead (Brookfield and Preskill, 1999). I believe that conditions are more egalitarian online because everyone has an equal chance to participate.

Freedom from Temporal Constraints

The online class is available 24/7. In this way, when you or your students have a good idea or generally feel inspired, you know the class is available and receptive. We might not necessarily feel our best at the scheduled time that a class meets on campus, but online we can join our class with a flick of a switch, as soon as we have an inspiration, thereby grabbing the idea while it is fresh and exciting.

This also helps the less assertive students who might not have had the time to respond in the finite time frame of the campus classroom as others talked first, talked more loudly, or generally interrupted them. It also helps to alleviate situations that can arise on campus in which you, the professor, ask a question and because there is no ready response and because the silence makes you uncomfortable, you provide the answer. Online students have more time to be reflective and provide well-thought-out answers.

Being online also helps to alleviate those awkward situations that can arise on campus, in which a student asks a question that stumps you. Instead of resorting to saying, "Good! Let's discuss that next week," you can research the answer there and then, and log back on with an informative response.

On campus it is advisable to create a smooth transition from one class to the next by starting the new class with questions about the previous one, such as, "What are some of the most important points we learned last week?" or "What surprised you most from last week?" (Brookfield and Preskill, 1999). Transitions are of less concern online because there are no discrete time intervals between classes. In fact, you can continue to have discussion about a previous topic, even as you open a new forum to consider the next topic. I should also add that even though this is an asynchronous model and students log on at their convenience, you still want to move them along to new topics as a group, to ensure meaningful interactivity.

Freedom from Cultural Constraints

Different cultures have different norms of what is considered respectful behavior. For example, Americans consider good eye contact to be important in demonstrating active listening, whereas other cultures consider a person to be more respectful when demure and distant from the professor. This latter type of response can be misinterpreted in a campus class here in the United States, but these kinds of confusions do not exist online.

We must be mindful, however, of the design of our online class, in terms of language and graphic representations, so that students of other countries do not feel confused. A U.S. mailbox, clearly understood by American students as representing e-mail, can look like a rubbish bin to students of some other cultures (Cassidy, 2002). Generally speaking, however, students of various cultures enjoy the increased opportunities that online discussion allows.

Some Obstacles to Participation in Online Discussion

Despite freedom from the constraints mentioned, there can still be inadequate participation in online discussion in some classes. We should first consider what is meant by silence online. Brookfield and Preskill (1999) tell us not to fear silence, although they are making this comment in reference to the campus class. I know from my own campus teaching, or observation of courses on campus, that a question thrown out to the students only to be met by silence is a pretty scary thing, and often gives the instructor the feeling that things are not going well. Often the instructor overcomes the discomfort by filling in the silence and answering the question instead of waiting to see if a student will do so. I think, on campus, it is important to remember that silence does not necessarily mean a lack of student interest, but could, instead, mean that students are thinking and constructing their ideas, and what the instructor should do to allow time for thought is to perhaps rephrase the question. But what does this mean online? What is silence online? It could be defined as no new responses after a significant amount of time, such as a day perhaps, or even half a day, if it is a large class.

Richardson and Turner (2001) concluded, after sampling online courses in their university, that effective communication cannot happen online, as it leads to fragmentation and isolation of all online participants. According to them, students reported missing the "visual, kinesthetic and sound cues that facilitate communication." One student said, "It seems unnatural that we have to think about what we want to say, rather than just saying it" (2001). In regard to this particular student, I cannot help wondering if he or she does not feel some necessity to think before speaking as well. Richardson and Turner report that another student said he was uncomfortable that, after having posted a comment, no one responded to it, but instead the conversation "dragged on without anything useful being said." Let us investigate why students might not be participating, apart from experiencing technical problems, and then let us look at what can be done to improve the situation. I would like to suggest the following reasons why certain students are not participating in an animated online discussion.

- The absence of visual and oral cues can initially confuse some students (Rohfeld and Hiemstra, 1995).
- The asynchronous format could make the discussion feel disjointed if there is a time lag between responses (Rohfeld and Hiemstra, 1995).
- They are not highly motivated students. A student might feel moved by certain responses, but nevertheless, for reasons of time constraints, laziness, discomfort, or possibly inertia, remains silent.
- Your class has not engaged them, perhaps because your questions are too vague, or your class does not yet feel safe to them.
- Students are confused by the tangled threads of the threaded discussion format. At best, they can only see the immediate message to which they are responding, but what about the buildup of conversation leading to this last response? And, if they read through all new responses before adding any responses of their own, they might be lost and unable to find their way back to the key messages to which they wanted to respond.
- Student postings are excessively long and therefore create a disincentive for discussion.
- Some students might not own computers, and are therefore at a disadvantage, as they might need to endure long waits for an available machine in a computer lab, whereas those who own a computer can happily click into their class at any time.
- If the class is relatively large, and if you have required students to respond in every forum, is this possibly introducing an artificial element into the normal evolution of conversation? In the traditional class, does every student join in with discussions on every topic? If there are over 20 students, for example, might it become repetitive, as there is nothing original left to say about a topic?

Suggestions for Overcoming Lack of Participation

I would like to turn attention to what can be done to stimulate a hearty, intelligent discussion. As Dan Eastmond stated in 1992, "A healthy computer conference carries an aura of excitement. The topics are engaging, comments build upon each other, and everyone participates." A thoroughly involved and interactive discussion is desirable because it is an important pedagogical tool that helps to promote thinking (Berge and Muilenburg, 2000). I believe that it is not inevitable that communication becomes fragmented and students feel isolated in the online setting, as Richardson and Turner stated. Many online students reported that they became better acquainted with their classmates online than in any campus classes. They also said that they disclosed information of a much more personal nature than they could imagine sharing in a face-to-face situation. But how can we promote the conditions for all students to want to participate? I think this can be done in the following ways.

Circumvent Problems before They Occur

If you are teaching a hybrid class, students should be clear from your course description that the course will include a Web component. I would advise that students be told they need a computer if they want to take a hybrid or a fully online course. Studies are increasingly showing that students who do not own a computer enjoy the online class less than those who own one (Benson and Wright, 1999), although certain exceptions apply—one of the most enthusiastic students in my online class does not own a computer.

At registration, students also should be informed that if they are taking an online course, it is not a "soft option"; the course requires independence and maturity in reaching goals. It might also be fair and honest to let students know that participating in an online class takes more, not less, time than a class on campus.

Ask the Right Questions

Asking the right questions is crucial in stimulating a good discussion. In fact, Berge and Muilenburg (2000) state, "In a constructivist learning environment, the instructor always needs to keep in mind that when facilitating online discussion, asking the right questions is almost always more important than giving the right answers."

Design High-Level Questions

You should attempt to promote the right conditions for constructive thinking in the online class. As mentioned in Chapter 3, this is thinking that (a) constructs knowledge from personal experience and prior learning; and (b) subsumes concept formation, creative problem solving, and shared social meaning through collaboration among the members of the class group. In so doing, you should attempt to design high-level questions that are as interesting as possible, with topics that are controversial, and stimulate thought and a variety of ideas. In other words, your aim should be to make the class an incredible experience, one that the student would not want to miss.

Many types of good questions can initially stimulate online discussion. They can be thought provoking and hypothetical (if you were _____, what would you see?) or evaluative (what do you think is better, x or y?). They could tie into whatever is topical at that point in time. They can be controversial. They can involve a case study, role-play, or synthesis of elements already learned (Berge and Muilenburg, 2000).

Types of Questions to Avoid

Avoid asking questions that are too vague. If the class has not yet become a safe place, an open-ended question such as "What do you think?" or "Who wants to start us off?" or "Are there any questions?" could be met with no response (Brookfield and Preskill, 1999). I think this might especially be the case in the online class, when at the beginning of the semester every aspect of the class feels so new. A student might fear asking a question, in case it seems too stupid, and then the stigma seems indelible.

Avoid questions that require a yes or no answer or that ask for one specific fact. I once worked with a history professor who asked questions such as, "When was the Battle of Waterloo?" and then was disappointed that he had very little student participation. So he redesigned his class to include higher order questions that, given certain facts, asked students to make comparisons, make predictions, suggest causes.

This provoked constructive thought and opened the gates for meaningful discussion. Avoid, too, asking students for their opinion, as this is a lower order of thinking; but if the student is asked to substantiate why he or she feels this way, this entails constructive thought.

Encourage an Informed Conversational Style

One thing to warn against is student postings that are too long and sound more like essays than informed conversational remarks, as this makes them harder to respond to than in a face-to-face discussion in which interruptions or rebuttals are more common, stimulating, and expected. This definitely points to the advantage of keeping postings succinct and informal because if they are excessive in length they are not likely to be critiqued, implying that students would gain knowledge by accumulation instead of by argumentation (Wegerif, 1998).

Encourage Conversational Development with Full Participation

Perhaps not every student can answer every original question posed by the instructor and still contribute an original thought. My hope is, however, that the conversation resulting from the original question will lead in many exciting directions, so that every student will feel inspired to contribute to discussion at some point. Berge and Muilenburg (2000) feel it is important, if discussion is thriving among the students, for the instructor to step back, and let it happen. Then when things start to wane, the instructor can either weave together different student remarks to summarize what has been said, or "give up the chalk" (Patenaude, 1999), which translated into the online context means letting students do the weaving of discussion threads.

Even if the instructor weaves and summarizes, this does not have to be the final answer. From this summary more questions can emerge, prompting the students to explore the topic yet more deeply. Examples of good follow-up questions include: What reasons did you have for saying this? Can you please elaborate? How do you define x? What do you think might be the implications of your previous statement? Are there any alternatives to this approach (Berge and Muilenburg, 2000)? In this way, the instructor "nurtures the conference to accomplish objectives and create a productive experience for all participants" (Rohfeld and Hiemstra, 1995). This pivotal stage, which Salmon (2000) calls "Knowledge Construction," is vital for collaborative learning. She provides a nice quotation from Rowntree, who in 1955 wrote in the *British Journal of Educational Technology*, "What [students] learn, of course, is not so much product (e.g. information) as process—in particular, the creative, cognitive process of offering up ideas, having them criticized or expanded on, and getting the chance to reshape them (or abandon them) in the light of peer discussion. The learning becomes not merely active, but also interactive" (quoted in Salmon, 2000, p. 32). In this way, students are more involved with knowledge construction than knowledge dissemination.

Ask the Students to Become Discussion Leaders

An interesting option to try later in the semester is that instead of the instructor asking questions from the readings, the students are asked to develop discussion questions. To assist them in asking pertinent questions, the instructor can tell the students to imagine that the author of the piece they are reading is going to visit the class and ask them what questions they would like answered. The students are encouraged to read critically and look for omissions, unsupported assumptions, and so on (Brookfield and Preskill, 1999). I think this activity can work nicely online. If the class is relatively small, each student can evolve a few questions; but in larger classes, group work may be beneficial. Students can compare questions asked and look for commonalities and differences. They can then think about ways in which they could respond to these questions.

Ask Students to Complete the Sentence

The activity of completing a sentence is another means to stimulate discussion. This idea was mentioned as an icebreaker activity that can be used in the "Virtual Lounge" of your class, as a way to encourage students to become acquainted, but it can also be used for discussion of course-related materials. You could initiate discussion with a sentence such as, "What most struck me about the book we are reading is. . . ." Once the students (either working individually or in groups) post their completed sentences, they are ready to begin discussion by asking each other about responses that have captured their interest (Brookfield and Preskill, 1999).

Playing Devil's Advocate

We cannot forget the idea of playing devil's advocate, which can be fun and work effectively online. This activity helps students to consider things from a different perspective and learn how to substantiate an opinion. One useful technique by which students can substantiate an opinion is to ask them to find relevant quotations to illustrate important parts of their reading or affirm or challenge the points made.

Consider the Layout of Responses

Is the way the responses are displayed on the discussion board a disincentive for contribution? This, of course, depends on the software program used, but I think with a threaded discussion layout, as opposed to laying out responses in chronological order, there is the potential for some confusion to arise. I also think there is the very real danger of a student not reading all the responses, especially if this student has not logged on for some time, and now is faced with an overwhelming number of new responses. We want students to read everything, to make sense of the discussion as a whole, and truly to replicate what happens in the traditional classroom, where presumably everyone hears everything that is said.

If you are using a software program that has a threaded discussion layout, I have a few suggestions that you and your students can use to make conversation strands easier to comprehend:

- Change the title of your message to a few words that capture and reflect what you are saying. This will provide a clear and easy reference for readers.
- Mention people by name and give a brief synopsis of what they said before responding, so that it is clear to which response, or even which part of which response, your message is referring. In other words, do not post, "Yes, that's true!" because when read in isolation as a new response it makes little sense and does not stand alone. Formulate a response such as, "Yes, Bill. When you mentioned that ethics in the workplace is sliding, I agree, as I see a huge increase in cut-throat competitive practices."
- When opening a new discussion forum, do not ask many questions within one message, but post a separate message for each question. If an instructor asks, for example, three separate questions all in one posting, the students are likely to answer all the questions within one response, which would make that response extremely long. We all know that a response that spans several screens is daunting, puts many people off reading it, and is not conducive to discussion. If posted separately, however, each question forms the start of a separate thread of a discussion, and student answers will be shorter as they will only be addressing one question at a time. This practice will increase the likelihood of interaction and continued discussion.
- Many software programs have a search function, which you can use either to search for a particular person or a keyword or phrase. It will then display all responses containing the name or words you requested.

Be Encouraging to Students Who Remain Quiet

If you have tried these strategies and the student is still not participating, then you could try to lure him or her into the discussion forum, never by nagging, but instead trying to encourage responses by a friendly word privately expressed through e-mail, phone, or tweet, or in person.

Remember that students have a variety of learning styles and so might feel comfortable with different activities and at different rates. Furthermore, students who have previously taken an online class might more quickly establish a level of comfort, and they might either assist or intimidate students who are taking their first online class. I suggest that you refrain from calling on a particular student or students who have been quiet for some time, as the objective is not to embarrass anyone, and, furthermore, they might not be online to see they are being called.

A few students might continue to hold back and barely participate, even after you have sent encouraging e-mails or made enthusiastic phone calls. As Fisher (2001) asks, how much should you continue to try to encourage a quiet student to participate? Does this expose the student's lack of knowledge, causing him or her psychological harm, or will it enhance learning? Practically speaking, if students continue not to participate and prefer to "lurk" (a word I actually dislike, as to me, it conjures up images of men in dark alleys, wearing raincoats with collars turned up), should we continue to do anything about this? After all, are not our students responsible, mature adults who should be aware of the consequences, as long as you have spelled out your expectations and requirements at the start of the class? If a student did not appear in the traditional classroom, would we be as concerned? Why should this be different?

For most students, however, free of many of the constraints of the campus class, the online environment truly pushes back the classroom walls. Even the students who are hesitant to participate in online discussion because of fear of poor writing skills grow to appreciate that good written communication is important to every aspect of their lives; and the more practice they have at writing, the better they become at it. Furthermore, whereas in a campus class, the spoken word can evaporate into the air, the online class, by contrast, has a perfect written record of all that has transpired. In this way, every student has a complete and thorough set of class notes.

Using Social Media Such as Twitter, Facebook, Blogs, or Skype to Stimulate Online Discussion

Despite your best efforts to show students the way around your online class, some might find the format of the online discussion forums in software programs such as Blackboard or WebCT unfamiliar and hard to navigate, and this factor might be limiting their online participation. If you suspect this is the case, it might be best to start with Twitter, Facebook, blogs, or even Skype, all of which are technologies with which they probably have more familiarity. And if you do adopt one of these, I would recommend that you link it to your class Web site.

If you have set up a Twitter account with your class, it might prove a useful tool in encouraging students to participate in online discussions. Walsh (2010) mentions many ideas as to how Twitter can be beneficially incorporated into education. For example, Twitter could be useful as you could send students class announcements and reminders as tweets they will receive on their cell phones. This can be advantageous as undergraduates nowadays are often more likely to look at their cell phones than check their e-mails. Your announcement might be something as simple as reminding students to log on at the start of the semester. You might even want to use Twitter when the semester begins by creating "Twitter Pals" in which you pair students to tweet to each other so that they can interview each other in short but plentiful little messages, and in this way become acquainted. They could then be ready to present profiles of each other to the whole class on the discussion forum of the online class (see "Students Interview and Intro- duce Each Other" in Chapter 6). This could be especially helpful and partic- ularly exciting if the online class is team-taught, bringing two groups of students together, possibly even from different geographical locations, as it would be a terrific way of students getting to know each other. Some people might be cynical about how much can really be achieved when restricted to messages of 140 characters, which is the maximum length of each tweet; however, it should be noted that telegrams were also a terse medium, but despite their brevity they were effective communication tools in their day.

Then, as the semester unfolds, you could tweet announcements about particular special discussions taking place in the online forums of your class, or about the arrival of an online guest speaker, or about some other event. And in general you could use Twitter to stimulate discussions. For example, you could tweet a "Tip" or "Word" or "Concept" of the day, and ask students to respond to it, or you could ask students to tweet a succinct reaction to reading some material, or even ask them to tweet comments as they progressively read through the assigned material. The small number of characters allowed per tweet might actually help focus students, and encour- age them to strive to make every word significant. And, depending on the discipline of the class you are teaching, you might ask students to follow certain political or academic figures on Twitter, or keep abreast of news stories as they unfold, as Twitter streams can have huge social and political ramifications. In fact, a tweet was sent about the killing of Bin Laden before this was broadcast on the news media channels. And because so many people are now tweeting, and all the more so when there are specific events that are politically important (such as unrest in the Middle East) or that capture public interest (such as the death of Michael Jackson), Twitter has been known to "crash" because it is being used beyond capacity. But this is relatively rare.

Tweets can also be used to send URLs of useful Web sites, using the Twitter application "Twhirl," if necessary, for abbreviating the URL to fit within the 140 character limitation. And Twitter can be used for students to brainstorm together, develop ideas, and help each other as they know they will receive almost immediate feedback. They could even tweet to capture an inspiration succinctly as it occurs. And, to avoid the tweets becoming confusing if many arrive simultaneously, the Twitter application "Tweetree" can be used to group conversations together. There is also a Twitter tool called "QuoteURL" that allows for many tweets to be posted on to one Web page. In all these cases, when discussion fires up, you might want to give students the option to transfer over to your online software discussion forums if you are teaching an online class or hybrid, and continue their online conversation there.

As Sorrell (2011) said about his writing class at Rutgers, Twitter can be helpful for students who are not participating much, not because of laziness or irresponsibility, but simply because they are not native speakers and are therefore not yet comfortable writing a longer response. Twitter could also be an immense asset to a beginning language class, in which learning such phrases as *"Quel age avez vous?"* might be the most the student can manage at one time. As Sorrell said, the lower the level of student competency, the more valuable it might be for that student to use Twitter. Students might then be able to build up skills and confidence in Twitter, before migrating to the fuller discussions in the online discussion forums.

Another social networking site that has considerable potential for use in education is, of course, Facebook, as students are likely to be familiar with the practice of conversing through this medium. Indeed Sorrell (2012) says he uses Facebook more than Twitter for most writing classes, as it is more like a Web site, and has photos and links. It can encourage collaboration and might be conducive to students continuing their class-related discussions on Facebook after a campus class is over. Facebook can essentially be used in all the same ways as Twitter, as discussed previously, thus increasing the potential for good interaction between teachers and students and offering the means to engage students; but Facebook has the added advantage of not being restricted in terms of length of the online post, and it is not as linear as Twitter. Thus assignments can be posted on Facebook. And, as with Twitter and online discussions in general, Facebook enables shy students or nonnative speakers to better communicate with their peers and teacher. Also it is easy for students to post Web sites on Facebook or use multimedia, as this is familiar to them; it is also easy to manage this site so as to create groups.

Runyon (2009) speaks of how Abilene Christian University in Texas has been using Facebook with the adoption of a Facebook application called "Schools," which sets up pages for each course in which a student is enrolled so that students can hold online discussions with their professor and classmates and submit assignments. Facebook can also be used for marketing courses, and even for prospective new students talking to existing students about particular courses. And even before actually starting at a new college, students can go to Facebook, once they know the dorm in which they will reside and who their roommate will be, and "meet" everyone on their floor before they arrive. That is what my own son did before setting out on his academic adventure. And this kind of online communication, both before and after, and in and out of class, can reduce tension and increase the potential for engagement and academic achievement.

Another alternative form of online discussion that may be familiar to some students is blogs. Twitter is basically a micro-blog, but a full blog itself, without constraints on length of online response, could be helpful to some students. The main blogs platforms from which to choose are Blogger, which is a blogging Web tool from Google, and WordPress.com. However, if students are blogging, I would recommend that you do not allow them to blog anonymously, as you will want to know what each student is contributing.

Also possible, although not text-based and not asynchronous except for its chat function, is Skype, which facilitates users being able to see and hear each other in real time over the Internet. Technologically, what's needed, besides downloading Skype, is for each student to have a microphone and a webcam hooked up to his or her computer. Alternatively, iPad2 has a built in camera and microphone, so it could easily be used for Skype sessions. Skype might be useful at the start of the semester of a fully online class to speed up the process of participants becoming acquainted, and might have other specific uses as discussed in the sections "Synchronous Online Tools," "Online Guest Lecturers," and "Virtual Field Trips" in Chapter 8.

Fluctuations in Rates of Participation

Do not be worried if participation in online discussion lags at certain points of the semester. This could be due to a holiday or midterms. I have sometimes found that a lag in participation occurs about two thirds of the way through the course. At the beginning students have a lot of energy, especially because they are inquisitive about the newness of the environment, then there is continued high participation as everyone becomes familiar with communicating this way, and then, before the push toward the end of the semester, students sometimes seem to fall away a bit. There are various methods by which you can revitalize your course, and these will be looked at in more depth in Chapter 8.

How Do We Speak Online?

Just as it is said that our eyes are the windows to our soul, then maybe it is fair to suggest that our words are the windows to who we are online. This is especially true if we only teach online and never meet the students, but even if we do meet with them on campus as well, our words are what convey who we are when we are interacting online.

Style of Online Writing

For us, as teachers, I would like to suggest that there are two different styles of writing. There is our more formal style, which we employ in our lectures; and there is the other style, the one that breathes life into the course and sustains it throughout the semester, and this is our voice in the discussion forums. As academicians, I think we are probably all used to writing formal pieces of work, and for these we might well compose in our word processors, with its barrage of tools such as spell and grammar check. The other type of writing within the discussion forums might be new to some of us. It is the quotidian writing of asking questions, responding to student comments, and asking more questions.

This conversational writing style mimics the way I would speak if I were sitting with my students in a seminar. It is for this reason that I compose my words directly online, as opposed to first typing in the word processor, as I want the immediacy and the excitement, and not the psychological jarring, of switching between computer programs.

Is There a Relaxation of Standards?

Most of us have come across e-mails, even some sent by fellow academicians, in which there is a tremendous relaxation of the usual rules of spelling and grammar. E-mails are generally sent off quickly, as often there is a felt need to respond promptly, which could account for some of the casualness of style. In a captivating interview on New York's Public Radio WNYC (December 2001), Brian Lehrer, the host, asked Dr. David Crystal, Honorary Professor of Linguistics at the University of Wales, and author of the book *Language and the Internet,* whether the Internet is responsible for "ripping the English language to shreds." Should we be pitying the English language, Lehrer asked, because on the Internet complete sentences are reduced to three-word phrases, "capitalization is dying on the vine," and not many people use formalities such as "Dear" when they write to each other?

Crystal argued that far from depleting our language, the Internet has enriched, extended, and enlivened it. He said that with the introduction of any new technology, people are initially a little worried, as no one wants to make a change, and it is a break with the familiar. Therefore, people pay extra attention when using it, and they make concerted efforts to make it work for themselves. He drew an analogy with the rise of broadcasting in the 1920s, saying that people were fearful then that language would be detrimentally affected, yet conversely it has grown since then. The same, he feels, is true of the Internet.

Writing on the Internet Is in a Constant State of Flux

In his interview with Lehrer, Crystal stated that, prior to the availability of the Internet, people had two main ways of communicating: by speech or by writing. He feels that the Internet provides an extra new and exciting dimension. He said that it is not like writing because if you are reading a written book and decide to stop at page 10, you know you can return to page 10 and it will remain the same. With the Internet, however, things are in constant motion. If you stop at a particular screen and return later and refresh it, things might have changed, as the Internet is animated and dynamic rather than fixed and static.

Crystal said the Internet is like speech—it can be either formal or informal, depending on the relationship between speaker and listener. He added that the Internet can presuppose quite an intimate forum of exchange, and as such there can be more of an elliptical construction of word usage, and the users "can get away with it." Similarly, he has seen, as I am sure we have too, some very long sentences and messages on the Internet.

Language, according to Crystal, is our means of communication, and the Internet lets us do just that all the time. It can be convenient and flexible, and can even allow us to speak to many people at the same time, not only as in a group e-mail, but also in an online class.

Online Expression of Emotions

During the broadcast, the subject of how to express emotions was introduced because we are devoid of body language, facial expression, and tone of voice when we communicate on the Internet. It was noted that people generally use more exclamation points and that the colon and semicolon are in danger of becoming an "endangered species."

There is also a growing usage of emoticons such as smiley faces. Crystal was asked why smiley faces had not been used before the Internet, and he answered that written language has its equivalents in the exclamation point or question mark, developed hundreds of years ago. He said these were the attempts, then, to capture the melody and inflexion of the speaking voice, and compensate for what letters alone could not convey. He also said that emoticons (which I must admit I do not like) are not used extensively. In a huge sample of e-mail messages that he analyzed, fewer than 10 percent used them.

New Internet Words and Abbreviations

Interestingly, about 2,000 new words have been introduced since the Internet came into existence, such as putting "e-" in front of words, or "dot-com." Amazing abbreviations have also evolved. I was musing about a humorous online exchange I had in the 1990s with my niece who is in England. We were using instant messaging, so this was taking place in real time, and I had made an off-the-cuff remark and had received back from her the perplexing message "LOL." When I asked her to explain what that meant she replied with the even more perplexing, "ROFL." My teenage sons translated for me: LOL means "laughing out loud" and ROFL means she had reached such a high degree of hilarity that she was "rolling on the floor laughing." Other examples of abbreviations are X!, meaning "typical woman," and Y!, meaning "typical man." What is most incredible, however, in terms of the Internet, is the sheer rapidity with which new words are diffused among the population. Crystal said that because of the profusion of electronic connections, a new word can go round the language faster than anything in linguistic history.

Is the Language of the Internet Robbing Us of Our More Complex Language Structure?

Lehrer asked Crystal if, in all these ways, the Internet is creating a mass popular language, and is indeed robbing children of knowing and using a more complex language structure. Crystal answered that he conducted a study of school children to investigate whether they would think that it was so "cool" to communicate in the way they do on the Internet that they would apply it to all other social settings. But he found that this was not the case, and that in the classroom they spoke in a more sophisticated manner. Crystal's conclusion, therefore, is that not only does the Internet not lower standards of language in general, but also that it widens the range of stylistic abilities that children and indeed older people have previously had.

A logical next question, then, is what happens when a class exists on the Internet? I do not know if Crystal has studied this, but I can say from my experience that it seems, in the vast majority of cases, that the fact that it is a classroom supersedes the fact that it is being held on the Internet. Seldom have I seen students relax academic standards of articulation and expression. I have seen a small sprinkling of emoticons, but generally that is the extent of it.

The Importance, for the Instructor, of Being a Role Model for Standards of Writing

Even though we want spontaneity and a conversational tone, I think messages should be reviewed before posting. They should again be reviewed immediately after posting, and any changes can be made using the edit button. I have heard some instructors lament the absence of spell check in the online setting, but I personally believe that spell check is never enough as work needs to be read through. "Witch way? Write over their" would be ignored by spell check (although the grammar check might pick this up).

Why do I suggest this time-consuming exercise of reading and rereading our responses when posting, when we all know that teaching online already takes a long time? I recommend it because the instructor is the role model for the students. How will students feel about an instructor who makes spelling mistakes, or whose sentence does not make grammatical sense? In the first place, reading a response containing plenty of mistakes can detract from the sense of the message. Then there is the danger that the students' respect for that instructor might decrease. Obviously, the occasional mistake can slip by unnoticed, and also I do not mean to suggest that the writing within the discussion forum should become laborious and lose its spunk and spontaneity.

Keep it sounding like you. Remember, too, that you as instructor also set the tone. If your work appears sloppy to students, how can you expect much but sloppiness back from them? Or perfect answers, neatly typed, with a degree of disdain perhaps? We, as instructors, certainly do not want to risk that.

Besides looking at writing style in a general sense, I think it is important to detect individual differences. For example, does each student feel comfortable in self-expression, or is there discomfort because of differences of gender, race, religion, or age that might inhibit a student from speaking? We have talked about the democratizing nature of the online environment— how the instructor, free of visual cues, reads each student response equally and with an unbiased approach. But what of the students themselves? Because they are disembodied, do they lose inhibitions they might experience in the traditional classroom?

Scope for Misinterpretation

We need to be mindful of how our words might be interpreted, although sometimes it is impossible to anticipate every pitfall. One student mentioned how sad she was when she wanted to thank her mother for having sent her a gift, yet her mother read her words, "Thanks a lot," as being sarcastic, as if implying that she hated the present. An instructor bemoaned a situation in which she sent back a piece of work, and her word "resent" was misunderstood to mean that she felt resentful, rather than that she "re-sent" the work.

Critiquing Work

I think it is important, if critiquing a student's work, to remember that without facial expressions and voice inflections, criticism of work can sound rather harsh when laid out in text. Therefore, critiques should be handled tactfully by mentioning the positive points before making suggestions for change and improvement. In this way, the critique should be seen as helpful and constructive, rather than demeaning. And if you are teaching a class in which you invite students to critique each other's work, advise them to follow these same guidelines.

Using Humor Online

Humor can reduce stress and help students to feel comfortable to respond. It can minimize frustration and promote a healthy atmosphere in which to enhance learning and increase students' receptivity. Furthermore, humor can unite students, decrease the potential for prejudice, and give the class a genuine feeling of camaraderie, as trust and rapport can result and everyone can share the universal experience of laughter. Instructors who are fun, energetic, and imaginative have the potential to motivate students and tap into their creativity. Perhaps many of us have attended a class that we anticipated would be dull, maybe because of the subject matter or the time of day, and instead felt energized and engaged because the instructor used an amusing and imaginative presentation style.

On campus, humor in the classroom can take different forms. Perhaps the instructor tells a funny story that is of relevance to the material being taught, or maybe has a spontaneously amusing reaction to ongoing discussion. Either way, the instructor indicates to students what is considered appropriate. This permits them to share amusing, subject-related experiences of their own. As we know, body language can also communicate or enhance humor, such as smiling or leaning in certain ways, as can tone of voice and laughter (Fall, 2002).

What of the silent, sightless online class, in which laughter cannot be heard and people cannot be observed? What of the fact that good timing is often crucial in relating something funny? How can this work in an asynchronous setting? I am sure many of you have had the experience of trying to describe a funny incident to someone, and, on finding that it could not be explained well, resorted to saying, "You had to be there to appreciate it!" Does this imply that the online class has to be devoid of humor? I do not think it does. Just as there can be amusing books, so too can there be effective use of humor in online classes. And just as in the campus class, it also can energize and it can unite. It can draw students to log on to the class. It can ease them over stressful situations. Knowing that one of the biggest potential problems of the online class is feeling overwhelmed by numerous and lengthy new responses, just think how much easier it would be to read good, content-rich material that is sprinkled with relevant humor, rather than screens and screens of dry, stuffy text.

Words of caution are needed, however. As we know, the group dynamic is different each semester, so something that amused students in a previous semester might promote a different reaction next time. This points to the importance of knowing your students and being sensitive to their ideas. This could be a problem whether online or on campus, but there are additional concerns about the use of humor in an online class. For example, it might be even more possible to misinterpret written words that are meant to be amusing than it would be if these same words were heard. Furthermore, it might be harder in an asynchronous setting to detect if someone was inadvertently offended, and it might be more difficult to do some timely back-pedaling or offer quick remediation. Remember, as Hudson (1999) warns, an instructor should not use humor just to make students like him or her, as the primary function of the instructor is, of course, to teach.

I recommend that you be yourself, and let humor spring naturally from your thoughts. It might be wise to pause a little before submitting your response, to anticipate the impact of your words on each of your students, but I would not recommend that you thrash it around in your head for so long that it has lost all of its humor, even to you. The goal is to create a positive atmosphere in your class, and being naturally funny might be a good way of achieving this. Remember, good humor is contagious, and if you set this tone, students might feel that they can use humor, too. We lack the oral and visual cues and the immediacy that is present in a campus class, but online we have the power of our words.

Gender Differences

Some interesting studies have been performed to explore whether there are gender differences among online learners. Blum (1999), an author from a university that remains nameless to protect confidentiality, analyzed 149 online messages posted in an online university course, to determine male and female preferred learning styles, communication patterns, and participation barriers; the findings were in turn compared with results in the traditional face-to-face class on campus.

The study shows women experienced more technical barriers and asked more frequent technical questions than men. In general, they had had less previous experience with computers than their male colleagues, although this might well have now changed since the time of Blum's study. The study cites dispositional barriers, which relate to self-perception and confidence, and again refers to the fact that men are more controlling than women, as they tend to dominate the online environment, which, the study says, is not dissimilar to what happens in the class on campus.

Observations from my own teaching, however, have been different, although I generally have more women than men in most of my classes. Even so, I have never found that men dominated the online discussions. Whereas in the traditional classroom, male students sometimes have a tendency to interrupt female students and want to dominate the discussion, I predicted and then evidenced that such a thing cannot and does not occur within the elasticity of virtual time in the online classroom because everyone has an equal and uninterrupted opportunity to respond. The only area in which male students might dominate, although I conjecture about this with some uncertainty as I have used it less often, is the real-time chat feature of the online class. It will take more observations over time to see if there is equality of opportunity for the genders in terms of responses there, or whether this more closely mirrors the behavior patterns of the traditional classroom. (For a more complete look at real-time chat, see "Suggested Uses of Synchronous Tools" in Chapter 8.)

In addition to looking at issues of domination and insubordination, Blum (1999) analyzed style of communication, with interesting results. She found, for example, that women displayed greater eloquence of phrase, substituting a word such as *got* with a fancier one such as *acquired,* whereas men stuck to *got.* Second, the tone was found to be different. Men posted shorter messages, had more certainty of tone, and were more likely to do online shouting (using all capitals).They tended to use fragmentary sentences, such as "Hey guys. Need help," whereas a woman would be more likely to say, "I would appreciate some help, if anyone is able to do so. Thanks!" Men were often seen to use more slang, tell more jokes, and be more assertive than women. Women's style of talking was more often personal and related to self or family members, whereas men's messages were more impersonal and abstract. Women more often added tags at the end of their sentences, such as "Don't you agree?" If a woman gave advice, she would generally write a follow-up comment to the effect, "I hope that helped." Women were generally more polite, with a frequent "thank you" added to their response. Blum's findings on style of communication are generally corroborated by my observations in the online classes I teach. However, I should add that in some instances, the instructor cannot tell from the name alone whether the student is male or female, and sometimes not even the style or content of the posted response offers much of a clue to the gender of the student.

In general, however, if it is true that women adopt a more personal and possibly helpful tone, then it can be inferred that many of them are involved in building connections, whereas men remain quite separate in their learning. In the women's responses that Blum (1999) analyzed, she determined that they were more empathic and collaborative, rather than competitive, which was more frequently the behavior trait exhibited by men. These trends reflected those of student behavior in the face-to-face class. This view was also echoed by Kramarae: "Computer-mediated communication is not a neutral medium. Women and men interact in different ways in Internet classes. The patterns from the traditional classroom (including men engaging in more argumentative conversations and women in more open-ended conversations) carry over to the distance learning environment" (2001, n.p.).

The implications for the online environment are important. Even if we see similar trends to those displayed in the campus class, it can be inferred that the collaborative potential of distance education would be effective for female learners who enjoy interaction and sharing as their primary learning style. Any women who are initially hampered by low confidence levels in their academic or technical abilities might benefit from having an online mentor or student partner to help them over the hurdles. The online instructor, therefore, has the job of both encouraging the collaboration between women and also the independent work of men. This could be a hard task, but it seems that perhaps students in the second half of the semester could be given a project and could choose either to work in pairs or individually.

Another important obstacle for learning experienced by many women is, as Blum (1999) suggests, "situational barriers." These are brought about by the fact that women often shoulder the extra tasks of being the primary caretakers of their children and having greater domestic responsibilities. This was the topic of an interesting report, entitled *The Third Shift: Women Learning Online,* by C. Kramarae for the American Association of University Women (AAUW). Kramarae found in her 2001 study, in which over 500 students were interviewed, that over 60 percent of online learners are females older than 25 years of age. She says that online courses allow women, already juggling home and career, an opportunity for a "third shift" in their busy days (and nights), to be online learners. As so well stated by Jacqueline Woods, AAUW's executive director, "Technology does not create more hours in a day, but leaves women—who shoulder most of the family and household responsibilities—improvising to squeeze in education" (Kramarae, 2001). In addition, Kramarae states, "In this respect, technology hasn't freed more of women's time, [it has] only created a third shift in the home" (2001).

This kind of flexibility, although it opens up possibilities for lifelong learning that otherwise would have been harder to achieve, often comes at the cost of sleep or time with the family. Although women might need to deal with their feelings of guilt that they should be doing something other than what they are doing, they are generally committed learners in pursuit of a degree for their own advancement. However, it has been thought that the more roles and obligations a person has, the more psychologically healthy they are because if something is not going well in one role, chances are that things are better in another role (Galinsky, 1999).

Kramarae (2001) found that women particularly favor online learning as it gives them much needed flexibility in their juggling acts, it cuts the costs of commuting and child care, and it provides a realistic way in which they can achieve their educational goals. As an extreme example, I once had a student who unfortunately had a complicated pregnancy and was ordered complete bed rest. Had she been taking a class on campus, she would have had to drop the course; but because it was an online class, she took her laptop to bed with her and the only remaining question was, what would come first—the baby or the end of the semester? Luckily the student submitted her final paper on the date it was due, and a day later gave birth. This student was obviously highly motivated, and motivation helps students to succeed.

For busy women to successfully complete their online class, they also need much support at home and work. Despite the fact that online learning provides tremendous potential opportunities for women, Kramarae (2001) mentions that if a class is a hybrid, some women who truly consider their education as a "third shift" might have a hard time completing deadlines or coming to campus meetings in real as opposed to virtual time. It might be supposed that if indeed women are the primary caretakers, these types of constraints of real time meetings might be harder for them than for male students.

Racial Differences

Packer explores the assumption that totally online classes (as opposed to hybrids) "could be delivered to an invisible, ether-based audience, and so could be 'colorblind' in the truest sense of the word" (2002, p. 265). She wondered, too, assuming that this is true, whether preexisting race-based educational imbalances could be overcome. It had been expected, says Packer, that, "freed of the constraints of the material body, people would embrace and accept one another for whom they really were, rather than for what they represented through their physical form" (p. 265).

Packer states that it was not intended that online classes would be blind to personal appearance, but that this was the way they started out because, in the very early days of online education in the early 1990s, the classes were not yet on the Web, but instead were purely text based and contained within the DOS operating system. Thus it was impossible to include photos or other images. This "deficit," however, was perceived as advantageous by the early pioneering online academicians, as they thought that this would guarantee more educational equality. I agreed and frequently talked of how the online class provides the potential for a meeting of minds, uncluttered by any prejudicial baggage.

Gradually, however, I have come to question this opinion that I had so strongly held. It started one day when I was talking to a colleague who teaches campus-based classes about racial diversity. When I told her that if she put the class online, no one would know anything about anyone else's racial, ethnic, or religious characteristics, she replied that these were the very facts that she wanted to be known and made explicit and that they should not "dematerialize." I could see her point, although thought perhaps this might be specific to the course she teaches. Packer says,

> Few people considered the fact that psychological identities develop around one's physical persona, and that this persona includes race, among other things. Few people considered the fact that complex intellectual, artistic, political, and philosophical positions accrue around race, and that dismissing its existence could simultaneously dismiss the importance of these positions. (2002, p. 266)

I certainly do agree that one's fundamental character is very much a product of racial background, and just because a person is not seen, it cannot mean that all personal attributes are literally whitewashed. In other words, it is not right to assume that we can pretend these factors are not important just because they are not perceived.

However, even at the time in which it was thought that online classes would do so much to promote educational equality because of the invisibility of its participants, there were some people, myself included, who were concerned that because participation in an online class depends in part on computer ownership, then online classes could widen the gap between the haves and have-nots. This, in itself, was not so clear-cut; whereas indeed many African Americans were less wealthy, even those who were more affluent were less likely to own a computer, according to Packer. This has led to the creation of the situation called the "digital divide." However, with the advent of smartphones, and their increased ownership among many people throughout society, the digital divide is lessening.

Packer (2002) talks about the importance of personal introductions at the start of the online class, and how, as we all know, these are generally even more important and even more extensive than introductions given in the campus class, in an effort to overcome any dehumanizing effects of cyberspace. She says that because the class held totally online can and does attract students from literally around the world, students generally say the place in which they live, to give some exciting information as to the location from which they are logging on. But, says Packer, "in practice next to no one identifies him- or herself by race without first alluding to place" (p. 267). She goes on to say that the posted names of each student give some indications as to race and ethnicity, but there is certainly a danger of making the wrong assumptions from these alone.

What is particularly fascinating in Packer's study is her discovery that now that the technology has advanced, and photographs can be easily attached, some students of color made special use of this feature. However, as she also says, we do not know how many students of color did not post photos, or even whether those who did posted authentic pictures of themselves. Packer conducted personal interviews with some of her students, and found in these cases that the photographs were true likenesses. She concluded, therefore, that the act of posting a photograph "seemed to be a way to express discomfort about erasing race entirely and with being forced to adopt an invisible online identity" (p. 271). It was also revealed through these interviews that students chose to show classmates what they looked like, as they thought that "people presume that someone is white unless they specifically state otherwise" (p. 271). Packer also found that it seemed to be liberating for students of color to post their photos, that once they had done so, they started to participate actively in the course much more than before. However, I am uncertain as to what this means, as I do not know what time frame Packer is considering. Would not most students post their photo near the start of the semester to accompany their personal introduction?

Interestingly, the only other students to post photographs of themselves were students who were performers of some kind, such as actors, dancers, or singers. In contrast, those students who identified themselves by place instead of race generally did not post photographs, yet posted information on the special attributes of their community. These students who talked about place were active participants in discussion from the start of the course, Packer says, which makes her believe in the importance for students of revealing some personal information, whether about race or place, as it correlates highly with increased comfort levels in participating in online discussions. Packer sees "something liberating about reuniting with one's physical form and with revealing who one really is" (p. 272). This seems to imply that we are untrue to ourselves if we try too much to dissociate mind from body.

Although Packer is not an instructor of color, she is Jewish, and her first class was on the psychology of religion. She quickly realized that none of her students were Jewish, and she started to feel uncomfortable about the fact that she was from a minority religion and that she was the instructor in a position of authority. Packer struggled with the issue as to whether she should tell her students, and thought that she should as she did not want students to make the wrong assumption as to who she was.

She said, "Still, I was surprised by my own trepidations at facing a class of 'others,' and I was even more surprised by the relief I felt after addressing the issue directly and encouraging students to share their own experiences" (p. 273). Packer includes this personal experience of hers, as she states how, in Hitler's time, Jews were considered to be a race, and she felt and empathized with the associated discomfort of this. So she thought that by describing herself in terms of race, she could liberate others in her class to reveal more about their racial identities, and thus increase their comfort level in terms of participation.

On the basis of the interviews Packer conducted, it was found that most students and instructors, surprisingly, did not consider the issue of race in online classes, but those who did included American students of color, Asian Americans, Germans, and any students who came from racially torn cities. Perhaps still more work needs to be done in terms of defining individual identity in the online class.

How We Show We Are Listening and Caring Online

Who Cares? Listening and Caring

One of my sons remarked to me how it seemed to him to be so hard to advertise perfume on the television, as the particular fragrance could not be conveyed. This started me thinking, by analogy, as to how hard it may seem to "listen" online, as listening implies that we can hear, and of course, online, the only sounds are those in our imagination. Not only that, but it seems to me that listening implies some sort of encouragement on the part of the receiver of information—by a smile, a nod of the head, a leaning forward of the body—to impart to the speaker that the words are having an impact, and that the talking should continue.

Also, as previously discussed, a crucial element in encouraging students to participate in online discussion, and to post responses to which we should listen, is to establish a feeling that the online class is a safe place. According to Fisher, "Willingness to take risks concerning safety in self-disclosure grows in part from whether teachers or students interpret vulnerability as a danger or an opportunity" (2001, p. 152).

But does safety mean the same thing to everyone? As with the question of freedom, safety has a twofold manifestation. It is both safety from certain things and safety to do certain things.

In other words, the instructor should attempt to set up the class in a way in which students feel both *safe from* abuse or ridicule according to the rules of civility established at the start of class, and *safe to* fully participate in class discussions and activities, as the instructor has promoted a benevolent, interested, supportive atmosphere with plenty of positive affirmation. The instructor should, at all times, express a keen sense of curiosity about each student (Vella, 1997). In the act of free expression, however, there is the possibility that conflict or disagreement could arise; but as long as this is handled in a civil manner, it might actually be beneficial and thus move understanding to a deeper level.

Once the students feel safe to express themselves initially, it is vital that they feel listened to, as this will encourage them to continue to respond. Listening, Daloz says, "is a powerful intervention, perhaps the most powerful we have as mentors. It is not a passive process, for the good listener is always alert for things of special significance" (1999, p. 205). Although Daloz is referring, when talking of mentors, to the teacher in the campus classroom, I believe his ideas translate to the online environment. In addition, it is not only the instructors who need to listen attentively, but also the students, who need to pay attention to each other and their instructor.

Daloz (1999) suggests that listening should include, on the part of the instructor, the active process of providing support, challenge, and an ultimate goal or "vision." Let us look at each of these categories in turn, and consider how efficacious they can be online.

Support and Caring

The giving of support can make the class feel like a safe place in which to be. Caring, of course, can be addressed with regard to issues that range from the impersonal to the highly personal. Impersonal cares might be more likely to occur at the start of the semester, when, for example, a student does not know how to find a book, but as the semester progresses and a feeling of trust is established, caring might reach down to a more personal and private level, especially if the preferred mode of teaching is to encourage the collaboration of education with experience (Fisher, 2001).

The way to establish trust is for the instructor to be attentive to each student, so all will feel individually noticed. This is so important when working remotely. The optimal way to convey to students that they are noticed is for the instructor to mention each student by name when acknowledging a response. I think it is also beneficial to make each student feel special in some way. Being closely listened to and receiving supportive feedback can be rare in today's busy world, so by doing this, you provide the potential for the student to flourish.

It has been my observation, and the observation of many of my colleagues, that the online environment seems to encourage the discussion of highly personal material. I think this occurs because students have greater pause for deeper reflection when they respond online, and as long as the instructor creates a welcoming tone and the feeling that it is safe to share thoughts, substantiated opinions, and relevant experiences, this will lead to greater intimacy.

Students also might feel in part protected by the anonymity of their computer screen, rather than feeling embarrassed about making a certain remark when others are watching them in a campus class. As an extreme example, one student who took a class on campus with me and who had worked at the World Trade Center, sobbed uncontrollably when talking of her anguished flight from the building on September 11, 2001. She kept apologizing for crying, and actually told me privately after class that she wished the class had been held online to spare her this embarrassment.

Additionally, I feel intimacy can evolve online because students are not interrupted when formulating a response (as they might be in real time in the campus class) and they all have the chance to respond at whatever time best suits them. Unlike the class on campus that meets at a predetermined time, which might well have little to do with when students are inspired or even at their best for discussion, the online class offers the possibility of continuous caring and contact.

Fisher says that the traditional classroom structure "resembles ordinary life, in the sense that most people have limited opportunities for . . . talk. . . . The students and I are aware of the time frame in which we operate . . . because it may become oppressive to any or all of us (too long, too short, too crowded between other activities)" (2001, p. 41). If that is the case, it can be argued that the virtual classroom expands the normal opportunities of "ordinary life," and also provides an element of choice as to when is the optimal time to log on so as not to be crowded between other activities. This can really expand the potential for good, active listening and discussion.

Generally, the caring mostly emanates from the instructor, who can project compassion. Fisher says of listening and caring on campus, "Caring requires patience and the carer's willingness to project herself into the world of the one cared for" (2001, p. 120). Daloz (1999) makes a similar point in suggesting that the instructor can give support by empathizing with each student, and by trying to see the world as the student sees it. All this points to the fact that learning is not just cognitive, but also affective, in the sense that it can produce an emotional reaction (Pardouly, 2001; Vella, 1997).

How aware are we, as online teachers, of the emotional reactions of our students? If we are remotely situated from our students by working with them online, would we even know if a student was upset, hurt, afraid, or angry? I think we would in most cases be able to tell if we read their words sensitively and empathically, and I would like to suggest that this might even be easier to establish online than on campus, as there usually is less of a hierarchy in the virtual classroom, and the online student is apt to reveal ideas and thoughts to a greater extent than in the campus class.

I think it is also important that students are encouraged to listen accurately to each other. We have talked earlier of the quiet student, but what of the online student who writes excessively long posts that might become trite, anecdotal, and irrelevant? I believe that this could be discouraging to conversation of the group as a whole, so I would recommend advising students to keep to the point, and to try to relate what they are saying to factual knowledge and information generated in the class. As long as a student can accomplish this, then I think every other student should be a respectful listener and be open to learning as much as possible from each other. They might not necessarily agree, or even need to agree, but at least they should give each other's remarks the focused attention they deserve.

The question of anonymity sometimes comes up, as some software programs allow students to post anonymously. This is especially relevant to our considerations of safety. Does it protect the students if they post their responses anonymously? First, I see participation in discussion as an important part of the grade, so this is one reason why students should post in their own name. I think much greater bonding occurs once students come to understand the issues with which each of them is grappling. It is harder to care for someone who does not identify him- or herself. Second, if students are stripped of their name they might, instead of feeling protected, actually feel a loss of identity and an erasure of their own voice.

However, there might be cases in which some students are fearful of the indelibility of their online responses in particular topics under consideration, so if the issue is private, a student could have the option of sending an e-mail to the instructor rather than posting on the discussion board. Alternatively, it might be beneficial to break the class into small groups, which might lessen a student's fear. What I also do in some online classes is ask students to keep journals, which they submit to me privately by e-mail; then I select a few to post to the class. I never post before first asking the student if he or she is comfortable with me doing this (see "Journals" in Chapter 8).

Once the student has expressed an issue of concern, it is important for the instructor to show the student that he or she is attentive to this. That might not mean providing immediate healing or all the answers, but showing that he or she has read the student's troubling issues carefully and has asked a few pertinent questions to help the student try to resolve this.

Challenge

It seems that there is an inverse relationship between *challenge* and *support*. It is a question of finding the right balance that is crucial. With too little support, students are unlikely to feel heard or to be keen on learning more. And if there is too much challenge, insecure students might drop the course. The right amount of challenge can produce just enough tension to motivate the student to learn more and think in fresh, new ways.

Sometimes feelings of confusion can lead down paths of new exploration and understanding. But how can challenge be given online, especially when words may sound more harsh than might be intended? I maintain that challenge can certainly be given online, especially if it is done in an exciting way. This might include you playing devil's advocate and questioning commonly held assumptions, or you might introduce some contradictions to encourage students to consider a new perspective. You might even want to introduce an element of mystery in assigning a particular task. The idea of online role-playing comes to my mind, but there could be plenty of other mysterious assignments that could be done online as well (see Chapter 8).

When promoting challenge, I recommend that you encourage discussion as much as possible, as it is here that students can listen and learn from each other and thrash out difficult ideas in a multiperspective fashion. You might need to remind students of the rules of civility at this point. Daloz (1999) suggests that, when discussing controversial issues, a student should summarize the previous speaker's opinion before expressing a new point of view, to ensure accurate listening and understanding. This could be beneficial in the online class as well, and the student would therefore summarize the message of another student when responding in the online discussion.

Another way in which Daloz suggests presenting challenge is to set high expectations for student assignments, as these become positive self-fulfilling prophecies. This can certainly be feasible online, and can include not only assignments but also parameters for online discussion.

Vision

By *vision,* Daloz (1999) means that the students have gained greater understanding. He suggests we look closely at language as a clue to assessing levels of understanding: "The words we use and the way we use them are powerful indicators of how we see, of our particular vision of reality" (p. 227). He suggests there is a continuum from elementary writing styles to more "contextual" levels, in which there is varied sentence structure, less clichés, and more qualifiers such as "assuming that." In this case, teaching online puts us at an advantage, as we are in a position to more closely look at and remember the words of our students than if we were listening to them in the campus class.

Daloz (1999), like Socrates, suggests holding up a figurative mirror to students, so they can better see their thoughts and hear their voices, and thus create a greater self-awareness. This leads to metacognition, which is the students' ability to think about how they are each thinking. A mirror, in the online setting, could be virtually held up by providing the students with much feedback on their learning style. Mirroring could also be done online by asking students questions to try to further their discussion points to their ultimate conclusion, thereby providing scope for them to fully understand the implications of their thoughts. Another way in which students can become aware of their thoughts and the thoughts of others is for the instructor to create a good role model of being nonjudgmental. Fisher states that "nonjudgmentalness is not simply a matter of withholding criticism or passively taking in the other's words. It requires active listening [and] trying to understand" (2001, p. 37). To achieve the condition of being nonjudgmental online, it seems important to establish an attitude of cooperation. I believe this can be brought about by an explicit concern for each other's feelings, which certainly can be apparent online. The best way, I believe, for a student to know that his or her feelings matter is to provide clear indications that they are taken seriously. This occurred in one of my online classes, as demonstrated by the following dialogue between two students (with fictitious names).

ANGELA: Samantha, oh no, I didn't mean to sound like I was directly disagreeing with you. It was just my opinion that the story and the outcome would have been extremely different if. . . .

SAMANTHA: Angela, I didn't think you were directly disagreeing with me, I hope I didn't come across as defensive! I was just making my point in response to what you said.

ANGELA: Samantha, I love this class so much, and I think one of the reasons is that we are so concerned about each [other's] feelings! That's the only drawback with the online courses, that we can't see each other's expressions or hear the tone of our voices. I don't want you to feel bad, and believe me, I don't feel bad either, I would just feel bad if you felt bad!) Now does this make any sense?

SAMANTHA: Yes, I think you must be right. . . . I am glad too that we care about each other's feelings. It's funny, but I have had so much more of a communal feeling in my online classes here. I wonder why that is.

September 11, 2001

No one might have predicted that a book of this nature could include a section on the tragic events of September 11, 2001, but I include it because it provides an extreme example of the special need at that time to care and listen to our online students. The tragedy happened at the start of the new academic year, a season usually of new beginnings; of our children back in school; of our teaching just starting; of anticipation of newness, excitement, and learning.

It was inevitable that this event had to be discussed to some extent in our classes. I think the existence of the online component provided a very real connection between our students and we as the faculty during that traumatic time when contact with others, especially when classes were canceled, provided an opportunity for comfort. Kempster (2002) states,

> I think more than anything else that I have realized that the classroom is an essential safe environment that students really need at a time after 9/11, where they feel that they can talk about things even if they don't really understand it, where they won't be intimidated to ask the questions or express the views that they have.

At that time, in those early weeks in September, I asked myself how long we should devote to discussions of this tragedy. I recognized that they could obviously go on for a very long time, as we all needed to go through the natural stages of shock, grief, anger, and ways in which we wanted to see this settled. We could not completely go against the grain of what was occupying the primary place in our minds, but at the same time we had a syllabus to cover. I decided that we should move on when it seemed natural to do so, being cognizant of the fact that the terrorist attack was a topic to which we might return in different contexts and within different topics throughout the semester. To do otherwise would be to deny that it occurred, and this was something we could not do.

I saw so many online instructors who were frequently there with a sensitive response, and I think this provided great reassurance for their students. My own personal experience was that in one of my online creative writing classes, which started immediately after September 11, students opened up and told of their experiences, fears, and nightmares; and against this backdrop they produced work that is among the finest I have ever seen. Their writing seemed to touch the core of their souls. One student wrote,

> I live on the upper west side of Manhattan, and see the procession of construction trucks and heavy equipment being hauled away each night. I found out I live across the street from Con Edison's "nucleus" building that supplies all of Manhattan with electricity. It's a nameless, nondescript, windowless structure. I thought it was an ABC TV bldg b/c my neighborhood includes all the TV studios. After the Con Ed bldg was photographed by a "suspect" and it received threats of a truck-bomb, the bldg is now surrounded by cement barricades, cops. It's a constant reminder when I look out my window and see cops on its rooftop. I packed a "run away" bag and keep it in my closet. One of my friends in the bldg (who is 72) packed one as well and says she'll put her dentures in her getaway bag each night . . . just in case . . . I never thought I'd have to think of things like this while living in America.

Another student, closer to Ground Zero, wrote,

> Until January of this year, I lived on Duane Street, between West Broadway and Church. It was extremely difficult to watch the destruction of the towers, and to see how it affected my old neighborhood. I had to stop watching the television for a while after the attack. Thankfully, my former roommates are all okay, and one is living with me temporarily in my East Village apartment. We still smell the smoke at times—it depends on which way the wind is blowing.

In answer, one replied,

> I have been so shocked and frightened since 9/11 and haven't been quite able to get myself back into the mindset of work and school. My boyfriend

and I stood on the roof of our east village apt. that morning and watched the towers fall and then our neighborhood was barricaded and we, too, were packing emergency bags to keep by the door. The whole thing has just been overwhelming for me.

I found their writing so expressive, so lyrical, so genuine, as in this response:

Doesn't normality feel almost weird though, at times? As I cycled home 2 nights ago from my mid-town studio, down the Hudson bike path, I could see the smoke, STILL, lit up at Ground Zero. It was a beautiful night; the air smelled fresh and rivery; a cricket was cricking; and I thought, Doesn't it know what happened? The discrepancy between the horror and Life Going On as before, is so huge. . . . I live on the lower East Side and my husband and I watched from our roof. I'm thankful though that I didn't see the collapse in person, I think that would have done me in. Friends of ours live very close, and saw the whole thing, people jumping and all. God how awful. . . . I do have a sense of optimism about it, but am afraid it might take Armageddon to get there. One positive thing that does seem to be enduring though is my gratitude to all the amazingly brave and committed people working down at the site. I find myself saying "Thank You," aloud and under my breath, every time I see a fire truck or police vehicle. And it feels good not to get irate with complete strangers about nothing any more.

As the semester progressed, and the bonding between us grew ever stronger, I started to see a change of attitude in some students to external events. One student wrote how she was nearly run over by a negligent car driver while crossing the road. She said,

When my friend and I walked away I reflected that even as we are afraid after the WTC, and wondering if we should buy gas masks. War casualties, nuclear bombs, etc . . . there are still valid dangers in our daily lives. I guess the lesson is—stay alert, watch where you're walking/driving these days. Our world events have probably caused a lot of people to lose focus on what's in front of them.

To which a fellow student answered,

I've had similar thoughts coming back a few weeks after the WTC. . . . Not any brushes with collisions, like you, but reminders that, after an initial phase of extreme tolerance towards my fellow man, there are still some who rub me up the wrong way. . . . Noisy neighbors and people in restaurants being rude to wait persons etc. . . . And learning to accept the fact that that will probably always be the case! It's oddly disturbing though to come back to those feelings when you want to keep open-hearted towards everyone.

Never before have I witnessed such bonding within an online class, so much support and caring. One student had to fly to Los Angeles, and she wrote as follows:

> I'm flying to LA tomorrow and am nervous about the JFK–LA flight. I've been trying to tell myself that I just can't live that way though. Trying to tell myself that I could be hit by a car on the way to work today or even that where I work, in Union Sq., could be attacked by anthrax but that I can't just stop going to work because I'm scared. It's kind of helping but I was already afraid of flying—even though I do it about ten times a year— and I just can't imagine what kind of thoughts I'm going to have on that 6 hour flight tomorrow. But the only thing I keep hearing over and over in the news and from friends and family is that we can't just stop living our lives. This is all just going to take a lot of getting used to.

It turned out that the day she made that flight was the day America first bombed Afghanistan, and I think we all held our breaths until she logged on again and said she had safely arrived at her destination, and we all gave an even bigger sigh of relief when she was home again. But her fear was real, and was manifested in nightmares that came to her after her trip, as she wrote:

> I thought that I had been feeling better lately about Sep. 11. The week afterwards I had such a horrible succession of nightmares, the likes of which I had never before experienced. And after those subsided I had a few shortlived anxiety attacks but then I eventually started feeling better. You know, I flew to LA and back and was fine and even this anthrax doesn't seem all that scary. But then last night I had such a terrible night- mare. I dreamt that I was at a friend's house in Brooklyn with a really close view of the city and that hijacked jetliners just started crashing into build- ings all over the city. Then there were cropdusters flying over and releasing horrible chemicals. My friend and I were screaming and watching it all through her big windows. I was trying to close the windows and turn off her ceiling fan and get a towel to breathe through. And it seemed that some of the cropdusters were spraying acid because buildings just started melting. It was so horrible. It seemed so real too. There was a strange

moment in the dream too where I was running down the street and I heard a girl crying and screaming and I started looking around so that I could help her but I didn't see anyone and then I finally realized that it was me screaming. I woke up and just started sobbing.

To this, a student replied,

I'm so sorry about your horrible nightmare. I understand how you feel, I've had my share of awful scary nightmares with planes crashing and bombs exploding and being separated from my loved ones. . . . It's awful and so disturbing. During the following weeks of 9/11 I would just burst out and cry and cry. . . . I heard a young girl on the news (she was in Ohio or something) and she said that the air just felt sad. . . . I thought that that was the truest thing. *Feel better . . . we are all here for you.* [Italics are mine.]

Tension because of the instability of world events remained high throughout that semester, as exemplified by this student's remark:

I broke a tooth two weeks ago because I've been grinding my teeth so hard at night since 9/11. I haven't had heart palpitations like ___. But I have had strange pain in my left arm since 9/11. So have two of my other neighbors. On 9/12 I figured it was the beginning of a heart attack, but decided against going to the emergency room. You know, they always tell people that don't "look" like they're at risk for a heart attack the symptoms are from "gas." My friend is going to the doctor for her mystery left arm pain. But I think mine is that I'm so tense these days I forget to breathe properly.

Throughout this period, what was striking to me is that the tension did not distract from the work these students were doing. On the contrary, it enhanced their efforts, making their work stunning and outstanding. I was also struck by the frankness and candor with which students were able to discuss their concerns. One student wrote that she was afraid as she was a Lebanese American, and that for the first time she felt that she was going to experience more racial profiling than her boyfriend, who was African American. Everyone sympathized with her, and was accepting of her. In short, it was a most extraordinary class, and the students, feeling able to unburden themselves when the need arose, and being so expressive and full of caring and support for each other, left room to be exceptionally alert to analysis of the course content.

It might have been the particular mix of students, it might have been the time frame, or it might have been the potential for intimacy offered by the online environment (we all debated the factors a great deal), but certainly we came together online to experience one of the most fulfilling academic ventures that I have ever known.

Pedagogical Loneliness

Pedagogical loneliness, a phrase coined by Fisher (2001), describes the feeling you, as instructor, might experience when a particularly tremendous class is over. It came up in conversation with an online class I once taught, in which I could not ask for a better group of students—lively, alert, engaged, insightful—that it can be sad when this shared classroom experience is over. We had originally been talking about why people read, and from there, we talked about how sad it can feel, if you love a book, to reach the end of it. I wrote to them,

> I might also add that I feel that an online class is very much like reading a book; at first you need to get to know the characters in textual form, then you start to flow along, knowing people and looking forward to hearing from them, and then, when the class is over, I miss everyone just as I miss the characters of a good novel.

I was fascinated to receive several comments from my online students in response to my statement. Two of these follow:

> I also wanted to comment on what you had said in relation to what I had said about the ending of a book is like saying good-bye to a very close friend. You had said you felt this same way about the online classes. I have only taken one other, and as you know, it was your last class. And you are right . . . I did feel this way! I really felt so lost and saddened when it was over. I had become so attached to EVERYONE! I couldn't wait for this class to begin. The feeling can be similar in a campus course if it is really an absolutely amazing and stimulating class, but this feeling of loss when the class ends does not seem to be as intense as the online classes.

> When I took my first [online] class last year I had the strangest feeling when the class was over. While I don't see anyone, there is a great sense of security knowing that any time of day I turn on my computer I can be surrounded by classmates and a stimulating discussion. The next morning, after the "classroom" was turned off on the last day at midnight, I went back to see if it was there. When I couldn't get past the home page I felt like my whole classroom experience never existed and it had all been a dream. It reminded me of "The Lion, the Witch and the Wardrobe"

because there had been access to another world in the back of the closet. It also reminded me of a Russian movie (with French subtitles) called "A Window to Paris," where there is a magical hole in the wall of a dismal Soviet apt. building. The hole leads to Paris, but it remains active for only a short period of time, and the people must decide to stay in colorful Paris, or return to a miserable life. Last semester I decided to stay awake all night so I could watch the site "go off," and not feel like I woke up from a strange dream. I stayed up until 3AM and then couldn't take it any more and went to sleep.

I savor these comments. The first, I thought, was interesting, as this student points out that for her, the online experience is "even more intense" than the campus class. And I really enjoyed the second, especially when she said what she had loved about the online class was the "sense of security knowing that at any time of day . . . I can be surrounded by classmates and a stimulating discussion." I think, perhaps, this speaks to the point about intensity made by the first student. I also loved how the second student felt that it was like a dream, or that she had traveled to another world, especially terrific for me to read, as the subject of this class was children's literature.

That this can occur in an online class, possibly accounting for the intensity mentioned by one of my students, leads, in turn, to the sadness and isolation when a riveting class is over; but there is one comfort, perhaps. Whereas students might not always stop by your office to see you after a campus class is over, however wonderful the class, there is definitely a greater opportunity for students to remain in touch with you in an online class, assuming they continue to have Internet access. I still receive wonderful e-mails from students from many semesters and sometimes even many years ago. We remember each other, remember even each other's particular likes and favorite topics. It minimizes the pedagogical loneliness, perhaps.

Overcoming Problematic Situations

We talked earlier in the chapter about ways in which to encourage participation in discussion if some students are not posting responses. In this section, we discuss other problems that might arise, and make recommendations as to what the instructor should do if they occur. The problems that are considered include heated online conversations, absent or late students, and issues of honesty.

Heated Online Discussions

Most software programs provide the facility to edit or delete responses in any of the discussion forums. If a student has posted a highly offensive remark—offensive because it attacks another class member, uses inappropriate language, or both—this gives rise to the thorny decision as to whether it is justifiable for you to remove the response.

I believe there are several reasons why the offensive response should not be deleted or changed. First is the issue of freedom of speech. To remove the response seems in some ways dishonest, as if it were a pretense that the remark was never there. If the same offensive remark were made in a campus class, everyone would have heard it and might feel compelled to address it. There would be no way in which the remark could be made to seem as if it never happened. It takes on form in our minds and memories. So, in similar ways, I think the same process should be allowed to exist in the online class. Because we all work asynchronously online, there also is the chance, however frequently you, the instructor, log on, that some students might have already read it before you see it. If you remove it, it seems that you are falsifying the history of the class discussion. However nasty, disgusting, and even polluting of the forum that response appears to be—and yes, comments can look harsher when they are in textual form only—it is important for the class as a whole to try to understand the root cause of the disagreement and provide incentive for it to be resolved, rather than camouflaged or glossed over. After all, often after a crisis (a rather strong term) comes a new synthesis, resolution, and understanding. Very great insights might be fathomed if there is honesty to explore the issues. Ehrmann (2002b), in a posting to the American Association for Higher Education and Accreditation listserv in a discussion about stages of faculty development, used the term "flaming" for when two or more students "get into a reactionary confrontation stemming from a misconception, miscommunication, or disagreement," and wondered whether it could be "converted from a hazard into a teachable moment. . . ." Researchers in the Derek Bok Center for Teaching and Learning said, "Often when things get most hot, people are most capable of learning at a very deep level, if the exchange among students is properly handled" (Salley, Wadsworth, Terry, and Richardson, 2002).

I think this is true, but the question is how to properly handle the online exchange between students, how to make most use of the "teachable moment." One method that Salley et al. (2002) suggest for the campus class is to ask students to step back and see what positive elements can be gleaned from this heated discussion. Because timing may be crucial here, this could be harder in the asynchronous online environment, in which a number of heated responses could have already been posted since you last logged on. I would suggest if you need immediate intervention that you e-mail or phone the particular students most involved; if your class is a hybrid, and you will be meeting your students on campus, it might be helpful to also discuss these issues face to face so that you can more accurately read each other's expressions and gather more meaning from the tone of voice. Even if your class is only held online, I believe it could be helpful for the whole class to thrash out a provocative issue, so you should encourage this to occur.

Of course, heated and passionate discussions should not be rude or hurtful if there are areas of disagreement, but should be exciting and respectful of the opinion of others. In other words, the exploration should not be emotional but strictly intellectual in its pursuit of knowledge (Ehrmann, 2002b). Salley et al. (2002) also state that if a student has made a particularly charged statement in a campus class, that you stop the class and then ask students to research the implications of this statement as homework, and come to the next class prepared to discuss it. How can this be done online? Even if you log on at the right moment to stop the discussion as soon as the charged comment was made, how can you stop the class? The only way you can do this is to immediately lock up the discussion forum so that no new responses can be added, and then wait a few days or a week to open a new forum to discuss the implications of the heated exchange. I like the idea of giving the students some time for consideration, rather than just discussing impetuously and emotionally. You could remind the students that discussion on this topic should be thoughtful, and it is very likely to be just that, as we already know that asynchronous discussions often tend to be impressively reflective. Salley et al. (2002) suggest that, within the discussion, you ask students to explain why they hold certain opinions. I think this can be performed well online, as students should always be encouraged to be articulate and prepared to substantiate their viewpoints. When a heated discussion is encouraged, rather than hushed up, as long as it is kept safe in the ways discussed, it can be a thrilling occurrence, with you and students alike feeling that you cannot wait to log back in to class to see what has now been said and to add new thoughts of your own.

I should add that even though I would not use the delete function to remove an offensive response, should it occur, I do see one pragmatic use of this function, and that is if a student clicks several times on the submit button, so the response comes through multiple times. I have sometimes seen this happen at the start of the semester. I feel that the delete function can be used to remove the multiple submissions, accompanying this with an e-mail to the student about what you did for the sake of housekeeping, and perhaps giving a brief and friendly reminder about the technique of submitting a response. I have found that the student is generally quite relieved that you have done this.

Furthermore, most software programs allow you to decide when setting up a new forum whether to allow students the ability to edit or to remove their own responses. If you do select these privileges for students, I would advise that you tell them that they should only edit or remove their own responses if done immediately after the initial posting. If not, and they return some time later to do this after the response in its original form has probably been read by quite a few people, then it would change the history of the conversation and could cause no end of confusion.

The Late Student

It has always been my policy to leave discussion forums open, even after we, as a class, have moved on to the next discussion topic. Many software programs have a mechanism to lock up a forum, thereby not allowing any new postings, but I have chosen not to do that, essentially because I marvel at the fact that in the online class, unlike in real time in the traditional classroom, time can be twisted this way and that; many topics can be discussed simultaneously, depending on the juggling skills of the students; and online class discussion topics can be enriched by the contributions of new thoughts and comments.

The Returning Versus the Late Student

I believe that it is excellent if a student returns to a discussion forum, after we have essentially moved on to immerse ourselves in new discussions in a newly created forum, because the student has continued to ponder or research issues and has new insights or information. This could deepen the discussion in important ways. In fact, I often create a discussion forum on basic definitions and encourage students to return to it throughout the semester, as their thinking on the topic becomes more refined and informed. If students do return to an earlier discussion forum, you might want to make an announcement to the class to look again at that forum, as exciting new conversation threads are being spun.

I realize, however, that my policy on leaving the door open on past discussion forums can also have negative consequences. The situation of a student returning to a discussion forum with new insights contrasts sharply with that of a late student who is only visiting a discussion forum for the first time, long after the rest of the class has moved on from that topic. Admittedly, there can be many reasons as to why this can occur, such as signing up very late for the class, experiencing technical delays, waiting for books to arrive, not fully understanding the expectations of the class (some students might be under the mistaken impression that it is a self-paced class), or just plain laziness and lack of motivation. It is important to remember, however, that on campus, if a student misses a class, that is the end. The opportunity no longer exists if that student did not attend that particular class at the specified time. Online, however, the lecture and discussion forum remain visible. At what point does this stop being an advantage and become instead a nuisance?

A lone student responding to all the questions in a previous discussion forum well after everyone else has talked together about the issues is going to represent more work for you, the instructor (and you might already be spending large amounts of time in your online class). This student tugs the class backward when it should be propelled forward, and chances are that the other students will not even return to that forum to read the new responses anyway, so interactivity is unlikely to be rekindled at that late stage. Furthermore, this late student could just be copying the responses already posted by others, rather than saying anything original.

What to Do about a Student Who Is Late

What should be done about the student who is late? We can try to prevent this from happening by advising students at the start of the semester that their participation in online discussion counts significantly toward the final grade; we can tell students that this is not a self-paced course despite its asynchronicity, convenience, and flexibility (see earlier in the chapter, "How to Facilitate and Stimulate Online Discussion"). We can elaborate upon what we mean by *flexibility,* stating that some students might want to participate at lunch time, and others at midnight, and others at any time in between, and others yesterday or tomorrow, but basically everyone should participate a minimum of three times per week, spaced evenly throughout the week. It is not effective if a student participates three times on a Friday, and not again until the following Friday, because it is crucial for everyone to be at approximately the same part of the course at the same time, to permit the online discussion to reach its fullest interactive potential.

We can even involve students in formulating a policy about rules of civility. In my class on ethics, I found that besides the usual suggestions about treating each other with respect (and the unusual ones of dressing appropriately!), there was a response from one student that all her classmates keep up with the course in a timely manner; and other students readily agreed. However, one student in the online ethics class remained absent from class discussions. I doubt that he even saw that a class code of conduct was being discussed. From time to time I would receive e-mails that his books had not yet arrived, but I assured him that he should nevertheless start participating in discussion immediately, as I start the class by giving a lot of basic information, plus a hypothetical ethical dilemma, so students are not required to have yet read anything at that early stage of the course. He did not. Then more excuses started rolling in. His cousin's computer, which he was apparently using, kept crashing. His boss was being very demanding at this particular time, and so he had to work late and had insufficient time for the course. Then he did receive the books, and e-mailed me enthusiastically about how he couldn't put one book down and would respond shortly in class, but still nothing.

What to do? Give him the benefit of the doubt? Tell him to drop the class; that, through no fault of his own, the unfortunate circumstances made it unrealistic that he could meaningfully complete the course? There I was, remaining undecided, when all of a sudden there was a sprinkling of responses from him, in the very earliest discussion forums, which the rest of the class had left a month ago. I was surprised, and also admittedly rather disgruntled that I had to go over that material again. What came as an even bigger surprise to me, however, was that some students seemed just as annoyed. I must admit to not having thought about the effect it would have on them, although clearly I should have. But naturally, any leniency I might show to the seriously late student would be perceived as unfair to the other students who did participate on time and did not have the luxury of having extensions.

Giving this matter a lot of thought, I finally came up with the idea that the fairest strategy—and one which balanced the needs of the class, the difficulties of the tardy student, and the time constraints of the instructor with the inherent need to teach and interact with the group and not with separate individuals—was to suggest to this student that he join in with the most recent discussion forum posted, and thereafter keep current with the rest of the class. This, of course, implied that it was then too late for that student to start posting responses in discussion forums from earlier in the semester, although he would have to work through this material on his own. Unfortunately this would negatively impact the student's grade, as participation in discussion counts significantly, but I felt that there had to be consequences, despite the excuses.

I believe that if a student wants to succeed in the course, it is his or her responsibility to find access to the Internet and thus to the class, by any means. By analogy, if a student is repeatedly unable to travel to a class on campus because of car trouble, then the student should find an alternative way of getting there. If it is a busy time at work, then the student must juggle the responsibilities. I have known students who have truly amazed me by having such extremely busy and hectic schedules, but, despite this, they are always the first to respond to online discussions and in a thoughtful, insightful way. If everything seems truly impossible, then perhaps this is just not the best time to take this course, and maybe the student should try again another time.

What I see happening in some classes is that whereas students mostly keep up with their readings and are ready to join in with discussions as new forums are posted, there is sometimes lateness when students are given more responsibility, such as working collaboratively with class members, making a presentation, or leading a discussion. The amount of lateness varies with the students; poor students are sometimes a week late, but even the good students possibly are a day or two late.

Why Some Students Are Late: The Relationship between Real Time and Virtual Time

I have been giving a great deal of thought as to why this time lag occurs, and have come up with a few possibilities. One is that the amount of real available time outside the online class, during which to get the work done, has shrunk as students have taken on yet more commitments. Another is related to the degree of motivation, although even students who are motivated and engaged, and who post stimulating, insightful, pertinent responses, sometimes are a little late, too. I also wondered whether the events of and since September 11, 2001, have distracted students, and I saw this as a possibility at that time.

Another plausible thought is that the setting of due dates might seem like an oxymoron in an asynchronous environment, in which the primary emphasis is on the fact that time is virtual, that it is theirs to fill as they want and when they want. For within the asynchronous online environment, the only expectation is that participation should be a minimum of three to five times per week, at a time that is convenient to them.

If we look more deeply, I think one definition of conventional time is that it is the interval between two events; but what is an accurate definition of virtual time? Can it still be thought of as a discrete interval, or does the fact that time is virtual make this interval much more elastic, much more pulled, lengthened, stretched, and maybe even coiled in on itself than in the real world with its steady marching forward with every tick of the clock, every swing of the pendulum? Does virtual time more approximate mental time, the time within our heads, rather than objective time as measured by the clock?

We all know that mental time does not always correlate with objective time. When we are enjoying ourselves or are immersed in an activity, it feels to us that no time has passed, although the clock tells us otherwise.

The asynchronicity of the online environment induces reflection and encourages one to respond when ready, when one has thought deeply, when one feels stimulated, when one is inspired. In this context then, does not a due date seem rather jarring? What are we to do because we must have dates by which activities are performed, groups work together, assignments are submitted? It is supremely disappointing if one or more students are kept waiting on a group project because other group members have not participated (see in Chapter 8 the sections on group work). Is it recommended that the instructor e-mail to students reminders when the date approaches for them to do a particular project? Or should this be part of the student's responsibility, to keep track, to log on frequently enough to the course to know what is expected? Should there be penalties for lateness? If so, how much leniency should there be? I prefer to encourage rather than be punitive, but it can certainly be discouraging if students are late with their own work in the asynchronous environment. David Hoover (2002) at New York University suggests that possibly the decrease in hierarchy and authoritarianism relaxes the class into thinking that they can more liberally interpret due dates. He also goes on to say that he dislikes being punitive for lateness:

> I have often thought that it is costly in several ways: it puts a very heavy emphasis on the due date, so that students may come to see punctuality as more important than quality (think of the difference in quality between a B paper and a C paper); it requires more precise bookkeeping than I am generally willing to perform; and it emphasizes and insists upon the gap between student and teacher.

Maybe the problem lies in telling students that they can log on "at their own convenience." Yes, students logging on at their own convenience is certainly advantageous in reflective online discussions. But perhaps we need also to let students know explicitly that there are, in fact, certain time obligations to be met, such as the date at which work from them is due to begin, or be submitted. Perhaps we need to be clear at the outset of the course that virtual time sometimes intersects with real time, and students need to pay attention to those points of intersection. It should be noted, however, that these problems are lessened in the hybrid, in which students and the teacher do meet in real time, too.

Academic Integrity

At nearly every conference I have attended on the subject of online teaching and learning, the question comes up as to how we know the students are who they say they are, and that their responses are original to them. I have even heard suggestions for such precautionary measures as retina screening to ensure integrity. My suggestion is that if we encourage students to participate fully in all discussions throughout the course, we should gain a fair idea as to the caliber, engagement, intelligence, and insight of each student, so that we should be better equipped to detect any sudden inconsistency, if this arises. Dishonesty can arise in many ways, but I will concentrate here on plagiarism and honesty of student remarks.

Plagiarism

Within academia, we are always talking and learning about new ideas, and it is essential to acknowledge at all times the source of that information. Plagiarism includes lifting information (text or graphics) from an original source without quotation marks (in the case of text), reference, or acknowledgment, as well as paraphrasing without reference or acknowledgment to the original source.

A Princeton pamphlet, entitled *Academic Integrity at Princeton* (2002), asks how this applies to the online environment where rules might be a little more relaxed and the writings in the discussion forums more informal. When a student submits a paper, whether on campus or electronically, we can define the rules to avoid plagiarism, but can the same be true in online discussions? My feeling is that, even within conversational online discussions on the discussion board, proper acknowledgments should be given. After all, if a student was speaking in a campus class and wanted to quote something, it would be expected that this student would cite the source, if it were a verbatim quotation. I once had an online student who copied an entire online review and pasted it into the discussion forum without acknowledgment, as if this were her own opinion. But little did the student expect that I had read the same review! There is absolutely no campus equivalence to that. After all, in the traditional class, a student would simply not be able to raise his or her hand, clear his or her throat, and then recite the words of a different author, without it sounding as if the student was indeed reciting, and without, if the passage was long, the likely necessity of looking down at the article. I insisted that the online student give due recognition to the original.

The Princeton article goes on to say that not citing the source of information is one violation to academic integrity, but there are certainly others. For example, a student might be unable to find the original source and instead choose to make up a citation. Another violation is if a student submits an identical paper to more than one course, without prior permission in writing from both professors. We can also step into murky terrain in regard to collaborative or group work, as it might be unclear who did what work (see "Online Testing and Grading" in Chapter 8).

As far as giving students advice about how to write good papers that do not run the risk of plagiarism, the Princeton article suggests telling students to take good initial notes and keep track of their references at the time, which is much easier and more reliable than having to hunt down source material well after the fact. In addition, the students should be told that secondary as well as primary sources need appropriate recognition, and any words that are from someone else should be put inside quotation marks. Students should also display citations properly and cite electronic sources. As we know, it is all too easy, mechanically speaking, to simply copy information from one Web site and paste it elsewhere. Hopefully with some clear guidelines and good ethics, this will not occur.

Instructors, when referring students to materials, should be careful not to copy and distribute copies without copyright permission. If a relevant piece of work resides on the Web, it is absolutely acceptable to construct a link to it, as it is in the public domain, but it is not acceptable to copy and paste it into the class.

Student Honesty

There is some debate within the Princeton (2002) article about students showing their written paper to a friend before submitting it. It can be a beneficial learning experience for both students if they bounce ideas off each other before writing, or if one proofreads another's paper for typing mistakes, but it is a violation if one student substantially rewrites large sections of the other student's paper. This occurred in an online class I taught a few semesters ago. On this particular occasion, I had a student who was a very poor writer, as evidenced in her online responses and journal entries, but then she submitted a perfect paper, which was eloquent beyond belief. This was such a jarring contrast to her previous work that I called and asked her about it. She was honest enough to admit that she knows she cannot write, and was also under a "time crunch," so she dictated her thoughts to a friend, who wrote them in proper structure and grammar (and possibly added some extra ideas of her own?). I asked the student to rewrite the paper herself.

The question of honesty within the online class can take different forms as well. I was recently involved in a discussion with some colleagues, and one of them remarked that in a face-to-face class, if a student says something that meets with a lot of negative reaction, the student might choose to deny ever having said it. This, he continued, could not occur online, as the remark would remain, as indelibly and undeniably as if it had just been said. He thought that whereas in a campus class, a student could say, "I didn't say that," in the online class, a student would have to say, "I didn't mean that." Whereas my colleague saw this as a possible negative factor in working online, I would like to turn this situation around as an advantage. I find it helpful to have a complete record of the exchanges, and I think there is nothing wrong in a student saying, "that is not what I had meant" and clarifying it further. Although a challenge, I think it helps us to seek clarity of expression, and I see this as being a better situation than denying a remark had been made.

This led to an interesting discussion in which another faculty member spoke of a campus class that she had been teaching and that was looking at the subject of nonverbal behavior. My colleague mentioned that one of her students gave as an example her reaction to men who are always touching their genitals. When this remark was met with laughter from her classmates, the student regretted that she had spoken, and retreated into an uncomfortable position in which she repeatedly apologized. My interpretation of the situation is that it was only the laughter around her in the classroom that made the student pull back and wish that she had never made that statement. When she first made the remark, this was something she felt motivated to say. In other words, I think her remark only became awkward as a result of the reaction of others, which seemed to come as some surprise to her.

So how would this situation translate to an online scenario, in which the student making the remark would not hear laughter, and any reaction would probably be less immediate? In fact, if a comment of this nature was read online rather than heard in the traditional classroom, would anyone feel like laughing? Why did they laugh in the campus class? Perhaps it was because some students felt relieved that someone had dared to express something that they themselves had not been able to speak about. Perhaps for others it jogged a certain memory. Perhaps for still others it was purely embarrassing. They each had their private reasons, but the student in question might have felt they were laughing at her, which could be why she kept apologizing.

As I was discussing these issues, a colleague said that she thought that a superb feature and advantage of an online class over a traditional class on campus is we have the ability to edit or even completely delete responses if we find that we do not like them. I strongly disagree! Just as in the previous discussion about what to do if conversations become heated (see "Overcoming Problematic Situations" earlier in the chapter), I feel that unless a response is edited or removed immediately so that no one else has a chance to read it, I definitely do not think it should be pulled away or changed later. If, for example, the student who made the troubling response had been working online rather than on campus, and other students then started to post disapproving comments (which incidentally I don't think their laughter was about), then it would not only be confusing if she deleted the remark, but also dishonest because the remark had been made and we should not pretend that it never happened.

I think it would be better, and actually more of a learning experience, if the online discussion board could be used in such a way that students could thoroughly delve into reasons why one said what she had, and why others reacted the way they did. I am not in any way intending to imply that there is less scope for misinterpretation and dishonesty in the online class than in the class held on campus. Indeed, it is possible that in a face-to-face situation, there are more clues and opportunities to understand meaning because of nonverbal behavior, and this can be useful information. Conversely, so-called clutter can also occur, in which prejudices might arise about a particular person for reasons of race or ethnicity, as well as for banal aspects such as someone being too old, young, fat, thin, whatever. In fact, sometimes I marvel at how accurate communication occurs at all.

Just as when we read a book and co-construct the meaning of the words in front of us by bringing in our experiences which affect our interpretation, this also occurs with the written text of the online class and during a face-to-face conversation. The hope is that in both environments, online or on campus, there will be clarity of articulation and respectful follow-up on the responses of others.

Suggestions for How to Avoid Feeling Overwhelmed

It is an irrefutable truth of the online class that it takes longer to teach than a class on campus. Of course, this depends on the discipline, but it is especially true for discussion-intensive courses. Class size and student involvement will make a huge difference as well. As someone once said to me long ago, "It takes longer to type than to talk, and longer to read than to listen." Besides this basic fact, I have also mentioned different methods whereby to stimulate and encourage online discussion, and I have talked about how communicating online gives every student, not just the more dominant ones, a chance to express him- or herself. I also have shown how virtual time is elastic and infinitely expandable. Each of these factors can increase the time spent in online teaching. Most instructors are probably already busy and quite overscheduled, so what happens if you have such a successful class, with very responsive students, that you feel that you are constantly running to keep up? In short, you are not infinitely expandable, and just because the online class is 24/7 does not mean that you are.

Previously in this chapter we talked about listening and caring. I mentioned the importance of responding to everyone, so that every student feels noticed, included, and heard. But could it leave you feeling drained and overwhelmed, and consume too much time? Could it therefore lead to burnout? First, take comfort in knowing that you have a marvelously full, stimulating course, in which you and your students are benefiting from a much deeper and more profound engagement with the topic than you might have thought possible. Sometimes the very best, most exciting and thought-provoking classes are precisely those that take up the most time. Is it best, therefore, to get caught up in the class to such an extent that you do not accurately measure the length of time it takes? Possibly, if the joy and intellectual excitement of a wonderful exchange of ideas is its own reward; but pragmatically speaking, it may not be feasible.

I think most of us have experienced frequent occasions in campus classes when several students want to respond to the discussion question, but there simply is not time to listen to everyone because we must move on to the next topic at hand. Speaking personally, I know there have been times when discussions have taken such interesting turns that I do not want to artificially restrict them, and under these circumstances, I will let them play out naturally and then have to be creative and flexible with the syllabus schedule. But this cannot happen in every class, or we will lag too far behind and will be unable to complete the entire syllabus by the end of the semester. Excessive amounts of lingering and lagging are not good. So what do I have to do under these circumstances? With much regret, I tell students that I can only hear the first five students and the others must put their hands down. I do not like doing this at all, nor do the students because if they are involved and excited, they want their say. I try to be fair and rotate students in an attempt to ensure that if they cannot individually respond to everything, they each can at least have a say in a minimum of one topic. I might also ask a student to be more succinct when the discussion is too long or becoming irrelevant.

What happens online, however, is a different matter. It is believed that, online, everyone can speak, unconstrained by time limits or interruptions. But is this so? It seems that perhaps the pressure of time limits is shifted off the students and on to the instructor, if the class is responsive. By this I mean, yes, every student can and might respond, possibly even several times a day, possibly in lengthy and numerous paragraphs, and consequently the online instructor finds it necessary to spend more and more time online. It is all too easy to become totally absorbed and immersed in the online class, and you can easily lose track of real time. So often I have told myself that I will have a quick check in to my online class, and then find that several hours have passed. The usual symbols of keeping track of time are not there. Sure, there is the clock on the computer, but for me it is easily ignored in the temptation of "just one more click." There also are no ready indications of the length of a text, as is true for a tactile object such as a book in which one can immediately gauge the number of pages. There is, instead, just a scroll bar, and then any number of links on which to click. So virtual time becomes elastic, both because of the constant availability of the online class and the temptation to avoid keeping track of time by the usual instruments.

While teaching one online class, which could only be described as explosive, I asked myself if it was truly necessary to respond to everything every student had said, the reason being that one day I logged into this class, after having not visited it since the previous day, and found 102 new responses! In general, this class generated at least 16 new responses a day, each one long and substantial, and which, in *Alice in Wonderland* fashion, seemed in my overzealous mind to contain a label, "Read me and Respond." Please do not think I am complaining. These students were a blend of the best I have ever had, as their responses were often phenomenal and their commitment and enthusiasm enough to warm anyone's heart. My only question was, how do I keep up? What is the equivalent of "hands down" online, and should it exist? If an instructor feels in danger of burnout, following are some suggestions for how to continue to incorporate caring for each student while teaching, without feeling overburdened or overwhelmed, and to most effectively rationalize the time spent online.

- *Remember to make time to care for yourself.* This is not only for your sake, but also because a less-stressed, better rested instructor (and online teaching can be very demanding) will have more to offer (Fisher, 2001). Try to set boundaries for yourself. Perhaps you can limit yourself to a certain number of hours a day; or say, for example, "Never on a Sunday" and refuse to go near your computer that day; or perhaps, if teaching a hybrid, you can transfer some activities, where appropriate, to the campus class.
- *Establish priorities and realize that it is not necessary to respond to everyone at once.* I will never ignore a student response entirely, as to acknowledge a student online is akin to having eye contact and showing you are listening in the campus classroom. It establishes a good role model for students to listen to each other. However, I will not necessarily respond to everything that everyone has said if there are a large number of long responses (I think I used to), but I will pick out the excellent, original thoughts, and comment on them. If some students have not said anything excellent or original, I will try briefly to find something of value in what they said so as to include them in discussion, make them feel good about themselves, and encourage them to perhaps think more deeply and contribute more next time. I know! This is yet another boost to generating a plentiful new supply of responses, but I think, when handled in the way I have said, it should be more manageable.
- *Ask students to keep e-mail to a minimum.* They should only use e-mail to ask you private questions or tell you about a personal matter, in much the same way as when a campus student will come to see you privately after class or in your office. Nonprivate questions should not be e-mailed, but posted into the online class discussion forum because they may reflect what others are thinking. By asking and

answering in the online class forum, you will be spared from answering the same thing to many separate individuals, and this will save you time. The discussion forums are the energy center of the online class and should not be eroded away by nonessential e-mails. By developing a collegial, collaborative atmosphere within the online discussion forum, you are establishing a truly learner-centered environment. In cases when students must e-mail you, be aware that they might frequently change e-mail addresses or have unusual e-mail addresses, either of which might involve you in wasting time determining the author of a message. I would recommend that you ask students to include their name at the end of their message, and also to give their message an easy-to-identify title. It might be helpful to keep e-mails from students in a separate folder so that they do not become lost among your other e-mail messages.

- *Establish agreement as to the nature of student postings in online discussions.* As the instructor, you can model what you see as a good type of response, in terms of its length, relevance, and succinctness. Excessively long posts from online students, or students who try to monopolize the discussion by posting too many times, could be discouraging to conversation of the group as a whole, especially if they start to become too trite, anecdotal, irrelevant, or elitist.
- *Delegate work.* By delegating work to students, you give them more responsibility for their own learning and lessen your burden of time. In other words, as well as having plentiful discussions corresponding with information that you have posted as a mini-lecture, you can also have other learning activities. This would be beneficial, too, as students learn in different ways from each other, so a variety of activities might provide all students with opportunities to excel in the online class.

A thorough investigation of alternative online learning activities is the focus of the next chapter.

8

INNOVATIVE ONLINE TEACHING TECHNIQUES

Give a man a fish and you feed him for a day.
Teach a man to fish and you feed him for a
lifetime.

—Chinese Proverb

It is important and beneficial to vary the learning activities in the online class. A semester is a long time, and it might become heavy and cumbersome if the entire time is spent opening up new discussion forums to correspond with new mini-lectures. There are many other exercises that might prove to be effective for collaborative work and that provide alternative ways for stimulating online discussion and effective learning. As with teaching on campus, it is beneficial to provide a variety of learning activities to match the different ways in which students learn and to challenge them to greater heights. Furthermore, it will be beneficial to you, the instructor, to be creative and to reinvent yourself (Blankespoor, 1996), rather than just pasting the same ideas into your online class from one semester to the next, as this will help the class to feel fresh and spontaneous.

It is crucial to provide learning activities that enhance reflective thinking beyond pure memorization. We saw in Part One how Bloom proposed the six developmental levels of learning: knowledge, comprehension, application, analysis, synthesis, and evaluation (Cameson, Delpierre, and Masters, 2002). In this chapter we look at a variety of innovative online learning activities, each of which appears at different levels of Bloom's taxonomy, and will investigate how each provides new perspectives and a change of pace, which help to keep students engaged, challenged, and fascinated by their online course. I should add, however, that timing is important; had some of these learning activities been introduced too early in the course, students might not have been confident enough to contribute, but with sufficient encouragement and modeling from the instructor, they find they can more easily slip into, enjoy, and benefit from some or all of these learning activities.

Group Work

Most software programs allow you to divide the entire online class into exclusive groups in which students only see the responses of their group members, with only you as teacher having global access. These smaller groups offer students a variety of ways by which they can communicate online with other members of their group. You can create an asynchronous discussion board for each group, or each small group can use real-time chat (see later in the chapter), or students can send e-mails to those within their group. Some students might also opt for the telephone or try to schedule face-to-face meetings, but the online environment seems to offer valid alternatives to this.

Group Hopping

Even though most software programs allow you to create exclusive groups, another option might be for you to create a new discussion forum for each group with *open access* to all, so as to enable students to see all the responses of everyone in the other groups as well as their own. If you do this, you should tell your students to hold discussions with their group members but also encourage them to "group hop," should they wish to do so; in other words, if they see some really exciting conversation going on in another group, they have permission to join in. In fact, students should be encouraged to always read the responses in the other groups, whether they contribute to them or not. Setting up online groups makes online discussion more manageable because there are fewer responses that they must respond to, but at the same time permitting group hopping suggests the value of reading all other student responses from all groups, and gives them the option to respond in other groups.

This has several advantages. In the first place, if some students are not participating in their group discussion, despite your best efforts to encourage them to do so and reminders that they have responsibility to their group members as well as to themselves, other students in that group do not have to be frustrated or hampered in their attempt to have an enriching online discussion. They should no longer sit idly and angrily waiting for their group discussion to ignite and for someone to respond to what they have written; they can instead hop to another group's discussion and join in. And what's more, they can group hop even if discussion within their own group is good, if they see interesting conversation also going on elsewhere. This often enriches a group's discussion still more by having other eager students contribute to it. Another advantage of having open access to all group discussions is that students have ample materials in the form of archived online discussions when it comes to writing their papers, rather than being confined to only the discussion raised by their group or by the group leaders representing the group discussions. In this way, with the core group holding its online discussion and the possibility of input from other motivated students, the group discussion becomes amorphous and amoebic, much like an improvised and nonprescribed hearty face-to-face discussion, and all can potentially benefit from its richness.

It should be mentioned, however, that open access to all groups is not appropriate if groups are working on such topics as preparing for a debate in which they are on different sides, or likewise if they are preparing for a mock trial. In cases such as these, you as teacher should set up exclusive groups in which only you have global access.

Optimal Group Size

I suggest that the optimal size of a group (depending on class size) should not exceed four or five people. This group size helps increase opportunities of participation because it creates a more intimate feel. It might also be a good idea to pair up the students and have each duo resolve an issue that has been discussed in class.

Implications of the Instructor Seeing Each Group Discussion

As instructor, whether or not you have created exclusive or open groups, you have global access to all the groups and thus can observe the discussions within them, a fact that I think you should tell your students. This should avoid creating any feelings that "Big Brother Is Watching You." But, and here I see enormous pedagogical implications, does your presence in their discussion change student behavior? Would this make them work more? Say less? How might it affect the final outcome? Certainly this ability as instructor to look into the work of each online group differs from assigning a group project in a campus class. If you did assign group work on campus, chances are that you would not necessarily be present as the group thrashes out their collaborative work, unless they spend some class time doing this, or you requested updates and scheduled deadlines for certain stages of the product.

Some students might initially feel resistant to online group work, being unable to conceptualize it, but in fact it is far more convenient to work asynchronously as a group online than it is in the real world, where there are all sorts of scheduling issues to agree upon.

Group Work in Large Classes: Case Studies and Collaborative Problem Solving

Group work can be especially helpful in:

- A very large class
- Case studies
- Collaborative problem-based learning

We talked about how one might feel overwhelmed in a very large class, or one that generates many responses. If this is the case for you, it might be helpful to divide the class into groups, and then have a discussion leader from each group present to the whole class. You can rotate discussion leaders throughout the semester so everyone has a turn. You can also rotate who belongs to which group so that everyone in class has a turn working with everyone else. Whereas you might only want to observe the discussion within each group (unless you need to intervene to solve a problem), I would recommend that you take a much more active part in the discussions with the group leaders on the class discussion board.

As in all discussion forums, I would not recommend that each group representative post only once, as this discussion would be flat and not reach its fullest potential, but that the representatives in a forum should become truly immersed and engaged in the discussion topic, at times checking back with their group to discuss ideas, and then returning to the class discussion forum to continue the discussion in depth. In addition to assigning groups for large classes, students can also be divided into groups to prepare a case study or solve a particular problem, both of which can then be presented to the entire class.

Assigning Groups

If this is a one-time project, the question then arises as to how to decide who should belong to which group. I would recommend that you assign students to the groups, rather than waiting for them to choose, as this could be lengthy online. Of course, this might be different if you are teaching a hybrid, and perhaps students can make their choices of online group membership in the campus class.

If you decide to make the selection, how should you go about it? Should you select students alphabetically, randomly, or on the basis of information you have already gathered about each student's work habits, abilities, and skills? It might be that you are likely to see better group work across each group if you mix students with varying skills and abilities so that they can learn from each other, but some online instructors say that they do not like mixed-ability groups, as they think the good students feel dragged down by those less talented, and they often feel that their grade could be compromised. Instead, they advocate choosing students who have a similar grade, as this is more equitable.

This could also be determined by performing a Myers-Briggs Inventory to match students on the basis of similarity and supposed compatibility. Certainly it might be an idea to put several strong students in one group, and have them present first, so that they can model to the other groups what is to be expected.

If, early in the class, a student expresses unhappiness with the assigned group because he or she feels overwhelmed or excluded or believes that there is little to learn from the other students, you should investigate the student's complaints. If these reasons seem valid, it might be better to transfer the student to another group rather than running the risk of hampering the student's learning.

Individual Student Roles within Their Group

Within each group, as they prepare for a case study or collaborative problem, it might be advantageous to assign each group member a specific role so that no student is idly waiting with nothing to do, or alternatively you could ask students to decide on roles for themselves. One student, for example, could be the organizer, who makes sure that the group works in a timely fashion and keeps relevant to the assigned topic. Another student could be the main researcher, and a third student could be the editor of the material who is responsible for putting the work into its final form. This means that the discussion leader from the group simply needs to paste the final document onto the classroom discussion board, but this student must have been involved in every step of the document's creation and understand it well so that he or she can competently answer questions that have been raised by the rest of the class.

The Instructor's Contribution to Group Discussion

The question arises that if you look in on online group discussions, should you contribute anything to the ongoing conversation? This should be determined by need, but if there is low participation in a group, it might be indicative of the fact that the students are not used to working together without your input, and might therefore benefit from a little nurturing, encouragement, or some useful information and suggestions from you. Also, you might want to offer some feedback or give them further questions to consider. In this way, the instructor's ability to more closely monitor online group work could create advantages for students over group work done on campus.

The Nonparticipating Student

It may still unfortunately be the case that one or more students are free riders in their group. Whereas in the class discussion forums, it is best if everyone is at approximately the same part of the course at the same time, for group work this is essential, as each student is also responsible to other group members as well as to himself or herself. The fact that you can observe group discussions gives you a good opportunity to monitor how much work each individual student is contributing. It might help students if you remind them about this. The grade for doing the work might be an added incentive to work well, but I imagine that the largest motivator might be in knowing that the group must present to the rest of the class. I know of some instructors who have pulled nonparticipating students out of their groups and put them in a new group together. I have mixed feelings about this, as I am against public humiliation and shame. I certainly think the first step is an e-mail or a call to ask why the student has not contributed to the group work.

Of course, some students do not like collaboration, as they prefer to work independently; these often are the good students who want individual acknowledgment for their work. I do not think we can ignore these feelings, as they are valid too, so what I suggest is that if you do have group work, vary these activities with other learning activities in the course, such as general discussions and papers.

Group Presentations

When it is time for each group to present their case study or problem to the class (which could be done online in the class discussion board, or possibly on campus if your class is a hybrid), every class member should listen to or read the group leaders' presentations and ask questions or make comments. It should be emphasized to the class that because comments can sound more harsh online, care should be given to making the feedback constructive and helpful.

The group work is likely to be at the application, analytical, or possibly even synthesis level, according to Bloom's taxonomy, and the reactions from the class to the presentation would be at the evaluation level, implying that group work, when carefully designed and carried out, can include high-level tasks and can encourage students to think at a very deep level.

Other Forms of Group Work

In the previous discussion we considered dividing the class into groups if the students generate an extremely high number of responses, or if you want students to do a case study or collaborative problem solving. Next, in a little more detail, we look at other ways in which students can work in groups, including role-playing, engaging in a writing game, and holding a debate.

Role-Playing

One area in which I have found that online technology holds hidden and unexpected advantages over face-to-face communication is in role-playing. This can be used, for example, to deepen analysis of a work of fiction, or as a tool by which to comprehend different case studies and scenarios, or for learning more intimately about different historical periods. On this basis, I believe role-playing is at the comprehension, application, and analytical levels of Bloom's taxonomy for those students who are participating in the role-play, and at the evaluation stage for the students offering feedback on the presentation.

Even though role-playing works well on campus, it seems to fit superbly into the online environment, possibly because it gives room for students' imaginations and comprehension to soar, while being unimpeded by the stage fright that some might otherwise feel. As with other asynchronous discussion, role-playing also leaves room for students to be reflective and deliberate.

I would like to describe two ways in which I have used role-playing in different types of online classes that I have taught, and then provide an example of role-playing in a hybrid class. In the case of the online classes, one was an online class on ethics in the workplace, in which I divided the class into groups and assigned each group a topic of study, such as "Loyalty to Supervisors" and "Issues of Confidentiality in the Workplace." The other was an online class on literary analysis of several short stories, in which I assigned each student a character role from one of the stories we were reading. In this way, each group was assigned a different short story, and each student within the group was assigned to play a character from that story. In the case of the hybrid, which was a writing class, we had read about a trial and I thought it would increase the students' understanding if they reconstructed the trial by role-playing assigned characters in the courthouse.

In all three cases, I waited until midpoint in the semester before starting the role-playing so that students were comfortable with each other and with the online environment. I created group discussion forums, which I entitled, "Backstage Rehearsal Area," and this was the exclusive space in which that group could prepare, for which I allowed approximately one week. After this time, each group had to put on their virtual play on the class discussion board, if it was an online class, so that it was visible to all class members, or acted it on campus if it was a hybrid. In the following sections, I provide more information as to the way the role-playing went in each of these three classes.

Role-Playing to Illustrate a Specific Situation

In the ethics class, it was truly fascinating for me to see the preparations of each group, which involved their creation of a scenario to illustrate the topic, and the assigning of roles among themselves. I present to you the following comments that students (with fictitious names), made during their preparations:

> LISA: Ladies, I have a case that really happened. I don't know if you want to work with this, but here goes. . . .
> JUNE: Sounds like a great foundation. Another scenario we could use would be. . . .
> BETTY: Hi J! I think the first scenario will definitely work because our topic is "Loyalty to Supervisors." Also, we have to decide who will play the manager, assistant, and coworkers. I'm willing to play anyone.
> DELIA: Hi ladies, I agree with the first scenario. I would like to play the role of the coworker. I am not comfortable playing the role of the advisor. Can we negotiate?
> LISA: I'll play the role of the assistant. I think I've played that role in real life. (smile) But after taking this course, I'm not going to play that role any longer.

What I particularly liked as I read these conversations was the way that students were relating education with experience, which, as Dewey ([1938] 1963) says, is the optimal path to true learning. When it came time to produce the virtual play on the class discussion board, each student, acting his or her part and using a fictitious name, posted responses interactively with each other in the asynchronous setting so that the virtual play took about three days to unfold. These plays were wonderful! Students compensated well for the lack of visual or audio cues by writing in "Ring, Ring, Ring" for a telephone; adding information about facial expressions, such as "Assistant frowns when she hears Sandra's voice"; mentioning when an actor is having an internal dialogue (something that might be harder to convey on campus); and detailing actions such as "They hug each other and sit down at a table" or "She is drinking her tea. In the meantime Kendra [her nickname] went to the lady's room."

Although students were asked to silently observe as the virtual plays were unfolding, one student became so excited that she posted a response right in the midst of the drama, and then, recognizing her mistake, immediately sent me an anxious e-mail to please remove it. She realized that she was being rude, like an audience member who claps before intermission.

Once groups completed their virtual plays, I opened up a new discussion forum for each group, in which members of the cast from each play shed the role they had been acting and became the discussion leaders of the topic that they had role-played. In this way, students who had silently been observing the play now legitimately had a chance to ask questions or express reactions to the topic. Lively discussions ensued, and many students commented that the role-playing helped them to become so immersed in the subject that they reached a new level of understanding, as well as being able to bring in and act through a lot of their own issues.

Role-Playing in Literary Analysis

The other occasions in which I use role-playing are in online classes I teach on literary analysis. Using the same format as in the ethics class, I created separate group discussion forums for several short stories that we were reading in class. In this case, students naturally did not have to create their own scenarios, but they had to collaborate with others as to how they were going to virtually stage their online play. When it was time for a group to produce the play for the class, I created a discussion forum, titled with the name of the story, and I asked each character to start a new discussion thread in which to post some initial comments—in the voice of his or her character—

about who he or she is, what he or she did, and how that behavior could be justified.

Once every student started a new discussion thread with these descriptive comments, I asked students to read each other's character postings, and then, maintaining the voice of the character they were each portraying, to interact with each other by posting responses within the thread of the character with whom they were interacting. In this impromptu and improvised way, the students were reenacting the story, and many commented to me later that by so immersing themselves in a character, they had a much deeper appreciation for that character's behavior and motivation. After allowing three or four days for the virtual play to unfold, I then opened a new discussion forum for the students to be themselves once more, in which they could discuss the story unconstrained by representing the role of just one character within it.

In both of these examples, students afterward told me that they found role-playing to be fun as well as educational, and in fact students who have taken a subsequent class with me have often asked if there will be any role-playing in the new class.

Role-Playing in a Hybrid Class

A hybrid format can also provide an exciting way in which to prepare for and then present a play because the rehearsals can take place online, and the actual staging can take place live in the classroom. This we did, actually quite spontaneously, in my hybrid expository writing class. We had read a piece by Beth Loffreda titled "Losing Matt Shepard," which was about the brutal murder of a gay student who attended the University of Wyoming. The piece discussed, among other things, the initial trial, and exemplified the complexity of the characters involved.

Quite coincidentally, we learned that Loffreda was coming to Rutgers to speak to the university at large during the evening of the exact day on which my hybrid had its scheduled campus class. Because she was arriving in the afternoon, we invited her to visit my class. I wanted my students and I to do something really special for her, and not just have questions and answers, as that was what she would be doing for her evening talk. So it occurred to me that it would be a great learning experience for my students, and hopefully enjoyable for Loffreda, if we staged a "reconstructed trial" of the real trial about which she had written.

What made things particularly exciting was that I only found out about Loffreda's planned visit to our class one week before her arrival, which meant that because my students and I were not scheduled to meet again until she would actually be present in our classroom, we would have to use our online component to prepare for our reconstructed trial. So in that campus class a week before the "big visit," I told students my plans and then asked them who would like to role-play which character from Loffreda's accounting of the trial scene. Fortunately there were many characters to represent because Loffreda had written that there was a large crowd from the media present in the courtroom, so this meant that everyone had a part, some larger, of course, than others. I decided that I would act as the judge.

As soon as that campus class was over, I opened an online Discussion Forum, which I called "The Backstage Rehearsal Area," and I posted the following message:

> This is the space in which we can plan and prepare for our superb staging of the "Reconstructed Trial and Media Event" surrounding the brutal murder of Matt Shepard.
> *Here is the list of who will be in the cast: [followed by the playlist]*

I also posted the following message:

> Let's plan among ourselves how this will take shape. We only have a week, so let's do lots of rehearsing. Remember, when you "play" your part, speak in the way your character would speak. You can even use direct quotes if you want, and if you think you will remember them, when this goes "live."

Throughout the week, students became more and more involved online, testing out what they wanted to say, what props they wanted to use, making suggestions to others as to what they might want to include and, in short, wondering about all sorts of aspects of this trial scene that they might well not have considered had they only been asked to read this piece passively to themselves. They discussed significant issues, such as hate crimes, the role of the media and whether it reported accurately, and even the image of the small town in which the university was housed. It emerged through online discussion that we would need a narrator to welcome Loffreda to the class and to tell her what we would be doing, and we democratically selected a very articulate student. We decided that she should also introduce each scene of the play.

The night before class, nearly every student was online at the same time despite the asynchronicity of the online component. After the week of busyness and excitement, many students reported being nervous. And I was nervous too; what if a student with a prime role was absent, or late for class?

What if they acted terribly once they were in front of the author of the piece? But, of course, I did not confess this to my students; instead I replied online that I thought that they were all great, and had planned this so well, and that I had great faith in them.

And all went terrifically well. All students were present in the campus class, and no one was late. Our narrator gave a gracious welcome to Loffreda, and we played a little music, and then the reconstructed trial began. The students acted absolutely impeccably. I was so impressed and relieved. And I could see that Loffreda was impressed, too. In fact, when it was over, she said she was amazed; she had been to the real trial, and thought that one of the students, who acted the part of the main suspect, was so close to the real person in looks, behavior, and even in the sound of his voice.

What was particularly rewarding was that, when it was over, a student said to me, "This proves that online communication works! We didn't see each other to rehearse at all. We did it all online! And when we came together to put on our play, it was great!" Even though I was delighted to hear this, and despite my nerves of the night before, I realized that all along I had believed that it would work. I think asynchronous online communication is a powerful tool allowing for engagement, collaboration, and for meaningful planning of ideas to ferment in a rich, reflective, and ultimately very productive way. It also shows how the online and campus components of the class could be seamlessly joined, with activities spilling over between the two environments. Although it is unlikely that the original author of the play will be among your audience, and certainly is not necessary, plays or reconstructed trials can be prepared online and presented in class, often to very great advantage.

A Writing Game

In a writing game that I have used in an online class, I divide students into groups of three, ask each of them to write a paragraph description of a person, and then e-mail it to one student in the group. Then I ask students to compose a paragraph description of a place and e-mail it to the other member of the group. Each student has then received a person description from one group member and a place description from the other group member. These short descriptive paragraphs are at the analytical level of Bloom's taxonomy.

Students are then asked to compose, like a collage, a short story telling what happened to the person described in an e-mail from one student, in the place described in the e-mail from the other student. In other words, they are synthesizing these separate pieces into a coherent whole new story.

Students then post this story to their group on the group discussion forum so that every member of the group can see it. Each group member hopefully has a fascinating time seeing how pieces of his or her construction fit into a whole new story, which provides an insight into the author's interpretation and creative abilities. Students also provide feedback to each other about their stories, which is at Bloom's evaluation level.

An alternative way of collaboratively creating an online story can be done by students using Twitter. Because tweets are short, students can form a chain, each adding a new tweet in turn to the evolving story. Depending on the amount of time devoted to this, the completed project might more resemble a "microstory" than a full length story, something that Walsh (2010) has referred to as creating "twittories," and what fiction writers call "flash fiction" (referring more to its length, and not the process by which it was constructed). At the completion of the microstory, students can provide feedback both about the process of its creation and the final product, and are therefore also working at Bloom's evaluation level of learning.

Holding a Debate

Cummings (1998) has done some interesting work on online debates. His technique is to divide students into pairs, and assign to each pair a subtopic. Within the pair, one student is the critic of the subtopic, and the other is its defender. Unlike a debate that occurs conventionally, in which typically the critic speaks first and then the defender rebuts, and there might be awkwardness as to who has the last word, the critic and the defender can both post position statements online simultaneously.

Cummings structured the course in such a way that he opened one discussion forum for all critics of each subtopic to post their views, and another forum for all defenders of each subtopic to post their views. When everyone had posted, critics were allowed to cross over into the defenders' forum and make a rebuttal statement to the critic's posted opinion on the specific subtopic under enquiry. Similarly, defenders were allowed to cross over into the critics' forum and make their rebuttal statement. Students were told that a rebuttal statement should look for inaccuracies, inconsistencies, and irrelevant statements. They were also asked to include a plausible counterargument. This, therefore, would be at the analytical level of Bloom's taxonomy. The third and final stage of this assignment was for every student to reflect on all the position and rebuttal statements of each subtopic of the main topic, and write a reflective paper, which would only be accessible to Cummings as the instructor, in which they take a position over the entire topic. This is at the synthesis level of Bloom's taxonomy, which clearly illustrates that high-level thinking is taking place.

Synchronous Online Tools

Although the software of online learning programs is predominantly an asynchronous model, most programs also have the capacity to hold synchronous online conversations, which are commonly referred to as real-time or online chat. Using this feature, all class participants can be online at the same time and can type messages to each other, much like instant messaging, although in this case it is not one to one, but one to many. In this section we explore the ways in which the online synchronous tool can be used, and discuss its psychological and pedagogical implications.

It is recommended that the number of participants within an online synchronous conversation not exceed five, as otherwise it can become confusing and some information might be missed. In addition, sessions should be no longer than 30 to 45 minutes because they demand a huge amount of energy and concentration.

Suggested Uses of Synchronous Online Tools

Suggestions for the possible use of synchronous online conversations include the following:

- *Group work:* Synchronous online conversations could assist students to work in groups, if they have difficulty scheduling face-to-face meeting times. Meeting online saves students from having to go somewhere (see earlier in the chapter). It should be mentioned that, just as the instructor can see the asynchronous group discussions, so too can he or she read the group's online synchronous conversations.
- *Role-playing in synchronous (as opposed to asynchronous) time:* As a possible alternative to role-playing asynchronously on the class discussion board, as mentioned earlier, students could use their group's online synchronous conversation area in which to stage their virtual play. This gives immediacy and excitement to their performance, as each student, maintaining a character role, interacts with others in the group in real time while dynamically creating their story. As a student

in one of my online classes remarked at the completion of a virtual play, "A challenge for me was . . . that I had to actually put myself in the moment and act upon reflex. . . ." Another student talked about the spontaneity and the sensitivity to each other by saying, "On a personal note, my attitude toward my 'brother' was not planned, it just happened. I think my two partners set the tempo. I saw their dialog [sic] and was able to sense the mood; thus, it was easy for me from that point." When their virtual play is completed, the instructor can copy the archived transcript and paste it into the class discussion board for all students to read (as they are not able to access each other's group areas), and a discussion can ensue as to the issues brought up in the role-playing. The writing and performing of the play involves students in at least the application and analytical stages of Bloom's taxonomy, and the subsequent discussion with the rest of the class might reach to the evaluation level. As one of my students said at the conclusion of the role-playing, "responding in 'real time' requires a quick answer . . . no time to think about what you are saying, or how you said it. In 'real life,' our responses to family members are sometimes the same—said without thought, not thinking about the effect our words will have on others." This was particularly interesting as the role-playing was on the topic of family dynamics, so I was especially pleased that the one replicated so well the conditions of the other, thus forming an accurate model for analysis. Many students seem to enjoy this type of assignment. A student from one online class said,

I cannot remember when I had so much fun as doing the role-playing . . . I found myself laughing with tears coming out of my eyes . . . I wish all classroom assignments can be that enjoyable. I felt so happy about the accomplishments of Linda, Robert [names changed for the sake of confidentiality], and myself that I insisted that my husband see what was said. I had to because he never saw me laugh when looking at a computer.

What seemed to be of particular value was that it truly fostered collaboration between the students, as seen by the following remarks: "I too had a blast . . . and was laughing. I didn't think I would have that much fun with the role-playing. We all worked very well with each other," and,

The virtual classroom was such a great idea, working backstage, putting ideas together with other classmates, then presenting it the whole class! I think I had it easy, as the other players kept me involved by their interaction. I complained to myself that it may be hard to understand an online class . . . now I want more . . . How easy [and fun this class has become!]

- *Virtual office hours:* If students find it hard to meet with you during your regular office hours if you teach a hybrid, then they might enjoy the benefit of a synchronous online meeting. This might be especially helpful to individuals or small groups of students prior to tests or exams, as it would provide them the immediacy of feedback and answers.
- *Online guest lecturer* (see later in the chapter): In this situation, it might be best if the guest lecturer posts information in advance in your online class, or you could have students read this person's book or article or distribute a handout, so the students could come prepared to the synchronous online conversation with worthwhile questions.
- *Demonstration of a Web site:* Most software programs have the capacity to demonstrate a Web site while being able to engage in synchronous online dialogue about it. Many software programs also have a whiteboard area to draw on or demonstrate certain concepts while engaged in synchronous online conversation.
- *Community building:* Because conversations are immediate and fun, this could be a good way to establish class camaraderie. It could also provide a useful space for students to ask questions of each other such as when an assignment is due or where to find a certain piece of information. A nice feature of many software programs is that if a student has missed an online synchronous conversation, this online conversation is archived and can therefore still be read after it has occurred. This, then, is superior to having missed a meeting in physical space and time, in which the communication that ensued is essentially lost, retrieved only from someone's memory or notes (which of course introduces an element of bias).

Faculty Reactions to Synchronous Online Conversations

Reactions to the use of the synchronous online conversation feature vary greatly. In this section I record several statements from instructors who were learning to teach online, and who were holding an online synchronous conversation with me to see how it felt. Many reported that it was fun, but hectic and disjointed. In general, they felt it would tend to favor fast typists, not necessarily the best students. One of the challenges of synchronous teaching and learning is that several different conversations can be going on at the same time because of the length of time it takes to type and because conversations can go off on different tangents according to individual interpretations. While typing you may feel as if you are missing out on what is happening on the screen, especially if you look at the keyboard while typing.

This situation has two implications. One is the feeling that you are interrupting each other, as we are not limited to the traditional conventions of spoken conversation in that it is understood that one person speaks at a time. But this does not have the same impact online as it does if we interrupt each other when face to face. In the case of online chat, we can still follow several threads of conversation because of the written record in front of us, which we can read and reread if necessary, whereas in spoken conversation, interrupted threads often get forgotten.

The second implication of missing what is on the screen as responses fly past is that the total conversation can feel disjointed. As one instructor said, "I find this way of communicating difficult because I can't easily follow the different threads of the discussion and like now, I'm answering a question you asked earlier and you're on to something else!" Another instructor said he was about to comment, but someone else preempted his remark. For all these reasons, it might feel as if it is hard to hold a thorough and cohesive conversation on any particular topic. To avoid this as much as possible, I think messages have to be fairly short; otherwise there is too much time lag. Also, others might post things in different tangents. A potential problem of this emphasis on speed, however, is that besides there being little time for deeper thinking, there is also little chance to correct spelling mistakes or typos. Therefore, are instructors providing an acceptable role model to students if their responses contain errors in format?

On the other hand, many faculty members who participated in the online training had positive reactions to the synchronous online conversations. One instructor likened the experience of the online chat to paying attention to several conversations at a crowded cocktail party. Many commented on how exciting it was. Time seems to fly when conversing this way, and as one instructor said, "Does everybody know that a half hour has passed? This stuff is like a drug." To this, another added, "I think I also enjoy chat better than the threaded discussion. I'm into instant gratification and enjoy haphazard discussion." He went on to say, "What is nice about chatting is that it is a fast response. This avoids the student who spends way too long thinking and rewriting."

Student Reactions to Synchronous Online Conversations

Certainly, to some students, especially those who are involved in a lot of online chatting, this probably feels familiar and easy, and because it is instant, it might provide a better way of keeping their attention. One of the instructors in the online training said, "Wow—this really is a medium for the MTV generation—so much for linear thought!"

Whereas the synchronous online conversations might fit in well with students' lifestyles and habits, is it applicable to learning, especially learning in depth, in a considered way? For example, sometimes in teaching it is important to allow time for silence, as one instructor commented, so that people can think about what was said and about how they want to respond, yet there could be limited opportunities for this in lively synchronous online conversations. This is where the more reflective asynchronous environment has a distinct advantage.

Furthermore, because many students take an online class because of the convenience and flexibility of working asynchronously, some might have scheduling problems that prevent them from attending an online conversation held in real time. Others might feel nervous. I heard from one student, who was an adult learner, how the mere thought of a synchronous online conversation made her feel so flustered that she dropped her keys trying to rush home in time, accidentally kicked the cat, and in her anxiety, could not remember how to log on! Others comment on feeling dizzy watching responses flying past, and find it hard to formulate thoughts, type, and read, all at the same time. We must take into account, too, students with disabilities, who might find synchronous online conversations to be an extra challenge. Many students, and not only those who are disabled, might be greatly assisted by voice recognition software.

Ground Rules Concerning Conversation Patterns and Flows

To maximize the potential benefits of synchronous online conversations, and to both make the conversation flow more manageable and try to guarantee that every student has a chance to respond, it might be helpful to establish certain ground rules. Of course, some might feel that making rules about conversation flows and directions introduces an artificial element into the discussion, and limits opportunities for someone with an inspired reaction to what had just been said from being able to respond. This could well be the case, but should you be interested in possible rules for discussion so as to avoid the synchronous conversations from getting out of hand, I would like to mention what Brookfield and Preskill (1999) tried in their campus class, as I think it can be very well adapted to online synchronous conversations.

Brookfield and Preskill established a technique called the "Circle of Voices." In this exercise, and with approximately four students at a time, the instructor assigns a topic, allowing students five minutes of "silent time" for reflection. After this time has elapsed, each student has five minutes in which to type in their comments, during which they cannot be interrupted by another student. Each student has a turn, by simply going around the circle. An advantage of this method is that it avoids the pecking order of the usual, favorite, dominant students going first and possibly overpowering the others. Even though it is possible that many people can speak at once online without interrupting each other in the conventional sense, the "Circle of Voices" could certainly introduce a beauty and simplicity of structure, as it avoids the hectic, rapid typing and possibly missing of each other's responses as the postings are hurling by.

Brookfield and Preskill (1999) suggest that once everyone has had their turn, students can react to what others have said, but, in an effort to maintain the streamlined approach already developed, each student can only react to the information of the student immediately before them, and they should do this by first paraphrasing the posting of that previous student's response. The authors feel that this has the further benefit of encouraging students to be respectful listeners, and I would add that this method allows for analytical thought processes to occur, according to Bloom's taxonomy.

This sequencing of events in the "Circle of Voices" allows for the synchronous area of the course to be put into good use, providing an effective and organized way to work collaboratively online. It might also be possible to change the positions of those within the Circle so that students have a chance of interacting with a variety of other students. It should be mentioned that it might not be up to only the instructor to lead the discussion in this way. Students working in small groups, for example, could employ similar rules for their discussion so that everyone can participate.

Should Attendance in the Online Chat Be Mandatory?

The question arises that if the instructor does include opportunities for using the chat feature, should attendance be mandatory? As mentioned, some students might find it hard to attend at a particular time, either because they are busy with other things or because they live at locations remote from the university or college, which might be on a different time zone.

In the case of collaborative group work, or role-playing, in which it is essential that each group member contribute significantly to the discussion, attendance is vital. Ideally, the group should schedule a mutually convenient time for an online synchronous conversation, and if all agree on this time, all should attend it. If scheduling problems legitimately preclude the opportunity for all students to attend a chat of their group, then they should find an alternative means, such as using the asynchronous group discussion board on which to work collaboratively.

The synchronous online conversation tool, while certainly being a great deal of fun, does not lend itself to a deep, complex discussion because it is too hectic. In fact, it strikes me as a bit of a jarring juxtaposition in an online class that is essentially asynchronous because asynchronicity lends itself more to reflection and thus the possibilities of deeper learning.

It is not completely without merit, however, and can be quite useful in community building, in holding virtual office hours, in meeting with an online guest, in small-group synchronous online collaborations, and possibly in preparatory work for a project that will continue on campus or on the asynchronous discussion board.

Using Skype as a Synchronous Online Educational Tool

Skype is an online application allowing users to make phone or video calls via the use of a microphone and webcam hooked up to the computer, or on the iPad2, which has a built-in camera and microphone. Skype can be advantageous in any teaching situation in which it is beneficial to have face-to-face contact. Thus it can be very useful, for example, in tutoring and online office hours in which it is thought that seeing each other's facial expressions and body language might facilitate comprehension. It might also be useful in oral exams, particularly those in a foreign language, speech, or music. For other uses of Skype, please see the sections on "Online Guest Lecturers," "Virtual Field Trips," and "Other Types of Student Online Presentations" that follow in this chapter.

Online Guest Lecturers

Sometimes, about two thirds of the way through the semester, online conversations start to dwindle as some students have moved beyond their initial excitement, yet are not ready for the final push toward the end of class. This might be an opportune time to invite an online guest lecturer. Just as in a campus class, a guest appearance introduces the intrigue of a new voice, possibly a fresh perspective, and maybe a welcome change of pace.

Even if you have a hybrid class, you might prefer to invite the guest to join your online component rather than come to your class on campus; this might be preferable for a guest lecturer who lives far away or is for other reasons unable to come to campus. This will save on travel and accommodation expenses. I have had guests from India and Fiji in my online classes, and it has been truly exciting and fascinating. All that needs to be done is to give the guest a user name and password to access your online class, and explain the basic mechanics of online discussions if necessary.

The Online Guest Makes a Scheduled Synchronous Appearance

There are two different ways in which an online guest can participate in the class: either synchronously or asynchronously. We talked in the previous section about having a guest lecturer join a scheduled synchronous online conversation, and how, because time is so short, it would be beneficial if the guest posted a lecture prior to visiting the online class, or if the instructor asked students to read a piece by or about the guest. In either case, the students could prepare questions in advance and post them during the chat, and the guest lecturer could provide immediate responses.

It should be noted that the guest could also join the online class via Skype. This would naturally save both the students and online lecturer from having to type in responses, as there could be immediate spoken interaction over the Internet. Even so, it is still advisable that students be very well prepared with good questions because time will be finite, and they should take notes during the session to remember what was said. Whether by real-time chat or by Skype, the immediacy of interaction with an online expert can assist students to reach the application and analytical levels of Bloom's taxonomy.

The Online Guest Spends a Week in the Class, Responding Asynchronously

Alternatively, the guest could devote a week to asynchronous postings of information and responses to students' questions in a specially created discussion forum. This would mean that the guest might log on to the class every other day for an hour or so. Working asynchronously with the online guest might allow for a more thorough, comprehensive, and reflective discussion, and thus it might be preferable to the guest making a onetime, synchronous appearance in the real-time chat area. Students might be able to move beyond the analytical level to that of the synthesis level as they form new conclusions and make important connections. If you know that you will be having an online guest lecturer, it is a good idea to inform students about this from the start of the semester.

Ideally, if your software allows it, it would be preferable if the guest only has access to the discussion forum in which he or she will be holding a discussion. I make this recommendation because there could be some courses in which personal matters are being discussed, and these students might feel as if it is a break in trust to suddenly have a newcomer look over their previous conversation. And because trust is essential to their learning, it should not be broken.

In my experience, students are thrilled to have a guest lecturer, and similarly, the guest is generally delighted to be there, not only to teach the material but also because it might represent the first time using online discussion. Most guests appreciate the opportunity to pick up a new skill.

Virtual Field Trips

An alternative to bringing an online lecturer to your class, or maybe a supplement to this, might be for the class to go on a virtual field trip. It's the next best thing to being there! You might consider sending your students out to Web sites that take them to places of interest relevant to your course. For example, I was once working with an art history professor, and she provided a link to the Louvre, from which the students benefited greatly. In a class I taught on D. H. Lawrence, I found a wonderful interactive Web site that took us on a virtual tour of his hometown, visiting the houses in which he wrote or that were represented in his works. The Web offers many exciting possibilities for these types of virtual visits. You might also want to consider using Skype for virtual field trips, for example, in giving access to a lab for scientists, or to a hospital for medical students to watch a surgery taking place, or to a concert hall for musicians. In other words, in skills-based classes, students might be able to better learn the necessary skills by watching experts and being able to hold discussions with them over the Internet.

If you provide your students with virtual field trips, they might be better able to comprehend what they are learning (comprehension level); apply what they have learned in new ways (application level); and, because they work at the speed comfortable to them, which affords them more opportunities for feeling in control and taking responsibility as active learners, they might be able to analyze the information well (analytical level) and synthesize this information with what they have already learned (synthesis level). Thus students are able to advance a long way through the levels of learning as defined by Bloom's taxonomy.

Integration of Web Sites

Besides virtual field trips, the Web offers possibilities of simulations, in-depth information, and analyses. These possibilities can enrich learning and advance students along Bloom's defined learning levels, in the same way as discussed for virtual field trips.

Because online teaching can so easily link to a Web site, this can be used to good effect. I often have the impression that online students are more likely to visit a Web site that is just a click away than campus students are if you provide them with the URL of that site. To facilitate this for online students, I think it is a nice idea to embed the link to a chosen Web site directly in the text itself, whether in a mini-lecture or a response, as in this way the Web site can be seen in context of your information.

Additionally, some software programs have a special area in which to list external links. I like to think of this area as an electronic library shelf. If you list the Web site there, it is a good idea to annotate it, to give readers a quick glance at what to expect when visiting that site. Certainly judiciously linking valuable Web resources can provide a good source of information and might mean that the students need purchase fewer texts. It might also decrease the need for assembling a course pack and will avoid the problem of seeking copyright permission, as a site on the Internet is available to the public.

However, some words of caution are needed. First, at the start of any course, you should check that the Web site to which you provide a link has not been removed. Some information on the Web is in a constant state of flux. Second, if a particular Web site is large and complex, I would recommend that you link students to the part of the site that you most want them to see. You want to avoid confusing them or having them wander off into cyberspace, and not returning to your course.

Guidelines for Students Doing Web Research

Some instructors also like to ask students to do a Web search for valuable material. Provide students with some guidelines as to how to best conduct

Web research; information on the Web is of variable quality because there are no standards of control as to what is posted. Guidelines are crucial because, as has been mentioned earlier, one feature of the digital revolution is that it enables such rapid retrieval of information. This easy access to information is clearly a wonderful thing, but is not without its challenges. Forni laments the fact that because students are online so much, they are not always able to make the distinction between what information is worthy and what is not. As he says, "The fact that one can as easily conjure up the Bible as *Mad Magazine* [on the Internet] erodes some of the difference between the two" (2008, p. 17). He stresses that it is important for teachers to show students that there is a hierarchy of values, even if all information is equally accessible.

Forni feels that the role of the teacher should serve as mediator between the students and the Internet, and I agree because teaching, as always, is about helping students learn how to become critical thinkers and judges of the value of information. Certainly it is true that in the pre-Internet days, we teachers could not let students loose in a library and expect them to come up with an impressive amount of research without any instruction as to how to use the possibly confusing and overwhelming card catalogue. We need to show them the way, and as Gopnik (2011) perceptively remarks, Google and other search engines are really the modern-day electronic equivalent of the library card catalogue. Then, as now, teachers, by communicating in a way that is insightful, challenging, and memorable, play a crucial role in essentially helping students know how to sort through mounds of information and judge its worthiness. Inviting research librarians to the class, as is done in the Rutgers Writing Program for the research classes, can also be an enormous help to students who are seeking information, as they can inform students not only about retrieval of materials in the library, but also how to find good online information as well.

Gardner (2011) thinks that students are likely to be skillful at finding information, but that the older generation of teachers, librarians, and parents should demonstrate how to interpret this information. As he says, "Ideally, one should blend the youthful ability to take in and store new information with the well-honed judging and evaluating capacities of older persons" (p. 164). He goes on to say, "Understanding the nature of claims and counter-claims, of rival forms of expertise, and of the changing nature of understanding, older persons can be in a privileged position to make judgments of truthfulness" (p. 175). This, it seems to me, is what good teaching is about. But how, specifically, can this be conveyed?

First, you can inform students of good search engines, such as Google Scholar or various online library databases. I also warn students to be cautious about using Wikipedia. As Gardner says, "How to determine what is truth—when a statement on Wikipedia about who I am and what I am doing can be changed by anyone at any time" (2011, p. 3)? He goes on to say, "No one has an explicit mandate to evaluate the truth of entries [in Wikipedia]. . . . Wikipedia simply represents the current consensual view of a subject—neither expertise nor truth per se enters into the equation" (p. 193). And Gopnik, who describes Wikipedia as "mob-made," sees its limitations and potential for trouble when he says it "is not the overall absence of smartness but the intractable power of pure stupidity" (2011, p. 2). However, I would like to qualify these remarks by saying that I do think Wikipedia might have some value in that it often displays links to other, more scholarly sites. In this way Wikipedia might be useful as a stepping stone in the pursuit of knowledge, rather than being the source of reliable knowledge itself.

Second, it is helpful to advise students to check the relative value of a particular Web site in comparison with other sites (Grassian, 2000). To do this involves, among other things, researching what other information is available, and determining the author or producer of the site to help ascertain the reliability and degree of expertise and to try to see if it is biased in any way. Other points of importance are whether there is contact information for the author, as well as the date that the Web site was produced, and whether or when it was last revised and updated.

Grassian (2000) also gives some thought to the design of the Web site, asking useful questions such as whether any graphic displays are merely decorative and distracting, or if they serve a pedagogical purpose. There is, of course, the very important element as to whether the text on the site is well written. Some sites are especially set up to address the needs of people with disabilities, by having large print and graphics, and audio options. Also some sites are interactive, welcoming online chats on a topic, or the possibility of doing simulations. It is important to determine how usable a site is, especially a site packed with information, as one can feel lost in a cyberspatial labyrinth, and be gasping for air and space if there are an excessive number of links. Grassian recommends that three clicks into a site, to find the needed information, is generally sufficient.

While on the subject of links, Grassian (2000) feels it is important to determine the balance between inlinks and outlinks (those pointing to areas within the site, and those pointing to other sites), and whether they are comprehensive and representative of the field. Important, too, is the consideration as to whether the links provide valid information that is not available at other sites.

Student Presentations of Their Discovered Web Sites

With these guidelines, it might be a good idea to ask students to explore the Web to locate informative Web sites on a particular topic. At particular intervals, they could each present their findings to the class by briefly describing the site and providing an active link to it. Students could investigate each other's sites and write brief reviews of them, and by the end of the semester, they could choose the two best Web sites, and write about them, giving reasons why they found them exemplary (Cummings, 1998). Writing papers on why particular Web sites were exemplary would boost students to the evaluation stage of Bloom's taxonomy.

If students write or present about the Web site they have found, it is important to tell them that they must not just copy and paste whole sections of text from the Internet into their papers, but should instead read the information carefully, possibly even printing it out and asking themselves questions as they read, almost as if they are having a dialogue with the author. They should write notes in the margins of the materials they read (hence the value in printing it rather than reading it online) and not merely underline or highlight; they should also identify key concepts and they should look for significant quotations. Furthermore, they should try to evaluate how the information on any one particular Web site connects with (supports, refutes, enhances and so on) other information that they have read on the subject from another Web site, book, or journal. Perhaps they would even be well advised to write a literature review documenting this sort of information for later use. Having gone through these processes, students should write about the topic in their own words. Incidentally, I think the requirement to write something in the students' own words even applies to students writing a definition of a particular term, and providing their own examples of usage, instead of merely pasting in the definition from dictionary.com. This is more active and requires more thought, which helps the students retain that information. Ultimately, then, we can help students learn how to think about the information they retrieve, and make good choices, so that they can move from accumulating information to thinking critically about it and developing knowledge and ultimately wisdom.

It should be noted that students nowadays seem to have great facility at surfing the Web, and I have found that they often spontaneously post to the online discussion forum certain Web sites they have themselves discovered that are relevant to the discussions we are having. You could, in fact, create an electronic library shelf in the online class, as mentioned in the section "Integration of Web Sites," specifically for this purpose, in addition to posting your own Web sites. Some students might also use Twitter or Facebook to share articles with the class by posting links to Web sites (maybe using the Twitter application Twhirl to abbreviate the URL to 140 characters, if necessary).

Other Types of Student Online Presentations

Today's technology allows students to present online using a number of different online applications, YouTube videos being an example. A very enjoyable moment occurred in one of my hybrid classes when I asked a student to prepare an online grammar presentation to give to the class, and he did this by creating two extraordinarily amusing and effective YouTube videos, one on "Singular and Plural Agreement," and the other on "Fragments." They can be seen (with the student's permission) at www.youtube .com/watch?v = duhJM2qJbf4 and at www.youtube.com/watch?v = Bocvi CanS-8 (Hani, 2010).

Twitter can also be used to link to videos. In his class in the Rutgers Writing Program, Sorrell (2012) takes short videos of himself presenting basic information, as well as posting grammar videos, using the program Jing. This technique could be used by students in an online language or music class to film their own presentations, or for watching online an oral presentation that the student has given in the campus class.

Alternatively students can give oral presentations online using Adobe Connect, which must be connected to your online class Web site. Students can use this to incorporate and narrate a PowerPoint presentation. Another effective medium for online oral presentations, especially if the student wants to demonstrate a particular skill, is Skype. When you use these programs you need to inform students that their presentations will be done in real time, and not asynchronously, which may introduce some scheduling problems. However, both the Adobe and Skype sessions can be recorded, and so their archives could be of use to students who were unable to attend, or for later use as a reference tool for all.

An alternative, less sophisticated, and possibly simpler way in which students can give oral presentations in the online class is for the teacher to create an asynchronous discussion forum on the discussion board called

"Student Presentations." The teacher can then open a new topic area within the forum for each student when it is his or her turn to present. The student posts the presented material in textual format, and other students read and respond to it asynchronously, with the student presenter essentially becoming the discussion leader of that topic by answering any questions or comments from classmates or from you.

Student Portfolios

Academic Writing for Students in the Age of the Internet

If you would like your students to write an academic paper, does the fact that they now generally do so much "out-of-class" writing by texting and on Facebook, Twitter, and so on, help hone their skills? Thompson (2009) does not necessarily think so. This might be because the "out-of-class" writing is socially interactive, often grammatically unstructured, and frequently emotionally charged ("Let's meet for a coffee," "See you after class," "Look at that guy's hairstyle"), whereas academic writing is usually more solitary and therefore might not feel so enticing. So, in their "out-of-class" writing, students are aware of their audience and to whom they are corresponding, whereas academic writing does not have this immediacy. It might help, therefore, to ask our students to whom they think they are writing when they compose their academic papers. Although most students, possibly incredulous at the question, say the writing is for us, the professors, it can be eye-opening and hopefully uplifting if we help students understand that their audience can be broader than just their professors. We could say, in fact, that the audience could be their classmates or even their friends who are not taking the class but who are interested in the concepts, or even a community of scholars-in-training. We could also say that the audience could be others who have read the same readings but do not fully understand them, so they should try to explain the topic to them.

However, because "out-of-class" writing is generally not critical but instead more likely to be full of banter, students should be prepared to take more sustained time with their academic writing so that they can generate complex ideas. After all, as E. M. Forster says, "How do I know what I think until I see what I write?" Seen in this way, academic writing could be very rewarding and even inspirational, especially if we recommend to students that they go beyond summary, and that, by virtue of juxtaposing various readings, their level of interpretation deepens and they arrive at exciting new realizations about these texts.

How many of us have had really uplifting discussions with our students face-to-face in a campus class and have been convinced that the papers they will write on this topic will accordingly be rich and replete with terrific information, only to find that we are disappointed with how "thin" they are? I think a possible explanation for this is that the students were so engrossed in the discussion that they did not take notes and simply failed to remember many of the great points that had been raised. Not so online! In fact many online and hybrid students have remarked that writing their papers is easier than if the class had been on campus, as all the online discussion in the forums is archived and available for them to read. Similarly, tweets can also be archived for a quick, handy reference.

One concern that some teachers now have is whether the student is truly the author of the paper that he or she submits. In a disturbing article in *The Chronicle of Higher Education*, Dante (2010), a pseudonym for a writer who makes his living writing papers for a custom-essay company, reveals the extent of student cheating. His story, which was more like a confession as he clearly makes money for something entirely unethical (although he says he intends to now retire), was made all the more remarkable by his inclusion of some e-mailed requests from students, possibly even at the PhD level, which are barely articulate. For example, he received this request: "'You did me business ethics propsal for me I need propsal got approved pls can you will write me paper?'" In the past year, Dante said he had written more than 5,000 pages of scholarly text in a variety of disciplines and at different levels of scholarship. He says that in this online company for which he and more than 50 other employees work, business is booming, despite the recession, especially around midterm and finals time. To emphasize the level of writing incompetence in his student "clients," he says, "They couldn't write a convincing grocery list, yet they are in graduate school." And certainly, whereas Turnitin and other programs designed to spot plagiarism work well, they are unable to detect this particular form of cheating. I recommend that, if you receive a paper that seems entirely beyond your expectations of what you think the student is capable of writing, you enter into a conversation with that student, not in a threatening way, but simply expressing interest and asking the student questions about certain statements and facts in the paper. If the student is incapable of answering your questions, this might be a strong clue that it was not the student who wrote the paper.

Dante says there are three main types of students who request his services: those who are not native English speakers, those who are literately deficient, and those who are rich and lazy and are used to paying to get what they want so as to excel. According to Dante, online students have even given him their login and password information, so that he can participate in online discussions and take online exams. How can Dante do it all? How does he not only perform the physical act of writing so many pages, but from where does he gain the knowledge? Again, he says it is simple. He does it all online, mostly using Amazon, but also Google Scholar as there are abstracts to most journal articles, and even Wikipedia. As we can see from what Dante says, this kind of cheating can occur in any kind of classroom, from online to hybrid to campus to lab. And he sees that the reason for it, besides the fact that obviously the Internet makes this easy to do, is that he feels that the emphasis in university education is on grades and not on learning. Hopefully, if we can be mindful of this, and make the acquisition of knowledge fascinating and worthwhile for its own sake and not for the sake of a grade, then this highly unfortunate type of cheating will cease to exist.

Use of Portfolios in Online Workshops

If you are teaching an online workshop, or would like students to peer review each other's papers or their online presentations about Web sites, you can create separate electronic portfolios for students into which they can post their work and then invite other students in to see this work and offer feedback. You, the instructor, can create each portfolio as a new discussion forum (e.g., Mary's Portfolio, John's Portfolio, and so on). This will be accessible to everyone and will also provide scope for students to post their feedback comments directly into the portfolio of the work to which they are responding. Twitter could also be useful here, as a tool for making brief comments, for example, on the effectiveness of the thesis statement or about other parts of the paper. Portfolios are not necessarily limited to individuals, as it might also be desirable to create a group portfolio in which groups can present their work to the whole class after having completed their preparations in their private group area, and then receive feedback from the class directly within the portfolio itself.

An alternative to creating separate student portfolios for peer review purposes, especially if there are many students in the class, is for you, the teacher, to create just one discussion forum and ask all the students to post their rough drafts into it. Then tell students whose paper they will review, and they can do so within this forum. Some software programs such as Sakai have a feature called "Quote," which enables student A to copy all of student B's paper into a new response box, onto which A can write comments and suggestions in a different font or color so as to distinguish his words from those of B. Alternatively, the students could use the "Insert Comment" function of Word; however, giving peer feedback directly in Sakai saves having to exit the program, and so might feel psychologically easier and more straightforward.

One thing to be cautious about, as in the traditional campus class, is that when reading through and reviewing each others' papers, students do not copy from each other. The line between collaboration and plagiarism can be very fine, indeed. Again, Turnitin is unfortunately unable to detect this form of plagiarism, in which students might copy from each other's papers, but this is where you as teacher must be vigilant. You might even openly permit students to gain ideas from others as long as they acknowledge the source and also use that idea in a way unique to their own work.

Comparison of a Master Class with an Online Workshop

An online workshop can be meaningfully compared with the concept of a master class. Ruhleder and Twidale (2000) believe that the master class concept, such as when students come with a prepared piece of music and perform it for the teacher and classmates and thus receive feedback on their work, is a sound pedagogical model for reflection and collaborative learning. Although it is an intensive, face-to-face experience, they were curious to research the implications of applying certain techniques to a spatially dispersed student body, as is the case in an online class.

Key Concepts of Teaching and Learning in a Master Class

From their observation of the master class, Ruhleder and Twidale (2000) derived the following key concepts of teaching and learning.

- The focus is on collaboration to achieve development of technique and skills on an ongoing basis, and is not individual work in solitary pursuit of a good final grade.
- Students are reflective of what they have learned from the group, and apply and incorporate this into their learning.
- The open collaboration of the master class helps students to learn and benefit from the successes and mistakes of their fellow students.
- Rather than learning in the abstract, students learn by doing, and this can be applied both to general topics and specific events.
- There is a process of "reification," in which all students can form concepts based on the current or previous performance of all their classmates.

Because the classes are generally taped, students can watch what occurred any number of times, which assists them in being reflective about their work and the work of others.

An Online Workshop

Ruhleder and Twidale (2000) then looked at an online class on interface design of information systems, in which students were asked to design a Web page. They thought that if this class were held on campus, the instructor would perhaps have students working individually on their designs, or would have them working in groups, but either way, the instructor would have to keep working his or her way around the classroom to look at everyone's work sequentially. If, instead, the class was to be held online, it could provide many opportunities for reflection and collaboration, leading therefore to the continuous possibilities of improving the work.

An online class was set up so that each student posted a first design draft in his or her portfolio, making this available to the instructor and other students in the class. Students and the instructor contributed their ideas and suggestions about each person's work, and what became apparent was the multiplicity of suggestions, based on subjective preferences informed by personality and previous experiences. This is not unusual in the field of design, or in anything creative. It is up to the student, with help from the instructor, to sift through the responses and make design revisions according to a careful discrimination as to the best advice. It is important that students not work over their original design, as this would have obscured their initial attempts, but instead produce a separate second, third, and possibly fourth draft, so that in this way they are keeping a permanent record of every stage of their work, and can therefore readily appreciate their development and progress. Each subsequent draft is also made available to the whole class.

Similarities between a Master Class and an Online Workshop

The online workshop class does not exist in real time, nor is it face to face as is the master class, but it does share many similar traits. Among them are the following:

- Importance and significance of collaboration are evident in both environments.
- Students' work develops and progresses, as their work is refined and improved from the first draft onward. This helps students understand

that design is an iterative process and that even experts are not usually brilliant on their very first draft.

- Everyone in the class can see and benefit from learning about the work of others, the ensuing discussion and the feedback.
- Learning can be from the general (broad design ideas) to the specifics of a detail within a piece of work. The instructor can relate both the general and the specific information to actual known examples in the field, to put these in context.
- Because both the students' designs and the discussions surrounding these designs are permanently available in the online class, meaningful understanding both of design and the design process can occur, thereby permitting reification to take place.
- Because there is a permanent record of all that transpired in the online class, students can be reflective about this collection of information, which in turn can inform their choices when making new designs or critiquing the work of others.

In other words, putting learning into active practice and seeing the work and development of others within the online class provides a tremendous learning opportunity. Posting work into the portfolio, whether it is information on a Web site, a creative short story, or designing a new Web site, is at the analytical level of Bloom's taxonomy, and class reactions to these works are at the evaluative level. Subsequent revisions to the original creative piece of work would allow the student important opportunities for synthesis, according to Bloom's taxonomy.

Online classes, Ruhleder and Twidale (2000) conclude, have the potential to establish "a robust and supportive learning environment driven by a collection of human users with a shared set of learning goals in mind." I think this is particularly true of a workshop type of class, facilitated by designing the class to incorporate portfolios for the submission, critique, and revision of each student's work.

Journals

You might consider asking students to write weekly or biweekly journals, which offers opportunities for reflection on, or writing about, experiences relevant to the course material. Because this is an opportunity for them to relate a number of ideas, journaling would draw on their level of knowledge, comprehension of the subject matter, application of that knowledge in other circumstances, and ultimately lead them to be able to synthesize ideas, thus placing journal writing at the synthesis level of Bloom's taxonomy.

I recommend that you ask students to e-mail these journals to you. After reading them and e-mailing back your comments, you could select a few of the more outstanding journals and ask the authors of these if they would be willing to have you post them to the class. You could create a new discussion forum expressly for posting these journal entries. In this way, their classmates could read and react to them. I have found that this is an area in which the students show impressive amounts of empathy and support for each other. It also assists classmates in reaching a new level of synthesis themselves.

Online Team Teaching

Advantages of Team Teaching

Many of us advocate collaboration among our students, but what about collaborating with our colleagues? After all, there is a lot of sharing of professional experience if we teach with a colleague (Cranmer, 1999). We might, for example, learn from seeing our colleague do something that we resist doing, or have expertise in something that we know less about, or learn about different activities to accomplish the same ends, or see a difference in priorities. Team teaching gives us someone with whom to talk about the class, as we have both shared the experience, so that we could discuss whether things are working well; and if there are unfulfilled needs, we can jointly decide on how these could best be resolved. When we talk of team teaching, we usually consider this to involve only two colleagues, but I have seen one or two classes in which there are as many as four teachers in the class. This might work well for a large class, or one in which students benefit from individual attention. Team teaching can be extremely rewarding. If team teachers work well together, then this can be a good model of collaboration to demonstrate to students. Team teachers can certainly learn a great deal from each other, not only in terms of content, but also style.

Potential Problems of Team Teaching

Team teaching is not necessarily easy. Some teachers might dislike planning a lecture together, or being observed. Cranmer (1999) makes explicit certain points to be aware of before embarking on team teaching, to lessen areas of potential future conflict. We will discuss these in the following paragraphs.

Although Cranmer is applying his thoughts to the campus class, I will draw on implications for the online teaching situation.

Concerns about Authority

In the first place, there is the question of authority, in regard to whether the teachers in the team have equal authority, or one is assumed to have more responsibility than the other, such as a student teacher who is there to learn some good teaching techniques. If the expectation is for equality, then problems might arise if both teachers have dominant personalities, or if either or both feel possessive of the class. At the same time, if both personalities are too deferential, nothing might be achieved, and the plans for the course to take shape might be indecisive and lacking in direction. Ideally, there should be an easygoing give and take so that teachers can switch back and forth from being in the metaphorical driver's seat to being in the back (Cranmer, 1999).

Team Teaching Colleagues Should Be Mutually Supportive and Considerate

Cranmer's (1999) second consideration about team teaching is that colleagues should be mutually supportive and considerate. Obviously, no teacher should ever embarrass another by pointing out a mistake in front of the students. There might be times when help is needed, and if so the teacher in need can send an e-mail or call the colleague. At least online there is the advantage of not working in real time (unless doing an online chat), so there are more opportunities for assistance than if team teaching face to face with students on campus. Cranmer cautions, however, that the team teachers should have absolute trust in each other and full respect as colleagues.

Concerns about How to Divide Responsibilities

A third consideration Cranmer (1999) addresses in terms of team teaching involves making decisions about dividing responsibility. Cranmer advocates that for true teamwork, not only should the course be planned together, but also both teachers should be present at all times throughout the semester. In contrast, if one teacher teaches while the other is absent, this is not *team* teaching, but *shared* teaching. Online, I have seen teachers alternating lecture topics, and I have also in one case seen teachers divide the semester so that one teaches for the first half and the other for the second half. I would definitely call this latter example a case of shared rather than team teaching.

I once team taught with a colleague, and we alternated topics, but we decided that when it was not our turn, we would have a minor voice within the online discussions on the topic so as to remain visible to the students, while leaving the main scope for the discussion for the one whose topic responsibility it was. We decided that it was important to establish the idea of the alternating major and minor voice because if we did not, we found that we might both swoop down on every student's response, and this could become overwhelming to the students and somewhat top-heavy. It might be beneficial for the teacher with the minor voice to also be conducting detailed observations about discussion flows and patterns, which could later be discussed with the teacher who has taken the major role for that topic.

How do teachers choose who will teach which topic? It might be that the teacher with the greater expertise (or interest or fondness) about a subject will choose that topic. If the course is team taught again, it might be feasible for teachers to swap topics, having learned from each other when observing in the previous semester.

Cranmer (1999) suggests that one advantage of team teaching is that it makes it possible for the class to be divided into two smaller groups, with one teacher leading each group. However, I would argue that this is more of a parallel experience than a team approach, unless the groups are divided by student ability, so that one teacher has the accelerated students and the other works with the remedial students. Even so, I would suggest that if the class is divided into two groups, then there should be interaction between the groups, such as making presentations to each other or holding a debate, to keep with the spirit of collaborative teaching and learning.

Intriguing Uses of the Team Teaching Concept

One of the most phenomenally exciting examples of online team teaching that I have seen is a class that spanned across the Atlantic and crossed international borders. This course was taught by Gerda Lederer at New School Online University, with Albert Lichtblau at the University of Salzburg, Austria, and with an equal number of students from both universities. The subject of the course was a study of the Holocaust two generations later. Each American student had an Austrian student partner, and they interviewed friends or relatives who had been alive during World War II, compared experiences and current cultural conditions in their respective countries, and discussed readings. Both teachers took turns posting information.

Also, as mentioned in the section called "Some Current Applications of Digital Technologies in Education" in Chapter 4, I team-taught an international online course in the Rutgers Writing Program with Chunyan Xu in Jilin University, China, in the fall 2012 semester, with 10 students from each university. Our subject was "The Ethics of Food." The students in China were very carefully selected for this course; they had to pass an exam to show their proficiency in English. All the students from both universities were very excited about this course, as exemplified by one of the Rutgers students, who said,

> This class is unique such that we get a chance that few other college students have. We get to interact with students from the other side of the world. Since so much of what we learn is in fact perspective, it is interesting to hear what individuals from another country and different cultures have to say in comparison to our points of view.

A student from China had this to say about the course:

> This class indeed provides a golden opportunity for us to exchange ideas with students on the other side of the world. Through our discussions and peer-review practice, I gained not only improvement in writing skills but also a more critical way of thinking by encountering various even opposite perspectives raised by different cultures. It is the first time for me to participate in a course via Internet, especially with students whose time of day and night is just upside-down to mine! Although it is not available for us to have a face-to-face communication, our exchange of ideas is not slightly blocked. That is exactly what I enjoy most.

Handling an Interruption or Unexpected Change of Direction

Of particular importance in my mind is Cranmer's (1999) point about what should happen in a team teaching situation if there is a sudden interruption or unexpected change of direction in the class, possibly brought about by a student's question or comment. This can be hard enough, perhaps, if teaching solo—although less hard online than on campus, as you have more opportunity for thoughtful reflection or research—but what impact will this have on online team teaching?

Assuming the teachers had carefully planned out their lessons and mutually agreed upon who has responsibility for what, then what happens with a sudden lurch in the direction of the course? As we know, there can be a time lag of varying length in online discussions because of the asynchronicity of the environment, and perhaps this spontaneous change needs to be addressed as quickly as possible.

The democratic and respectful thing to do is for the teaching colleagues to consult with each other and arrive at a mutually agreeable new lesson or response. But if the teachers are remote from each other, and logging on from different places, it could take needed time to reach each other, let alone discuss it. So in this case, if the matter is important and urgent enough, the first teacher who sees this spontaneous change should react accordingly to it. This is less likely to occur if you are teaching a hybrid class and you are on the same campus, but that does not stop this type of situation from happening. One instructor might log on while the other is in a long meeting, or away at a conference, or sleeping.

Team-Teaching the Hybrid Class

In hybrid classes, I have seen pairs of instructors teach their own separate yet parallel section to their students on campus, and then bring the two sections of students together online to hold particular discussion activities, visit Web sites, and receive online guest speakers. I have also seen hybrids that are team taught both on campus and online. The advantage of the former is that students are in smaller face-to-face groups, which might help opportunities for discussion and involvement, whereas the advantage of the latter is that both teachers are thoroughly familiar to the students, as they are seen in both teaching environments.

Grading

One topic that Cranmer (1999) does not mention in his article is grading. The team teachers should decide in advance whether they are both going to grade all student work, or if they divide the load. A possible problem in either scenario is if the teachers grade very differently from each other, so it helps if they are both working from the same grading rubric.

Online Testing and Grading

I include testing under the general heading of "Innovative Online Teaching Techniques," as there is always so much students can learn from being tested. We have spoken about students submitting electronic papers, reports, presentations, journals, and short stories, and if a variety of challenging and rigorous learning activities of this nature are given throughout the semester, then the students benefit from frequent feedback and gain a sound idea as to how they are performing in this course. This, in my mind, is true assessment. The word *assessment* is derived from the Latin root, "to sit next to," and although we do not physically sit next to students when we interact with them online, they can still derive the same benefits of learning if we provide dialogue and feedback.

Knowing a Student's Real Identity

A frequent question about online teaching is how we know that the students are who they say they are. If you are teaching a hybrid class, this doubt is presumably lessened because you could give some tests on campus and thus be present to proctor the exam. But if the class is totally online, or even if it is a hybrid but you want some activities to be tested online, there are many plausible types of online tests.

One important recommendation is to encourage participation in online discussion throughout the semester. This has several advantages. Not only is it beneficial for the student to be an active learner, but also you can grade each student's contribution to discussion. Because you frequently read student responses throughout the semester, any written reports or essays should not come as a surprise in terms of credibility and authenticity (see "How to Facilitate and Stimulate Online Discussion" in Chapter 7).

Grading the Electronic Essay or Take-Home Exam

An electronic paper or essay assignment is similar to a take-home exam. I recommend that, because the student has full access to all online lectures and discussions, as well as the reading materials, it is of relatively low value to simply test for memorization of facts. This is a good opportunity to design an examination that stimulates students to think at a very high level when constructing their essay, such as asking them to apply what they know to a different context, or to synthesize their findings and formulate a new conclusion, or to provide an overall evaluation. Any or all of these suggestions might help students to reach toward the highest rungs in terms of Bloom's taxonomy.

I think it is beneficial for students to receive their work back from you electronically, once it is graded, because online you have scope to make as many comments as you would like, as the electronic "paper" is infinitely expandable and your remarks are always legible. You might want to differentiate your remarks from the student's writing by using another color or putting your comments in [brackets]. I avoid writing my comments in capitals, as online this could be construed as shouting. Alternatively, you could use the "Insert Comment" function in Word, which allows you to write electronically on your students' papers, and appears in pink bubbles in the margin.

Remember also that critical words can sound harsh and upsetting online, so there is need for encouragement, tact, and suggestions for improvement. Sometimes it is a good idea to demonstrate to the class a good student's essay written either in the present class—in which case it is probably best to remove the student's name so as to avoid possible embarrassment—or from a previous class (see Chapter 10). This is easy to do online, as you could simply paste it in. Demonstrating the essay online is an easy and efficient way of making this accessible to all students. Some instructors display this model example in a specially created discussion forum, so that after viewing it, students and the instructor hold a discussion in that very forum about the merits of the essay itself, with the essay still visible by scrolling up to it.

Grading for Quality of Responses in Online Discussion

As for grading each student's participation in online discussion, I recommend that you count qualitative contributions to discussion as a significant percentage of the final grade (see "How to Facilitate and Stimulate Online Discussion" in Chapter 7). Emphasizing quality as opposed to a purely quantitative account of the number of student responses helps to establish to the students that you are interested in how deeply they are considering the issues under discussion, how much they relate the subject matter to their experiences and prior knowledge, and how much their competence in the subject matter is progressing.

If you grade the quality of online discussion responses, it is wise to let students know how they are doing on an ongoing basis, but be very careful about your timing. If responses are graded too swiftly, you may end the discussion, as students will not see a material benefit in continuing to discuss the topic. If grading comes long after a discussion has reached its natural conclusion, however, the topic is no longer fresh in students' minds, and you will lose the advantage of providing an incentive for students to respond to a topic in a timely fashion or else be penalized in their grade.

Grading Group Work

We now look at how best to grade students based on their group work. Should the group be assessed as a whole, with each group member receiving an identical grade? I would advocate against this. If you had been able to observe the group work, you will have derived a definite idea as to how much each student contributed, so it seems that it would be fairer to grade each student accordingly.

Another idea that I have seen used is that the students grade each other's work, and I think this could be a helpful indication, which possibly could be used in conjunction with your own assessment. Jackson (1999), while teaching at New York University, asked students to rank each other according to four dimensions: reliability, participation in group work, intellectual contribution, and contribution to the written project.

Students were asked to put these remarks in writing as a private e-mail to him. These dimensions provide concrete measures for grading, rather than being nebulous and impressionistic. Besides this, I believe another clear advantage of asking the students to think about each other's performance is that it helps them with the important process of evaluation and thinking about thinking, termed *metacognition* (see Chapter 3), which is extremely beneficial in advancing knowledge and understanding.

The student grades were then combined with Jackson's own assessment, and resulted in a good reflection of how each student was judged to be doing from a variety of perspectives. Jackson indicated that some students liked this methodology so much that they wrote to him to express their thanks. Although this technique was used with groups of students in the campus class, I believe it would also work well in the online setting. I would also recommend that you take into consideration the feedback from the class about each group's presentation.

Grading Synchronous Online Conversations

There is also the question as to whether each student's participation in synchronous online conversations should be graded. My feeling is that this should not be done in most cases. I say this because, unless using techniques such as Brookfield and Preskill's (1999) "Circle of Voices," it generally does not leave room for deep thought and reflection on the topic, as it emphasizes speed above all.

However, if the online chat is used for role-playing, the quality of each student's contribution to the overall virtual play should be graded. This should be combined with how well each student could discuss his or her performance in terms of the issues it raised and the quality of responses to other students' questions. Similarly, if the online chat was used for part of the preparatory work contributing to a collaborative group project, then I believe the quality of the final project should be evaluated, as well, perhaps as weighting the grade according to the participation of each group member in each of the stages of preparation. If the online chat involves interacting with a guest lecturer, it also might be a good idea to grade participation, as this indicates the degree of preparation each student did beforehand, so as to be ready to ask questions.

I think also it might be a useful exercise to have a student or students synthesize the conversation as viewed in the archived version of the online chat, in terms of extracting the main points of information, and present this on the discussion board. This can count as a graded assignment. Then, as a follow-up exercise, the student can develop this into a further asynchronous discussion or use it as the basis for a research paper. Alternatively, if the class is a hybrid, the students can present the synthesis of the online chat to the campus class, so that the class can continue to discuss the topic further in a face-to-face setting. This creates a good reinforcement of the online chat, provides opportunities for deeper exploration, and helps students with different learning styles. It provides, according to Bloom's taxonomy, opportunities to work at the analytical, synthesis, and even evaluative levels.

Grading Online Multiple-Choice Quizzes

Some instructors like to use online quizzes, and many software programs provide options for creating multiple-choice questions. If opting for multiple-choice tests, much thought needs to go into their design. Some instructors only reach the first level of Bloom's hierarchy in the types of questions they ask, which is recalling facts from memorization. In an attempt to make this test more rigorous, some online instructors do such things as make the multiple-choice test a timed test—something else many software programs allow you to do—so as to not provide students with sufficient time to look up the answers.

This is certainly one method of doing it, but perhaps a test aimed at a higher level of the cognitive hierarchy would be a better and more meaningful way in which to test true learning, rather than giving a timed test for the memorization of facts. Multiple-choice tests could, for example, be aimed at the comprehension level instead of the memorization stage. This assumes that students have the necessary knowledge and information, but now what is required of them is to demonstrate their understanding. Alternatively, the questions could try to determine each student's ability to apply both knowledge and understanding, and this therefore taps into the application level of the hierarchy. A nice example of a multiple-choice question at the application level is as follows (Cameson et al., 2002):

> Which one of the following memory systems does a piano-tuner mainly use in his occupation?
>   1. Echoic memory
>   2. Short-term memory
>   3. Long-term memory
>   4. Mono-auditory memory
>   5. None of the above

It is a question of application, as it tests how to apply the knowledge of memory systems, with the understanding of what each would mean. It is only when both knowledge and understanding are considered together that the student can choose which is the most applicable for the piano tuner.

Multiple-choice questions can, of course, go beyond testing application to testing analysis, and to be able to truly analyze, the students need the knowledge, the understanding, and the ability to apply to different contexts. Consider the interesting example of a multiple-choice question testing for application. Cameson et al. (2002) provided a table of data of three "mystery" countries arranged in rows and columns that displayed such economic data as population rate of growth; growth rate of the gross national product; and percentages of the population in agriculture, industry, and the service sector. By asking which country is A, B, and C, it implies that students must have knowledge of the economic situation in certain countries, that they comprehend the rankings, that they can apply this information, and finally that they are able to successfully analyze it so as to answer the question. This is quite challenging, and as such is a superb test of meaningful student learning.

The highest level of testing, at the evaluation stage, involves testing sophisticated judgments of the interpretation of information. For example, a short piece of writing could be displayed, and the students are asked if the writing is excellent, good, mediocre, or below average. Each level is clearly defined and specified, so that for example, "excellent" means that explanations are correct and the overall structure is clear, whereas "below average" implies that the explanations are unclear or irrelevant, and the structure is incorrect. By answering this question, students are making judgments according to their knowledge, comprehension, and analysis of the subject matter. In combining these elements, they are making their evaluation based on the specified criteria for each rank.

One word of advice when designing multiple-choice tests: at whatever level your questions are designed to test, be careful in your choice of language. Avoid colloquialisms, which might cause confusion for nonnative English speakers. In general, you will find that carefully designed multiple-choice questions, aimed at going beyond testing for rote memorization, are a good pedagogical tool. They encourage students to actively think about a subject and allow them the opportunity to learn from tests.

It is advantageous to make explicit in the syllabus how you will allocate your grades among each of the different learning activities and your expectations of students within each activity. This, I think, relates strongly to the goals and objectives you have set for the course, as an indication of whether these goals are being met, and consequently, whether the learning of the subject matter is being advanced. Furthermore, if students can see the range of learning activities at the start of the semester, then hopefully they will know how to pace themselves rather than cramming the night before the work is due.

We have talked in this section about how best to evaluate online students. But what of online education itself? How viable is it? Can meaningful statements be made as to the efficacy of teaching and learning online? These questions are addressed in the next two chapters.

PART THREE

ASSESSMENT

At first people refuse to believe that a strange
new thing can be done, then they begin to hope
it can be done, then they see it can be done—
then it is done and all the world wonders why it
was not done centuries ago.

—Burnett, F. H., (1911), 1987
The Secret Garden

Recent developments in the socioeconomic climate and in technology have
changed ideas about what is important for students to learn. We have
become an information economy. Boundaries between jobs are blurring;
there is an increase in collaborative teamwork and a need to think and reason
effectively in an effort to solve problems. Emphasis is often placed on speed,
as information is increasingly being sent electronically, and people must be
prepared to think and respond swiftly (National Research Council, 2001).
This points to very significant questions as to whether online education is
providing not only a means to a love of learning for its own sake, but also
whether it is suitably preparing people for this new work world. Since online
education is itself an electronic transfer of information, and since it works
best when students are encouraged to work collaboratively and interactively,
it would seem that online education could provide the very panacea needed,
but let us look into this question more closely. This final section of the book
will look at the following:

- Opinions about online teaching and learning
- Building a model of assessment of online education

9

OPINIONS ABOUT ONLINE TEACHING AND LEARNING

Appearances aren't deceiving, I think, but you
have to know where to look.
　　　　　—Smiley, J., 1987, *The Age of Grief*

As with any new paradigm shift, there are the naysayers as well as the
enthusiasts. The very same was true at the advent of the printing
press, when it was feared by some that this would mean an end to
Socratic learning. (See Chapter 10 for a more complete discussion on this
topic.) Skepticism and even cynicism about how well an online class can
teach students might develop, especially among those who feel uncertain
about technology. As Kahn wittily said, "For a list of all the ways technology
has failed to improve the quality of life, please press three" (quoted in Finch
and Montambeau, 2000). In this chapter I offer a sprinkling of the types of
comments made either against or in favor of online education.

Online Education Versus Correspondence Courses

Many of us are familiar with David Noble's (1997–2001) criticisms of online
teaching and learning in his series of essays, "Digital Diploma Mills." Noble,
who has studied the history of technology for more than 30 years, thinks
that being called a Luddite is not an insult, as he believes that technology in
teaching is distracting. (The Luddites were British weavers in the 1800s who
fought against technology.) Noble likens online education to correspondence
courses of the early 1900s, which claimed that they would personalize education, but in which standards dropped and eventually the programs failed. A
key difference, however, between correspondence courses and online education, is that whereas correspondence courses were a one-to-one format,

online education is many to many, thus providing scope for active learning within a highly collaborative framework, and resulting in the discovery of socially constructed meaning. Nevertheless, Noble thinks online learning is doomed because its students and instructors are not able to make use of all five senses; but it has been argued earlier in this book that this might indeed lead to fewer distractions and greater ability to concentrate purely in the realm of connections of thoughts and concepts.

Caring about Students You Never Meet

Another critic of online education is Carol Fungaroli Sargent, English professor at Georgetown University, who was quoted in the television program, *60 Minutes* (2001), as saying, "Education is like sex on the Internet. You can get it online, but it is so much better in person." She thought students were lured online, but that this was an "irresponsible, self-indulgent choice." She seemed to love teaching on campus, feeling that there was a great energy she could see in the classroom when a student was engaged. She asked how she could care about someone she never met in an online class. Furthermore, she had this to say about the hybrid class: "It sounds like the distance-learning camp had to resort to this compromise [hybrid courses] because its ambitions failed miserably." This book has argued that distance does not necessarily impede the excitement of good teaching and learning, and in fact many students have remarked how they felt they knew their instructor and each other better than had been the case in a campus class.

Exerting Quality Control Online

Chancellor Robert Burdall of Berkeley was shown on *60 Minutes* (2001) as saying that he worried about quality control if classes were offered totally online. Arthur Levine, president of Teacher's College at Columbia University, stated on the same program that the Internet allows scope for online teaching giants, equivalent to rock stars or athletes, who will be awarded huge sums of money and many other perks as all online universities will be bidding against each other for this superstar.

Overwhelming Aspects of Incorporating Technology

In a 1999 survey at the University of Michigan, Ann Arbor, many faculty members indicated that they wanted one-on-one instruction in using technology, and they wanted this help from someone they knew who was familiar with their work (Lynch, 2002). After all, it takes time to learn how to use technology most effectively, and it is important to make it specific to the needs of the course. As a result, incorporating technology can be understood as being stress inducing and frustrating for some faculty. Along with this is the very real fear for some instructors of a loss of control, as they feel the computer world with its army of instructional designers is intruding into academia. My belief, however, is that if pedagogy remains as the primary focus, and if instructors are trained to learn the basic technology only in as much as it will fulfill the desired pedagogical ends needed for their online courses, then they could take the responsibility of adapting their courses themselves for online delivery and therefore need not be afraid of any intrusions from the technologists.

Many believe, however, that academics are used to being in charge, and enjoy the feeling of power when strolling into a classroom, giving information, and seeing the students rapidly record it in their notebooks. Many professors shy away from technology as they would feel afraid of being in a situation that they do not know, not only in the design of their course, but also in the teaching of it through technological means. They might fear that the students know more than they do, which would mean that they were relinquishing their power (Lynch, 2002). Again, if the role of technology is deemphasized, and if professors are prepared to "give up the chalk" (Patenaude, 1999) so that teaching and learning take place collaboratively rather than hierarchically, then these fears too become unfounded.

Learning to Meaningfully Apply Technology in Education

Larry Cuban, a professor of education at Stanford for the last 20 years, addresses what he feels is "the mostly unfulfilled promise of technology in school reform" (quoted in Carlson, 2001). Cuban, in his book *Oversold and Underused* (2001), looks at the high amounts of spending on technology, yet indicates that it has been largely underutilized as tools in teaching and learning. The thrust of the book is that many teachers and administrators rush to incorporate technology on their campuses (see "Technological Stability" in Chapter 10), as they thought this would make teaching and learning more efficient. But Cuban asks, even though technology has reshaped the way business is conducted by promoting greater efficiency, is this a desirable end in education? I argue that what is of greater importance than efficiency is effectiveness, and I believe that online teaching can be very effective if done correctly.

Cuban also found that professors used computers less for teaching than they do in their own home, offices, or library. He says this underuse in the classroom, therefore, is not due to the fact that professors shy away from using them because they are technophobes, but because promoters of technology have little idea of its applied use in teaching. He believes that most software used in education was originally designed for business and it does not translate adequately to meet the very different needs of students and professors.

One Size Does Not Fit All

Along similar lines, one professor at the State University of New York (SUNY) Learning Network once remarked to me, "One size does not fit all," meaning that he thought it was restricting to work within one course template and expect this to suffice for classes on art and design, math, history, or writing, as if this was almost a "cookie-cutter approach." On campus a chemistry lab is necessarily designed differently from an art studio and from a seminar room, so the online environment should better reflect the physical environment of these different types of classes and the different kinds of activities that go on in each. Although I agree with his statement, I do think that most software programs offer a number of options for specific customization, so that courses in different disciplines can in fact look very different from each other.

Hidden Costs

In a fascinating yet controversial book entitled, *Let Them Eat Data: How Computers Affect Education, Cultural Diversity, and the Prospects of Ecological Sustainability*, Bowers (2000) looks closely at the consequences of technology on education. He argues that, much as with any form of progress, there is a double bind, meaning that there are benefits—which are usually talked about extensively—and costs—which are often ignored. As an analogy, Bowers talks of the Industrial Revolution, mentioning that it did indeed advance the wealth and standard of living within society, but it came with costs to the landscape in many areas in the form of blight and pollution, destroyed many individual and self-sufficient cultures, and set the world on the destructive path on which it finds itself today. The same is true, Bowers argues, in the advances in computer technology. We are persuaded through the media, in authoritative and euphoric tones, how marvelous are the latest innovations, so that any criticism is seen as "unwarranted and even subversive" (p. 7). Important questions to ask should be whether these technological advances will make for an "ecologically sustainable and culturally diverse future" (p. 7). Bowers thinks educators have done nothing to look more fully at the consequences of computerization and globalization, as they myopically value technology more than ecological and cultural well-being.

This leads inevitably to questions such as whether, in an attempt to preserve cultural diversity, we should keep our regional academic pockets of education intact, or whether it is advantageous to disperse knowledge and information over as wide an area as possible. Is the spread of information an opportunity or an intrusion? Is the so-called digital divide being widened? As with any new resource, if there are some who benefit and some who lose out, is it fair, based on a cost-benefit analysis, to proceed, thereby penalizing and heightening the relative deprivation of those without? Alternatively, is it fair to deny the spread of online learning, so that those who would have benefited are deprived of that opportunity? What is the most ethical outcome?

In the first edition of my book, I stated that my hope was that, similar to the advent of the telephone, there would be an eventual diffusion of computers throughout society. And this, I believe, is now being made possible with the advent of the smartphone and iPad. In this way, then, it seems that it is increasingly likely to promote the good of the disadvantaged, rather than deprive the advantaged (Navarro, 2000).

Additionally, students who do not own a computer, smartphone, or iPad can certainly use the computing facilities of the university (although admittedly, this does not always provide the same convenience and flexibility as possessing one's own Internet access). Navarro makes an additional valid point that computers can in fact increase the advantages of some previously disadvantaged groups, such as the old, infirm, or those living in very remote areas. In my experience, it can also provide advantages to those who are constantly mobile. For example, I have had a few touring ballet dancers and actors in some of my online classes who would log on from the next stop on their tour. As one student told me, this was not only the perfect way, but also the *only* way to complete her education.

To turn one's back on the possibilities of online education because of the opinions of its critics would mean losing out on potentially important opportunities, but at the same time, to paint only a rosy picture would be artificial and misleading. But what do instructors who teach online actually think of their experiences? I think that even though there are some negative aspects, there are indeed many outweighing positives.

Online Teaching Is Time-Consuming

A common complaint about online teaching is how much time it takes. Almeda and Rose (2000), in a survey of satisfaction levels of nine instructors teaching a broad range of topics in 14 online courses at the University of California Extension, found that some instructors mentioned that length of time was a concern. Smith, Ferguson, and Caris (2001), in a qualitative study of 21 instructors from the SUNY Learning Network and state universities in California and Indiana, found that instructors said that it can be an extremely lengthy procedure to set up an online class, especially as so much time needs to be devoted to the careful choosing of words to avoid misinterpretation, and the care given to know how best to design the course so that every part of it is in its logically best place. All mentioned having made extensive modifications on the courses they taught on campus, especially in terms of finding ways to motivate students.

Furthermore, once they start teaching the class, the long hours continue. In fact, one study showed that online teaching can take 40 percent more time than teaching in the traditional classroom (Ouellette, 1999). This might be all the more so as it is important for the instructor to be a definite presence in the class, so that the students are reassured that their comments are read and acknowledged (Smith et al., 2001). I think this points to the need to meaningfully increase the responsibility for students in their own learning process, so that, for example, students could sometimes be involved in preparing for debates or role-playing, leading discussion topics, or responding to each other's questions. This decreases the workload on the instructor, and, if done in a variety of exciting ways that meet the needs of many learning styles, can be a terrific educational experience for the students. Ironically, even though it is time consuming, Smith et al. (2001) found that most instructors actually looked forward to their time spent online.

The Value of Being Physically Present

Another difficulty with online teaching, as detected by Smith et al. (2001), is that some instructors did not like being primarily confined to a text-based environment through which to communicate to their students. Some even mentioned that a "life time of teaching skills goes by the wayside. They cannot use their presence and their classroom skills to get their point across. Nor can they use their oral skills to improvise on the spot to deal with behavior problems or educational opportunities" (p. 18). The instructors with whom I have worked, however, have said that they believe that having specific training in online pedagogy has made them thoughtful about teaching and communication in a way that they had not previously been, and that teaching online has actually made them better campus classroom teachers.

Teaching a hybrid would give opportunities for contact, and additionally by using Skype and other similar media, teachers and students have some supplements to a totally text-based environment. The ultimate goal, however, is to make whichever technology is used invisible, so that the focus is on the flow of ideas and knowledge, and the accompanying excitement of this flow, so that it is the transactional distance itself that is minimized. (See "Distinguishing between Physical Distance and Transactional Distance" in Chapter 1).

Advantages of Freedom and Flexibility

On the positive side of the survey findings, all of the instructors in Almeda and Rose's (2000) study commented that they loved the freedom and flexibility to be anywhere at any time when teaching online. They also mentioned that online teaching appealed to them, as they were interested in professional development to discover new and diverse ways of teaching and presenting innovative learning opportunities.

Richer, More Reflective Discussion

Many instructors in Smith et al.'s (2001) study mentioned the advantage of communication being through the written word, as this tended to enable students to become more reflective, and for learning to become more profound. They also felt that it was more inclusive, as asynchronicity definitely lent a helping hand to those students who might not otherwise contribute to discussion in the campus class. Instructors in Almeda and Rose's study said that there was generally very strong work from students, as they were "more prepared to stretch themselves online than in the traditional classroom" (2000).

Informality as an Online Asset

Interestingly, it was found that instructors thought that the anonymity that was probably felt by all online participants changed the perception of roles, and many students viewed their instructor in a more informal light online, which helped them to better challenge ideas and enable them to engage in a lengthier debate with their instructor than might be feasible on campus.

Online classes are not at all alienating, as might be assumed by those unfamiliar with them, but instead are a "labor intensive, highly textbased, intellectually challenging forum which elicits deeper thinking on the part of the students and which presents, for better or worse, more equality between instructor and student" (Smith et al., 2001, p. 19). Despite Aboujaoude's (2011) concerns that the loss of hierarchical structuring that can exist online erodes respect (see "Alteration of Interpersonal Relationships within Online Settings" in Chapter 4), it has often been observed that student participation in online discussions might often actually increase, which will ultimately help them in their learning.

High Satisfaction Levels of Online Students and Faculty

In a recent study by the Sloan Consortium, which is a consortium of institutions and organizations committed to quality online education, academics and instructional designers within the group reported that, generally speaking, both student and faculty satisfaction levels were found to be very high for those involved in online education. Many students reported that they had recommended online courses to friends, and that they themselves continued to take online courses. Faculty reported being pleased with online teaching, as they enjoyed this method of teaching with its high degree of interaction, enjoyed easy access to online reference material, and thought online teaching led to effective learning (Sloan, 2002).

These assorted comments about online learning have made me reflect upon a statement of Albert Einstein's, made more than half a century ago, and in a totally different context. He said, "It has become appallingly obvious that our technology has far exceeded our humanity."

Well, has it? It seems that this view is what has driven most of the arguments against online learning mentioned here. Chambers, of CISCO Systems, said on *60 Minutes* (2001), in terms of online education, that we have barely even made the first step as he thought it likely that there would be more technological innovations yet to come. Arthur Levine, on the same program, thought that in a matter of 10 to 15 years, it would be feasible to see holograms of the professor and all students there in the room with us as we teach and learn. As of this writing, it is now 11 years since Levine made this prediction, and although holograms are not in use, Skype permits us to see each other in real time. But the dominant mode, and also I believe the most effective, in online education is the text-based asynchronous discussion forums.

Certainly, however, new technologies are evolving with amazing frequency. With all of this comes enormous implications. Yet are technology and humanity mutually exclusive? I'd like to think they are definitely not. At all events, I believe that it all comes down to whether or not we believe that the medium is the message, as we discussed in "Can Digital Media Change the Way We Think?" in Chapter 4. We need assess with accuracy the efficacy of online education, and it is to this that we turn our attention in the following chapter.

BUILDING A MODEL
OF ASSESSMENT OF
ONLINE EDUCATION

It is the mark of an educated mind to be able to
entertain a thought without accepting it.

—Aristotle

T he disparate opinions as to the efficacy of online education, shown
both by vociferous criticisms and generally favorable attitudinal
studies, together with the fact that colleges and universities that offer
online courses claim that they are equivalent in terms of credit to their coun-
terpart courses offered on campus, call for a crucial need for a more rigorous
and objective assessment of this relatively new type of education to determine what and how much students are learning. Because the very structure
of the Internet permits diffusion of its use so rapidly, some academicians
might be using online teaching before really knowing how best to do so.

Formative research, which can immediately provide feedback to educators as to how to improve online education, if necessary, is an important first
step. Not only is assessment needed for assisting in teaching and learning,
but also in evaluating programs and determining how well online teaching
and learning, as a new form of education, is faring. Because assessment
involves reasoning from evidence, it runs the risk of being slightly imprecise,
but this chapter attempts to offer some alternative views on how assessment
can strive to tell the real tale.

Even though online education is, relatively speaking, still in its infancy
in terms of the number of years it has been in existence compared with the
vast span of human learning, like everything else in the computer world, it
has snowballed so rapidly that sufficient online teaching has now occurred
for there to be some notion as to its quantitative and qualitative success.

But first let us define what is meant by success. If we define *success* according to *Webster's New World Dictionary* (1990) as "a favorable result," what exactly does this mean in the context of the virtual classroom? Furthermore, "a favorable result" seems to be a comparative statement. Favorable according to what, and according to whom? As Ehrmann states, "Unfortunately . . . one can't ask, 'How well is this technology-based approach working, relative to the norm?' since there usually isn't a norm" (1995, p. 22).

Asking the right questions and knowing what to look for in regard to the effectiveness of online teaching is the first important step. It is a rather challenging subject with which to wrestle. Just because an online course is replete with PowerPoint slides, fancy animations, and other flashy displays does not necessarily make it a good course. We are not after a Hollywood production, but we should aim to teach a sound, rigorous course through the medium of the Internet, in which student learning flourishes.

But even if our primary focus is on teaching and learning, rather than technology, what should we be measuring? Any of us who have taught online know that it can be good; that we can feel excited, stimulated, challenged; and that we are doing something valuable and viable. We also know that sometimes we feel overwhelmed and frustrated. And we know that many students frequently rave about it, although some have difficulties. But how do emotional reactions translate into specific objective measurements of effectiveness?

Should we be looking, if not at emotional reaction, then at students' grades? Should we be looking at attrition rates? But what does attrition tell us? Unless we interview students who have dropped a course, we might be uncertain as to whether they did so because of some non-course-related impediment in their life or because of this new method of learning. If students dropped at the start of the semester, was it because they were "shopping around" for courses? If we look at grades and attrition rates, should it be a relative measure, as seen in comparison to the class taught solely on campus? Or is it possible to develop an accurate, objective, and specific measurement unique to the online class itself?

Factors to Be Considered When Performing Assessments

Interestingly, in 1978, when a new technical inroad in academia was introduced in the form of teaching by television, McKeachie said, "Unfortunately, there are some hidden traps enthusiasts for one method or another are likely to overlook" (p. 257). Although online education was unheard of then, I would like to apply what McKeachie said about teaching by television to online education, as both represent an important change and both have a profound impact on resultant pedagogy.

Emotional Reactions

McKeachie wondered whether, if students are taught by "some method quite unusual in their college" (1978, p. 257), which from here on we will interpret for the sake of the present argument as being online teaching, then the very fact that it is new and different might generate excitement; but this might be a reaction to the novelty, and not the educational experience in and of itself. If students in an online course experience tremendous feelings of satisfaction, is it to the detriment of a campus class because it might take more time and excite students more? Or does it have to be thought of as a balancing act, so that if the scale of satisfaction with online education goes up, the other scale of satisfaction with campus classes plummets? And, still on the basis of emotional reaction, McKeachie points out that some students, rather than feeling excited, might feel angry that they are having to compete with students from the more tried-and-tested status quo traditional campus classroom. What is more, emotional reactions might not only be experienced by students, McKeachie points out, but also by professors. He refers to how, in the face of exciting innovation, so many new professors might briefly enthuse about it, although only a few semesters later their enthusiasm, along with their courses, might wither on the vine. It is for these reasons that I feel that measurements of satisfaction might give some misleading results.

Are All Students Suited to Online Learning?

An important question to ask is, are all students suited to learning online? McKeachie (1978) believes that the students who opt for an innovative approach to their learning are more likely to opt for it again in following semesters than are students who have not yet tried it. I think this is less the case now as far as online learning is concerned, as I have detected some subtle changes in the students I have taught. At first, in the early 1990s when online education was brand new, I think there was a strong process of self-selection among students, meaning that students were generally highly motivated and terrifically enthusiastic. Over time, as more climbed on the band-wagon, I found that as the numbers of students swelled dramatically, the uniform high standard declined. Recently, however, I have noted an increase in bright, motivated students. Of course, this is my impression, but if it is objectively true, it makes intuitive sense as first there are the early experimental and adventurous students; then a big wave of students of varying talents and skills; and then, having experienced it, possibly those feeling overwhelmed and unable to perform well when needing to be self-motivated and disciplined who might opt for the campus again.

I believe that the ideal online student seems to be a curious mix of independence, in terms of being self-motivated, with a definite sense of affiliation and willingness for interaction and collaboration, rather than being a solitary worker. It is not only caliber that is an issue here, but also lifestyle. Levine, President of Teacher's College at Columbia University, believes that online learning is especially suited to the adult learner, who he says composes 84 percent of the student body (*60 Minutes*, 2001). Increasingly, we see adults returning to college and balancing their jobs and families with educational opportunities. These students, he believes, want the same relationship with their college as they have with their automatic teller machine; namely, great service, convenience, high quality, and even free parking (which, in my mind, amounts to easy access). Although Levine may well be right, I believe there are other not so strictly utilitarian attractions, such as the whole arena of personal attention and human contact missing from his stark comparison with another technological innovation, that of withdrawing money from a "hole in the wall."

As for the undergraduate student who is living on campus, online classes might be very welcome to those who have been typically used to very large lecture halls, as they might benefit from more personal attention online (Navarro, 2000). Hybrids, as opposed to the totally online class, also might provide wonderful opportunities for the discussion from the campus class to spill over online. Students might also enjoy the diversity of learning opportunities that each medium potentially provides. Lynch (2002) predicts, within about five years, students will come to expect online classes as a viable alternative from which they would like to select, and many would come to expect e-books, a 24/7 environment, and the possibility of being halfway round the world and still come to class. And, as shown in this book, these predictions are coming to fruition. However, I do not believe that online education should ever totally replace campus classes, as most undergraduates also benefit from the face-to-face social interaction that studying on campus provides.

Can Meaningful Comparisons Be Made between Campus and Online Classes?

If indeed there are differences in type and caliber between students who select a campus class and those who take one online, how then can comparisons be meaningfully made about the effectiveness of online education relative to teaching and learning on campus? Might this, in some sense, be comparing apples and oranges? What does it mean if it is said that learning effectiveness in the online class is at least as good if not better than the campus class? Isn't there a wide disparity of teaching and learning in both environments, online and on campus?

Comparative assessments, which can also be called "norm-referenced," can be informative up to a point, but they are limited as they cannot say how well a student is actually doing in an absolute sense (National Research Council, 2001). To gain an idea of how online students perform in absolute terms would require instead a "criterion-referenced" study, such as measuring the ways in which the students learned the subject and the degree of competence they acquired. It is impossible to have a control group against which to measure the success of online teaching. Even if a teacher teaches both in a campus class and online, the personality and skills of that teacher will have an effect on the success of the class. Perhaps what is needed is a large enough sample of teachers who teach both on campus and online to make comparisons and identify trends; but how can we limit for the personality and communication skills of every individual teacher? Or for the caliber, involvement, and intelligence of the students? Every teacher knows that two sections of the same course in the same semester have different student dynamics. To assume otherwise and to ignore these human differences would seem akin to assuming the purely predictable, robotic, rational man or woman, whereas we know in reality that human nature does not work that way.

Furthermore, is it possible to make a blanket statement about the efficacy of online education, in that it may vary according to discipline? Are there some subjects that lend themselves better to online education than others? My personal belief is that courses that are most readily suited to online delivery are those that have the most potential for discussion, such as courses in the humanities, social sciences, and writing. If an assessment is made of online education given on one campus or over one university system without distinguishing the academic disciplines, can meaningful interpretations be gained?

Impact of the Technology

Another key factor that will impact greatly on relative satisfaction levels of online students is the functionality and usability of the technology itself. Ideally the technology should be seamless and transparent once students become familiar with it. Careful determination should be given by the technical experts when choosing and customizing the software, so that the graphical interface (color, fonts, navigational elements), which affects the way the instructor and students perceive the course on the Web, should be user friendly and pleasingly aesthetic. According to government stipulations, access for the student who is vision or hearing impaired should be included (Sonwalker, 2002).

For some students, the following may impede successful learning: unforeseen technical hurdles of accessing the class, finding one's way around the online class, having a computer that keeps crashing, not having a computer at all, or repeatedly receiving error messages and broken links or unclear directions from the instructor that lead to ambiguities and uncertainties as to where to click. This points to the need for having a technical support staff who is able to give timely and reliable responses. It also points to how essential it is that the academic institution's server, on which the online classes are housed, operates smoothly, reliably, and with sufficient capacity to avoid delays for each individual user.

Other Possible Frustrations of Online Students

But it is not only technological problems that can lead to frustration. Frustration can also arise if some students do not read all the other student and instructor postings within the online discussion and thus it lacks meaningful cohesion, or if some feel overwhelmed by how time consuming it can be, or if some receive insufficient feedback from the instructor and thus they are uncertain as to how well they are doing in the class.

Hara and Kling (1999), in their observation of an online class, mentioned that some students felt visual deprivation, stating that if they were on campus, they could tell from body language, a nod of the head, or a smile if they had approval, which is reassuring. This fact highlights the need, mentioned frequently throughout this book, for the online teacher to be supportive, encouraging, and quick to respond. Otherwise student confidence can flag, which is detrimental, because if a class continues to present frustrations for too long, some students might be hesitant to ask questions and become even more lost and frustrated.

If a student fails to ask questions or express frustration, an instructor might erroneously assume that all is well in the online class. This is another factor that might therefore skew the accuracy of data on satisfaction levels (Hara and Kling, 1999). It is vitally important, when conducting an assessment of online education, to be realistic about the possibility of frustration that some students might feel, as it is only when the pitfalls as well as the benefits are taken into account that improvement and progress can be made.

Hara and Kling (1999) state that sustained frustration, which might be even more acutely felt when working remotely, can detrimentally affect both a student's cognitive and affective capacities. Cognition can be depleted by frustration as working (short-term) memory is distracted, and crucial inferences cannot be made; students can become far less motivated if frustrations continue.

Is Online Education Suitable for All Instructors?

We also need to ask whether online education is suitable for all instructors, and my feeling is that it is best suited to those instructors who enjoy writing and do it well, who enjoy a Socratic approach to teaching, who personalize education, and who are prepared to spend more time teaching online than they are used to spending in the campus class. Furthermore, it is best suited to instructors who have, or are prepared to develop, a comfort level and competence at using the technology so that technical frustrations are minimized.

Pragmatic Considerations of Accurately Performing Assessments

One other potential problem of performing assessments that makes intuitive sense is that the very act of observation could change the results (McKeachie, 1978). There is also potentially a problem with questionnaire design, as this could introduce an element of bias. Questions may contain words or expressions that are associated with a particular region and might be especially troublesome in terms of comprehension, given the possible regional and ethnic diversity of students from a global marketplace who are taking an online class (National Research Council, 2001).

Even if we were to overlook this point and take various statistical measurements, might we misinterpret the statistical significance of difference? We also must factor in the extremely large number of variables, as teaching is such a complex process involving interactions between many personalities and the subject matter of the class itself. There is the quality of the curriculum and the nature of the instructional materials to consider, as well as the experiences and skills of the teacher, the support the students receive outside class, the diversity of the student population, the class size, the opportunities for teachers to work together or to undergo professional development, public opinion, and media coverage (National Research Council, 2001).

So much depends on what is being tested. Some students may find certain tasks difficult whereas others find them easy, even if overall these students are of similar ability. This lends support to Gardner's (2000) views on multiple intelligences among students, as discussed in "Student Characteristics" in Chapter 2. Difference in ability to perform on these tasks could also be because of the prior knowledge each student holds (National Research Council, 2001). McKeachie (1978) referred to a stunning study by Parsons, Ketcham, and Beach (1958), which tried to compare the effectiveness of different teaching methods and found that one group of students who did not attend any classes at all paradoxically performed better on the exam than those who attended class, as the exam itself was based exclusively on the textbook! It was thought that those who attended classes of various types were distracted by other information beyond just the textbook, and so, with cluttered minds, they were less able to focus on questions related to the textbook alone. In this case, it seems that pure memorization and recall of facts were being examined, but as McKeachie says, "[O]ne cannot conclude that a particular method is superior in achieving all goals, if only one outcome has been measured" (1978, p. 260). I agree! If we think back to the six levels of learning identified by Bloom in 1956 (Cameson, Delpierre, and Masters, 2002), reliance on grades can be yet another variable that could muddle a straightforward comparison of effectiveness between online and campus teaching.

Furthermore, grade results might be inaccurate measures of assessment of online education as some students might strive to do well, even if the learning environment is very poor, as they are so motivated by the importance of excellent grades. In other words, they might do independent study to compensate. Even if the totally online course is considered equivalent to the campus class or hybrid class, in terms of the university recognition of the number of credits, can it really be so? Because students are learning in different ways, the exams must reflect this difference in learning and be suited to each learning environment.

Transference of Knowledge and Skills

Looking beyond the immediate education in a particular class to transfer of that knowledge to other classes, as well as to ultimate career success, can it be deduced that online students make more or less use of their knowledge and skills than those who were educated on campus? This is important as education, after all, should not end at the conclusion of the course. Ehrmann (1995), quoting from the findings of Pascarella and Terenzini (1991) in their 20-year study of the impact of college on students, mentioned that these researchers found virtually no correlation between grades and work achievement for campus students after graduation.

Why was this? Was this because of the "stickiness" of preexisting knowledge, even if it is misinformed? Are Pascarella and Terenzini's results an anomaly, or are they generally true? If this had been the case for students educated on campus, is it possible that online students will do much better? Is it possible to say, as some students take hybrid classes, some take a mix of online and campus classes, and some take their degrees entirely online?

A Criteria-Referenced Study: Assessment as a Measure of Achievement of Course Goals and Learning Outcomes

Rather than attempting to do a comparative study between traditional campus teaching and online teaching to assess the efficacy of online education, it would seem that a better approach would be to shift focus to a criteria-referenced study that concentrates instead on whether the course goals, explicitly stated at the start of the course, have been met by the course's completion, and whether the students have progressed throughout the duration of the course by having meaningfully acquired knowledge. This returns to the true meaning of the word *assessment*, derived from its Latin root as meaning "to sit next to," with the teacher and student sitting side by side, engaged in continuous and meaningful dialogue and feedback. This technique of investigating whether course goals have been met and of looking at learning outcomes is a method that could accurately assess a course, whether it is taught on campus or online. I venture to suggest that if this technique is used to assess the efficacy of a course, then elements such as level and quality of participation of each student and visibility of her or his thinking might become more apparent in the online class than in the campus class. Not only might it be possible to use this technique to assess a course once it is completed, but also it could be prescriptive in terms of providing indications as to how to intentionally and deliberately construct a course so as to include the following:

- A clear and explicit statement of course goals, along with a crisp, logical course structure, which enables students to comprehend the requirements of the course. This increases their chances for deep learning to occur and the course goals to be achieved.
- Discussion questions and techniques that will elicit upper-level thinking and reflection.
- A clear reflection of these discussion questions in the grading and assessment.

The Flashlight Project, created in the mid 1990s and directed by Steve Ehrmann, performs important work on assessment of online education. It would be useful to determine how their valid suggestions can be intentionally incorporated into an online course so as to assess at the end of the semester the extent to which the course goals have been achieved. Ehrmann (1995) believes that the goal for successful online education focuses on selecting "educational strategies for using technology to improve learning outcomes" (p. 26). These educational strategies include:

- Project-based learning
- Collaborative learning
- Learning through repeated revisions of written work
- Improved interaction between and among students and the instructor

Chickering and Ehrmann (1996) applied to the online context the model of "Seven Principles of Good Practice in Undergraduate Education," which was first published in March 1987, as a proposal to improve campus classes. They believed that "[i]f the power of the new technologies is to be fully realized, they should be employed in ways consistent with the Seven Principles" (p. 1). The principles are as follows:

1. Good practice encourages contact between students and faculty.
2. Good practice develops reciprocity and cooperation among students.
3. Good practice uses active learning techniques.
4. Good practice gives prompt feedback.
5. Good practice emphasizes time on task.

6. Good practice communicates high expectations.
7. Good practice respects diverse talents and ways of learning.

Let us look at each of these principles in turn and investigate explicitly their implications, both in terms of building specific learning activities into the online course and also in determining learning outcomes and achievement of course goals.

- *Good practice encourages contact between students and faculty:* This implies that knowing a few teachers well greatly helps a student to learn, which might in turn help the student to successfully accomplish the goals of the course. The online class can actually help this to happen in many ways. First, because the online class is always available, it offers the potential for much swifter and more continuous communication than in a class held once or twice a week on campus. Second, if students are dealing with a difficult matter, they might work better by putting it in writing rather than speaking about this. Third, because there is a very definite increase in part-time students and adult learners who have very busy, highly scheduled lives, the online environment offers extended opportunities to contact the teacher, whereas it might have been impossible for these same students to stay after a campus class to talk to the teacher. Fourth, it can help students who are shy, or those from cultures unused to conversing face to face with the teacher, to engage in dialogue, as it offers them time to formulate their response (Chickering and Ehrmann, 1996). Fifth, more intimacy can be developed among all class participants, as working online helps students to ask deeper questions because they are not being watched and they can become totally absorbed.

  This could result in online discussion that is not just formulaic, but sincere, exciting, and insightful. Each student's participation in online discussion is easily apparent, thus providing the teacher with a ready appreciation as to how well each student is learning. As the teacher, it is important to be highly accessible to the student without being overwhelmed, which can be accomplished by letting students know when they can expect to hear from you.

  In many online classes that I have taught, students have remarked at the end of the semester that they have come to know me, and each other, much better than had ever been the case for them in campus classes.

- *Good practice develops reciprocity and cooperation among students:* Good learning should be collaborative and social, instead of competitive and isolated (Chickering and Ehrmann, 1996; Wegerif, 1998), as this helps in the meaningful acquisition of knowledge and in achieving the goals of the course. Online discussion is a fantastically useful tool, whereby the sharing of ideas among the group can be readily facilitated. The teacher should avoid answering each student individually, as if playing many simultaneous games of ping-pong, but instead should try to weave together responses from many students, mentioning them each by name and acknowledging their contributions, and pointing out commonalities and differences of perspective among them. This woven tapestry of multiple perspectives can prompt the teacher to ask more questions and move discussion on to a deeper level. The questions asked by the teacher should not be mundane or ask for recall of memorized facts, but instead should be challenging so that they attempt to deepen enquiry and improve the opportunities to actively acquire knowledge.

  As well as discussion, there are other online activities that can stimulate reciprocity and collaboration. These can include any form of group work, such as working on case studies or role-playing, as well as giving feedback to presentations, journals, or writing assignments. Online discussions and collaborative online activities of this nature can reach the synthesis and evaluation stages of Bloom's taxonomy.

  Along with the teacher asking high-level questions, the tone in which these questions are asked and responses are given is also of utmost importance. By establishing an encouraging, enthusiastic, and supportive setting, the teacher can stimulate interaction and collaboration among the group members. This creates conditions for the development of shared multiple perspectives, which can lead to socially constructed meaning (Berge and Muilenburg, 2000; National Research Council, 2001; Wegerif, 1998).

- *Good practice uses active learning techniques:* This principle outlines how good learning is not a spectator sport (Chickering and Ehrmann, 1996), and does not take the view that students are empty vessels waiting passively to be filled with knowledge they must memorize. This is the lowest rung of Bloom's taxonomy. Instead, it asserts that the students will enhance their own learning process and be most likely to accomplish the goals of the course if they are active.

To establish the right conditions in which the students can be active, the teacher needs to ask high-level questions and set challenging tasks that stimulate the students to reflect upon the topic and to try to connect it to their experiences so that it feels meaningful. The asynchronous nature of online discussions allows time for this reflection and search for relevance to take place. If the students actively participate in online discussions and in all other online learning activities with deliberation and intentionality, and keep the course goals and objectives clearly in mind, it is likely that they will be motivated to perform to a higher level and will as a result retain the material for much longer as it has become more meaningful. It also could be conjectured that the very act of writing out thoughts as opposed to speaking them might further consolidate the acquisition of the student's knowledge and help each student to better retain it.

- *Good practice gives prompt feedback:* At the start of the class, it is helpful if the teacher can assess the competence and prior knowledge of each student, and then compare this with each student's competence by the end of each course as a way of assessing progress. This would provide a good indication of learning outcomes and the student's ability to achieve the goals of the course. As was discussed in Chapter 3, prior knowledge might either impede or assist in the acquisition of knowledge. As such, it is crucial that students allow their thinking to be visible to the teacher, as in this way the teacher can provide feedback to each student throughout the course and help to guide him or her accordingly. The online environment provides the mechanism in which thoughts are made visible, in the form of written responses to discussion.

Feedback to the students is important as it can help them to reflect upon what they have learned and what they still need to know (Chickering and Ehrmann, 1996) and help them with the skills of metacognition in which they can assess themselves and their progress (National Research Council, 2001). Giving feedback online is simple because there are permanent records of students' work and there is easy access to them. One other advantage of giving feedback to a student's online work is that it is an infinitely expandable space, in which instructor comments can be as extensive as needed, rather than being squashed into and around the student's writing on a possibly cramped sheet of paper.

Informative feedback can be helpful, if not inspirational, to many students. Students can more easily do repeated revisions of their work, taking note of each step toward improvement, and thus deepen their learning. Added to this, students can receive feedback from each other as well as from the teacher. Giving feedback draws on the highest level of thinking (evaluation), and incorporating feedback into making overall improvements of the work can lead to synthesis, which is also upper-level thinking. In this way, it can be appreciated that learning activities that encourage feedback can lead to deep learning.

Feedback can also be in the form of acknowledgment (Graham, Cagiltay, Lim, Craner, and Duffy, 2001). Acknowledgment can take the form of the instructor responding to each student by name in online discussions, so that everyone feels included as part of the group. Acknowledgment can also be given in the context of the teacher sending each student an e-mail to confirm receipt of any student assignment sent electronically, and it is tremendously reassuring to students to know that their work has arrived safely.

- *Good practice emphasizes time on task:* As Chickering and Ehrmann (1996) state, it is important to allocate realistic amounts of time so that effective teaching and learning can occur. Time means something different online than in the campus class, as the online class exists within the more elastic and subjective realm of a virtual dimension (see Chapter 3). This, however, can prove to be advantageous in that it does not call for immediacy; rather, because of its asynchronous nature, students have time to reflect and think deeply about issues before responding.

  The question then becomes that of how the teacher should optimally pace the course so that students are neither overwhelmed by too much too fast on the one hand, or bored by excessive periods of inactivity on the other. Optimal pacing of the course—along with a variation of stimulating activities that retain students' interest throughout, and a definite presence of the teacher who engenders a personalized, encouraging tone—might help in the ultimate accomplishment of the goals of the course and for students to move beyond mere memorization to much higher levels of thinking.

The online class can be timesaving in significant ways: it eliminates the need for commuting or parking, it provides easy access to references rather than having to go to a library, and it provides convenience and flexibility for those with busy schedules (Chickering and Ehrmann, 1996). On the other hand, we know that it certainly takes longer to teach and to learn online than in face-to-face classes. But the extended time online provides prolonged opportunities for thought and connection with the material, so that more learning can potentially be accomplished.

Asynchronicity can result sometimes in time lags in conversation topics, which can be frustrating. It is the job of the teacher to stimulate conversation as much as possible and make it explicit to students that they need to be discussing the same topic at roughly the same time so that lengthy time lags can be avoided and the excitement and benefits of meaningful interaction can occur.

- *Good practice communicates high expectations:* It is beneficial for the teacher to develop and post a syllabus at the start of the semester, in which the course goals and expectations are explicitly enumerated. As stated in Chapter 5, it is advantageous to post the syllabus online, as no students can claim to have lost it. Also, it might be helpful at times throughout the semester to paste key points of information from the syllabus into the announcement area so as to be eye-catching and to refresh students' memories as to what is expected of them.

The higher the expectations, the more likely it is that students will work to a higher level to try to achieve them (Daloz, 1999). Conversely, a course that does not make explicit its expectations, or that lacks challenging or rigorous expectations, could be creating a situation in which students are drifting, rather than feeling motivated or determined to learn deeply and well.

Stated expectations could include such managerial factors as frequency of participation, rules of civility in online discussions, and integrity. Knowledge of a teacher's expectations helps students to strive toward academic excellence. The right degree of challenge should be incorporated into academic questions and tasks so as to excite and motivate students but not to be so tough as to create fear in some students (Fardouly, 2001). One way in which fear might be alleviated, and in which inspiration might be given, is if the teacher demonstrates exemplary student assignments or responses, either from the present class or from a previous one (Graham et al., 2001).

This is easy for the teacher to do as it involves the simple act of copying and pasting, and it is also even more easily accessible to the student than if the work was read aloud in a campus class. This ease of accessibility might help the student to better comprehend what was done well in the demonstrated work and how best to learn from it.

- *Good practice respects diverse talents and ways of learning:* This is crucial, as it shows the fundamental importance of knowing your students. It is not only important to know the students in terms of their background and experiences, but also to be aware of the multiple intelligences that they bring to the learning environment (Gardner, 2000). Gardner drew up many distinct categories of intelligence, as discussed in Chapter 2.

Much greater accuracy of assessment can be carried out if we watch our students as they are learning throughout the semester to detect their strengths and intelligences than from a single standardized test at the end of a course. Knowing the students profoundly can be a good guide as to which are the optimal teaching methods to employ. Online teaching should never be canned. Even if you, as teacher, prepare your mini-lectures ahead of delivery, as long as they remain inaccessible to the students until the time they are needed, you can work on customizing them to best fit the learning styles and talents of the students who occupy your class that semester. Maintaining flexibility in teaching style by finding alternative ways to teach the same content to students of diverse needs and talents is therefore crucial for optimal learning to take place.

It might be conjectured that students who Gardner (2000) would categorize as having linguistic-verbal, inter- or intrapersonal, or existential intelligence might be very comfortable and learn well in the online environment, whereas students who possess logical-mathematical, visual-spatial, bodily-kinesthetic, musical-rhythmic, and possibly inter- or intrapersonal intelligence might learn better in a face-to-face setting.

This is where the hybrid class can provide strength, as it offers a diversity of environments in and of itself. It can allow for the types of hands-on teaching situations in which it is necessary, or beneficial, to meet face to face, such as in demonstrating art, music, math, or movement; and it can allow for those students who find the online class overwhelming to see their fellow students and teacher in real time. The online component, on the other hand, can help some students who are shy in a face-to-face class to find their voice online. It can also be beneficial to those who like to reflect and express themselves best through the written word. Different activities can be performed online and on campus so that these activities reinforce and supplement each other, and online discussion can continue after a campus class or can be used in preparation for the next campus class.

Online education can include many different types of learning activities, and the array will recognize the multiple intelligences and varying learning styles of the diverse group of students. Besides those mentioned in Chapter 8, such as various kinds of group work, journal writing, case studies, presentations, role-playing, debates, online guests, and virtual field trips, as well as using a variety of Web apps from the new digital technology, this could also include letting students choose their own research projects within the stipulated guidelines of the course. This would enable students to contribute their unique perspective and learn in a way meaningful to them.

When respect is given to the diversity of multiple intelligences and learning styles, and the teaching is modified accordingly, students can start to become responsible for their own learning and, as such, can meaningfully attain profound learning to the highest levels as identified by Bloom's taxonomy.

Technological Stability

We have talked about first deciding upon educational strategies and then making use of technology to reach the desired ends, namely, achievement of course goals and impressive learning outcomes. But what happens if the technology used to teach the online classes is replaced too frequently (Cuban, 2001)? After all, does there not seem to be a built-in obsolescence with many aspects of technology, and an assumption, as in the commercials of many products, that if it is new, it must be improved? Ehrmann (2002a) cautions that many academic institutions feel under pressure to purchase the latest technology so as not to appear to be falling behind, but that this is done at the expense of not necessarily allowing sufficient time to determine whether the previous technology led to benefits of its own, in terms of the accomplishment of stated educational strategies and goals. He argues cogently that more is needed in trying to improve online education than just improved technology.

There is a mix of other factors that plays a significant role, such as online faculty development, which allows for the diffusion of new information and course design suggestions among the educators who will be putting this technology to use. In using technology to improve educational outcomes, it would be beneficial, Ehrmann (2002a) says, to define the educational goals that one wants to pursue, such as improving research skills, collaborative learning and interaction, creativity, and the ability to transfer the knowledge and skills learned within academia to the work world. It would be helpful, knowing these goals, to select one goal that is of particular concern and determine if there is a technology that might help to improve this situation. If a new technology is selected, it should be chosen so that it is consistent with the progress that is already being made by the existing technologies in the achievement of the stated goals. In this way, a transfer to a new technology should be as smooth and seamless as possible, and education should not be disrupted. Furthermore, once a new technology is selected, it would be important to immediately track how well this system is working and thus maintain an accurate report, both of the progress and the pitfalls.

It used to be thought that an addition of new technologies in online classes would be somewhat disruptive because it had been assumed that teachers and students would be unfamiliar with them, necessitating time to learn them, and thus causing a distraction from focusing on the course content. However, as shown throughout this book, this is no longer true, as the iGeneration is so well versed in many of these new digital media. Referring to the Burnett ([1911] 1987) quotation (at the start of Part Three in this book) taken from her novel, *The Secret Garden*, when she speaks (albeit in a different context) of "a strange new thing" being done, she foretells that there will be gradual adoption, until ultimately "all the world wonders why it was not done centuries ago" (p. 269). I think this will soon be the general thinking behind the adoption of the new digital media in teaching and learning online.

I predict that the new digital media, if used wisely and always with the course goals and objectives in mind, will help facilitate a love of learning, precisely because they are such a familiar and often fun mode of communicating for the iGeneration. They will enable collaboration, and will increase the feeling of immediacy of the course because their use can enable students and teachers to speak in real time together, irrespective of distance between them, even allowing the online participants to see each other as they interact. Sound is also brought to the online class, as well as access to films and photos. This is not to imply that the new digital media should completely take over from the online asynchronous discussion forums, as I think the latter have already proved their amazing value. I have shown repeatedly throughout this book how asynchronous online discussion enables students to think deeply and richly, and it allows for all students to have their say and not be shouted down or dominated by others because of being shy, not speaking the same language, or being a reflective learner needing time to compose thoughts and ideas. So the asynchronous discussions should stay, but the new digital media can provide a very sound enhancement.

Additionally, use of the new digital media can be a very suitable preparation for students once they enter the world of work. Facebook, Twitter, texting, Flickr, Skype, and others are frequently used in many sectors of employment.

It is also apparent that use of the new digital media, as an enhancement to online asynchronous discussions, can produce positive results on each of Chickering and Ehrmann's (1996) "Seven Principles." They certainly encourage contact between students and teachers because of their huge potential for interaction and collaboration, which definitely enables reciprocity and cooperation between students. Because students in general enjoy using these digital media in their lives and are frequently doing so, this promotes active learning. Feedback can be given very swiftly through the digital media, not only from teachers to students, but among students themselves. These factors will also help students to produce their work on time. High expectations can easily be communicated through these digital media. And, finally, they absolutely produce diverse ways of learning, as shown throughout this book.

There is much that can be done and many new steps that can be taken to break down the barriers within traditional methods of education. As mentioned in Chapter 4, the paradigm of teaching and learning is starting to change. This is no doubt exciting, as the potential is vast. But as always, adoption of any of the new digital media as teaching tools should be used with deliberation as to the desired educational goal.

Concluding Comments about Assessment of Online Education

Learning as a Social Process, Impacted by Long-Term Memory

It is important to develop accurate models of assessment so as to gain as objective a measure as possible about the efficacy of online education. Prior assessment models as applied to traditional classroom teaching are outdated, as now it is better understood that learning is a social process, enhanced by discussion and interaction (Wegerif, 1998). Long-term memory also plays a crucial role in learning because it is used to reason efficiently about current information and problems (National Research Council, 2001). As stated in Chapter 3, it is important to understand long-term memory to see what students know, how they know it, and how they use that knowledge to answer new questions, solve problems, and learn new information.

The Assessment Triangle

The National Research Council (2001) states that assessment should consist of three crucial and interrelated components, which together comprise the "Assessment Triangle" (p. 44). Although this model was developed for application to face-to-face classes for grade-school students, much can be learned from this and applied to online education. The Assessment Triangle is as follows:

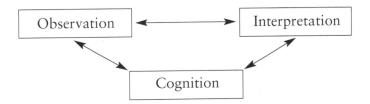

Cognition is the study of how students represent knowledge and develop competence. *Observations* are then made of student performance, and these in turn are *interpreted,* either by statistical or qualitative means. Starting with cognition is what distinguishes the National Research Council's (2001) approach to assessment from other previous studies. They state, "The methods used in cognitive science to design tasks, observe and analyze cognition, and draw inferences about what a person knows, are applicable to many of the challenges of designing effective educational assessments" (p. 104). This is in keeping with the criteria-referenced model detailed earlier in the chapter, which uses the methodology of the Flashlight Project, in which the starting point is the definition of educational goals and good practices, to design high-level tasks and learning activities and to draw inferences about learning outcomes and the achievement of these goals.

There is an important relationship among assessment, curriculum, and instruction: The *curriculum* should provide clear views of the course goals and objectives, *assessment* should be performed to detect the present state of the learner in achieving those goals, and *instruction* should be given to close that gap. Instruction should therefore be tailored so as to meet students' needs and talents, and should aim for high-level discussion and suitably challenging tasks to move students toward the highest rung of thinking and learning, as defined by Bloom's taxonomy. Assessment, then, is important not only to determine how well a system is performing, but also as a quest to improve education. It should be measuring how students understand and can explain concepts, how they can reason from what they know and transfer knowledge and skills to other areas, how good they are at solving problems, and how aware they are of their state of knowing so as to be able to self-regulate their learning (National Research Council, 2001).

The Value of Small-Scale Assessments

An important choice to be made is that of scale. Should assessments be broad sweeps at a large scale or should they instead be made at the level of the classroom? Whereas the large-scale approach can lead to public dialogue about the efficacy of online education and policy formation, it is thought that assessments might be most beneficial if made in the classroom. At the local level, cognitive theories can be more easily applied, and changes and improvements can be more readily incorporated, as long as the teacher has had some specific training in knowing how students learn (National Research Council, 2001). For example, as it has been previously argued, grading might be an inaccurate measurement of assessment of the efficacy of online education as it is not necessarily a true measurement of learning. Some students work hard to perfect their performance for a test at the end of the course yet have learned very little.

What is more important than simple measurements of right or wrong is to attempt, throughout the class, to see how each student is thinking. This can become apparent if a student is asked to explain his or her reasoning. The online environment lends itself very well to written responses of explicit lines of reasoning. Once an online student's thinking becomes apparent in this way, the instructor can identify areas of prior knowledge and, should there be any misconceptions, as illustrated by the film, *A Private Universe* (1987) (see Chapter 3), can structure teaching in such a way as to correct them. Alternatively, if the apparent thoughts of the students as written in online discussions reveal solid and correct prior knowledge in this arena, the teacher would be able to reinforce this and help students to expand their knowledge still further, to make more connections, and to build more schema. Furthermore, during the semester, students should be encouraged to develop their skills of metacognition (thinking about thinking), and in this way can identify which areas they feel less confident about and for which they would like some extra help (National Research Council, 2001).

The Impact on Analytical Skills and Knowledge Acquisition

It would be interesting and important to determine how a student's analytical skills and knowledge acquisition are affected as a result of being an online learner. In the campus class, the teacher is sometimes faced with the situation of wondering how much time should elapse before a student volunteers to answer a question. Because silence can be uncomfortable and the amount of material to cover is large, the teacher might provide the answer rather than continuing to wait. If so, the teacher does not allow an opportunity for the students to complete active formulation and expression of an answer, nor does the thinking of the students become apparent to that teacher. The online class presents an opportunity for every student to express him- or herself, thus giving the teacher the means to know the thinking of all students in the class. This is an advantage over the campus class wherein possibly, because of time constraints and other factors, only the thinking of the dominant students is revealed.

More research needs to be done in this area, but certainly it seems possible that online students, who by the very nature of the learning environment receive information in textual form, process it differently in their long-term memory banks and have opportunities to make connections and build schema differently than students in a campus class who receive new information through the spoken word. Information communicated online—in contrast to the campus class in which unlistened-to words are lost—remains available throughout the duration of the course, thereby increasing the opportunities for continued thought, reflection, and metacognition because each student can work to some extent at his or her own best pace. Extraneous distractions, such as noise or particular appearances, do not occur in the online class, and lapses of concentration do not mean that the chance of learning a piece of information has vanished, as would be the case in the class on campus. At the same time, however, body language and tone of voice, both of which help in the communication of meaning, are missing online, though they could be supplemented by the new digital media such as Skype.

Furthermore, possibly the act and increased effort of writing a response in online discussion, as opposed to speaking it aloud in a campus class, makes more of an impact on long-term memory and knowledge acquisition. Additionally, it is often the case that the generally slower act of writing rather than speaking allows time for new ideas, thoughts, and important connections to be made and communicated.

Preconceived Ideas about Innate Ability

What might also prove fascinating to discover is whether students cherish any innate beliefs about their ability to learn well in an online class. We know that students who hold innate beliefs about being good at a certain subject often do well at it, just as those who have a poor self-image in regard to a discipline often do poorly. This seems to be a case of expected realizations. But because online learning is relatively new, would students have already developed preexisting ideas as to their competence in online classes? Might some students, for example, imagine that they would not like an online class because of fear of technology or a preference to physically be with others rather than working remotely? Might some students imagine they would not be good at online learning as they think they cannot write? This area undoubtedly requires more exploration.

Transference of Acquired Knowledge

It is important to determine whether the previous factors not only affect an online student's learning in a class currently taken, but also on a student's ability to transfer this knowledge to other classes. In addition, it is important to determine whether online learning creates a lasting impression on long-term memory, so that the knowledge and skills acquired have future applications in terms of careers.

Additional Skills Acquired as an Online Learner

Besides the course content, students in an online class acquire and learn, as a byproduct, an important set of skills enabling them to communicate in cyberspace. The first skill is being able to express oneself with clarity in written form because online classes are primarily text based. It can be conjectured, and indeed I have witnessed among my online students, that writing, just as in any form of exercise, improves the more it is done. This strikes me as very advantageous.

As well as improved writing skills, students also gain the skill of working meaningfully from a remote location, which could impact positively on future possibilities in the workforce, such as telecommuting and conducting online research. Students are also developing skills of effective collaboration and interaction with others, despite the distance. These additional by-product skills yield marvelous benefits, which definitely should be factored in when assessing the efficacy of online education considered over the long term.

The Need for Frequent Formative Assessments and Student Feedback

As for the more immediate situation, it is beneficial for all online instructors to conduct their own assessments throughout the course, especially if they detect difficulties, such as a sudden, drastic decrease in the number of student responses. A single assessment covering many purposes is not necessarily accurate as it contains many compromises. A single assessment at the end of the course is even less useful, as the class is over and therefore there are no opportunities in which to make changes, if needed. Instead, a series of frequent, smaller formative assessments, each of which measure different factors, could generate a truer picture and lead to improvements in teaching and learning (National Research Council, 2001).

Asking for evaluations from students will help the instructor to avoid making wrong assumptions or misconceptions. Results of the evaluation should be quickly revealed to the students, and any consequent changes speedily implemented. If students realize that what they say in an evaluation might make a difference to the course they are currently in, then they are more likely to provide useful feedback than if the evaluation is executed at the end of the semester. If the evaluation is administered online, then just as with online discussion, students have more time to be reflective and generally write more complete and more helpful comments (Hmieleski and Champagne, 2000).

You could conduct this survey within your online classroom shell, and many software programs allow for anonymous postings, which would be of great use in evaluations. Questions to students could be specific if addressing a particular situation, or general, such as in asking them what they like about the course, what most helps them to learn, and if they have any suggestions for improvement. If you are teaching a hybrid, you could also ask students whether the online component meaningfully supplements the rest of the course, and whether any of their suggestions for improvements apply to the campus or online component of the class.

Ehrmann (2000) suggests that you also try to get to the heart of what the students might have to grapple with to work successfully online, as it is important to identify factors that might create obstacles to the possibility of acquiring knowledge and competence. Did all students take the orientation to learn about computer conferencing techniques, do any feel overwhelmed, do they like to collaborate with others in group work, or do they feel it is a waste of time?

Some teachers do not like evaluations and think that it is in their best interests to keep them as positive as possible, especially as they could factor in decisions about tenure or promotion. Marcus (2001), who teaches creative writing at Columbia, says that many students nowadays have the attitude that they are consumers. He finds that if he genuinely critiques the students' work and includes some negative comments, he runs the risk of receiving poor evaluations from them. Given this, Marcus admits to employing "dubious teaching techniques," which essentially amount to flattering the students so that they will in turn eventually flatter him in their evaluations. In other words, he concludes, this is a business model in which the customer is always right. Marcus asks whether more dissatisfied customers would mean a better learning experience because honesty and integrity in teaching would be exchanged for flattery. I agree and think that if you involve the students by first asking in the introductory comments what they hope to learn from the course and then conducting assessments throughout the semester, it shifts the emphasis from students being consumers to students being involved participants in their learning process. This should lead to a shared teaching and learning experience, and one that is conducted with integrity.

Feedback from Peers

As instructors, we are part of a larger community of teachers. As such, it is advantageous to discuss with others what went well as a teaching technique and what was less successful. This can be done as new teachers are being trained to teach online, during the teaching of the course, and at the conclusion of the semester. Peer review can be helpful, in which a team of teachers look at another teacher's online course and then collaboratively offer feedback. This practice is helpful to the teacher of the course being reviewed, and might inform the reviewers of sound and effective techniques that they might want to use in their own courses (McNaught, 2002).

Ultimately, however, to carry out valuable assessments of online education, there should be collaboration among educators, cognitive scientists, curriculum specialists, and psychometricians (National Research Council, 2001). In this way, online teachers could be appropriately trained to know how better to understand how online learning occurs in a social context and also how learning is affected by prior knowledge stored in long-term memory. They could learn techniques whereby to encourage high-level interaction and inclusion of all participants over challenging and rigorous learning activities, as well as learning how to detect what students know and their level of competence.

These factors help to promote conditions in which high-level learning can occur, as reflected by achievement of course goals and learning outcomes, which indicate that students have been thinking at the highest rungs of Bloom's taxonomy. A true collaboration among educators, cognitive scientists, curriculum specialists, and psychometricians would lead to a successful execution of the Assessment Triangle, and thereby help to foster the imperative relationship among curriculum, assessment, and instruction.

I believe it is possible for online education to be rigorous, challenging, and comprehensive. However, it is important to realize that to focus exclusively on technology is insufficient when considering including it within one's classes. As Ehrmann states, "If you are heading in the wrong direction, technology won't help you get to the right place" (1995, p. 22). The primary focus has to be on the teaching, and any decisions should be pedagogically rather than technically driven. It is essential to give thoughtful consideration to explorations of meaningful ways of promoting good teaching and learning through the electronic medium.

Online learning together with the popularity of the new digital media today, especially among undergraduates, signifies an impending change to the educational paradigm. Ouellette (1999) believes that traditional classes have an artificial learning environment as a result of the scheduled times for learning to take place. Online education, in contrast, provides an opportunity for renewal of this paradigm. As stated emphatically by Lynch,

> We also must expand our definition of teaching and learning. That calls upon us to open our minds—and our schedules—to asynchronous learning, to the notion that students can learn as well in front of their computers as they do sitting in our lecture halls. . . . Appropriate delivery—no less than content—makes a difference. (2002, p. B16)

Lynch (2002) believes that the convenience and flexibility of the online class might well increase learning effectiveness as students log on when they are ready to learn. Learning potential is also increased by interaction and collaboration, as well as by giving students more responsibility for their own learning. Students have greater opportunities online for reflection, and a chance to find their own voice (Rohfeld and Hiemstra, 1995). Not only are the pedagogical benefits of online learning there to consider, but also, Lynch states, students today increasingly expect the availability of online educational opportunities.

What is essential for instructors in this endeavor, besides familiarity with the software program, is a sound training in online pedagogy as well as information on how students learn. Then, once the online course is taught, there should be frequent assessments as to how well it is accomplishing its educational goals. Assessments need to be conducted with integrity so that any areas of difficulty can be noted and suggestions for improvement made. Ehrmann states, "Without asking hard questions about learning, technology remains an unguided missile" (1995, p. 26). Asking hard questions about learning is exactly what this book has set out to do.

REFERENCES

60 Minutes. CBS. July, 2001.

Aboujaoude, E. 2011. *Virtually You: The Dangerous Powers of the E-Personality.* New York, London: W.W. Norton & Company.

Almeda, M. B., and K. Rose. 2000. "Instructor Satisfaction in University of California Extension's On-line Writing Curriculum." *Journal of Asynchronous Learning Networks, 4* (3 September).

Anderson, S. 2009. "In Defense of Distraction." *New York Magazine* (May 17). Retrieved from http://nymag.com/news/features/56793/

Anderson, J. A., and M. Adams. 1992. "Acknowledging the Learning Styles of Diverse Student Populations: Implications for Instructional Design." In *Teaching for Diversity: New Directions for Teaching and Learning,* eds. L. Border and N. V. N. Chism. San Francisco: Jossey-Bass, pp. 19–33.

Anderson, J. Q., and L. Rainie. 2010. "Does Google Make Us Stupid?" *Pew Internet & American Life Project* and *Elon University's Imagining the Internet Center.* (February 19). Retrieved from http://pewresearch.org/pubs/1499/google-does-it-make-us-stupid-experts-stakeholders-mostly-say-no

Aristotle. 384–322 B.C. Quoted from http://www.quotationspage.com/quotes/Aristotle/

Arnone, M. 2001. "Philosopher's Critique of Online Learning Cites Existentialists (Mostly Dead)." *The Chronicle of Higher Education* (March 15). This article evaluated the book, H. Dreyfus. (2001). *On the Internet (Thinking in Action).* London: Routledge.

Baldwin, R. 2000. "Academic Civility Begins in the Classroom." *The Professional & Organizational Development Network in Higher Education. Essays on Teaching Excellence: Towards the Best in the Academy.* Retrieved from http://www.cte.umd.edu/

Bauerlein, M. 2008. *The Dumbest Generation: How the Digital Age Stupefies Young Americans and Jeopardizes Our Future (Or, Don't Trust Anyone Under 30).* New York. Jeremy P. Tarcher/Penguin, A Member of Penguin Group (USA) Inc.

Baum, L. F. (1900) 2000. *The Wonderful Wizard of Oz,* Troll Communications LLC.

BBC News Technology. 2010, November. "Facebook Revamps Messaging System." Retrieved from http://www.bbc.co.uk/news/technology-11743524

BBC Sci/Tech News. 2002, February 22. "Turning into Digital Goldfish." Retrieved from http://news.bbc.co.uk/2/hi/science/nature/1834682.stm

Bell System Advertisements: "Human Desire to Connect with Others." Retrieved from http://www.porticus.org/bell/bellsystem_ads-1.html

Benson, A., and E. Wright. 1999. "Pedagogy and Policy in the Age of the Wired Professor, *T.H.E. Journal* (November).

Berge, Z., and L. Muilenburg. 2000. "A Framework for Designing Questions for Online Learning." *DEOSNEWS*, *10*(2). Retrieved from http://www.ed.psu.edu/acsde/deos/deosnews/deosnews10_2.asp

Blankespoor, H. 1996. "Classroom Atmosphere: A Personal Inventory." In *Inspiring Teaching: Carnegie Professors of the Year Speak,* ed. J. K. Roth. Williston, VT: Anker Publishing Co.

Bloom, A. 1987. *The Closing of the American Mind: How Higher Education Has Failed Democracy and Impoverished the Souls of Today's Students.* New York: Simon and Schuster.

Blum, K. D. 1999. "Gender Differences in Asynchronous Learning in Higher Education: Learning Styles, Participation Barriers and Communication Patterns," *Journal of Asynchronous Learning Networks, 3* (1, May). Retrieved from http://eec.edc.org/cwis_docs/NEWS_ARTICLES_JOURNALS/gender%20differences%20in%20asynchronous%20learning.htm

Boettcher, J. 1999. "What Does Knowledge Look Like and How Can We Help It Grow?" *Syllabus Magazine* (September).

Bogost, I. 2007. "A Professor's Impressions of Facebook." Blog. (August 19th) Retrieved from http://www.bogost.com/blog/a_professors_impressions_of_fa.shtml

Bowers, C. A. 2000. *Let Them Eat Data: How Computers Affect Education, Cultural Diversity, and the Prospects of Ecological Sustainability.* Atlanta: University of Georgia Press.

Bowman, J. 2008. "Is Stupid Making Us Google?" *The New Atlantis,* Number 21. (Summer). Retrieved from http://www.thenewatlantis.com/publications/is-stupid-making-us-google

Bromell, N. 2002. "Summa Cum Avaritia." *Harper's Magazine,* (February): 74.

Brookfield, S. D., and S. Preskill. 1999. "Getting Discussion Started." Chapter 4 in *Discussion as a Way of Teaching: Tools and Techniques for Democratic Classrooms.* San Francisco: Jossey-Bass.

Bruce, B. 1998. "Dewey and Technology." *Journal of Adolescent and Adult Literacy* (November). Retrieved from http://www.readingonline.org/electronic/jaal/Nov_column.html

Burnett, F. H. (1911) 1987. *The Secret Garden.* New York: Dell Publishing, p. 267.

Cabell, B. 1999, September 8. "Technological Help Lets Students Concentrate on Learning." *Cable News Network.* Retrieved from http://www.cnn.com/US/9909/08/classroom.2000/

Cameson, J., G. Delpierre, and K. Masters. 2002. "Designing and Managing MCQ's." Appendix C: Bloom's Taxonomy in *University of Leicester Castle Toolkit.*

Carlson, S. 2001. "Computers Have Had Little Impact in College Classrooms, Stanford U. Professor Argues." *The Chronicle of Higher Education* (November 8).

Carlson, N. 2011. "Goldman to Clients: Facebook Has 600 Million Users." *Business Insider,* (January). Retrieved from http://www.businessinsider.com/facebook-has-more-than-600-million-users-goldman-tells-clients-2011-1

Carnevale, D. 2001. "A Researcher Says That Professors Should Be Attentive to Students' Approaches to Learning." *The Chronicle of Higher Education* (June 29). Retrieved from http://chronicle.com/article/A-Researcher-Says-That/109171/

Carr, N. 2008. "Is Google Making Us Stupid?" *The Atlantic,* (July/August).

———. 2010. *The Shallows: What the Internet Is Doing to Our Brains.* New York, London: W.W. Norton & Company Ltd.

Carroll, L. (1871) 1997. *Through the Looking Glass.* London: Puffin Books.

Carruth, G., and Eugene Ehrlich. 1988. *The Harper Book of American Quotations.* New York: Harper & Row. Edgar Allan Poe, *Marginalia.* 1840–1849. p. 35.

Cassidy, P. S. 2002. "Translating Cultures: Bridging the Next E-Learning Gap." Educator's Voice (September 27). Retrieved from http://www.pearsoncollege.com/Newsletter/EducatorsVoice/EducatorsVoice-Vol3Iss9.learn

Chickering, A., and S. C. Ehrmann. 1996. "Implementing the Seven Principles: Technology as Lever." *AAHE Bulletin,* (October): pp. 3–6.

Chinese Proverbs. Quoted from http://www.quotationpage.com/quotes/Chinese_Proverb/

Cohen, D. 2008. "Digital Note-Taking Gains Respect among Adults." *Reuters.* (November 26th).

Coupland, D. 1991. *Generation X: Tales for an accelerated culture.* New York: St. Martin's Griffin.

Cranmer, D. 1999. "Team Teaching." *British Council's Journal,* 10 (April). Retrieved from http://www.britishcouncilpt.org/journal/j1016dc.htm

Crystal, D. 2001. *Language and the Internet.* New York: Cambridge University Press.

———. 2008. *Txtng: the gr8 db8.* Oxford. Oxford University Press.

Cuban, L. 2001. *Oversold and Underused.* Cambridge, MA: Harvard University Press.

Cummings, J. A. 1998. "Promoting Student Interaction in the Virtual College Classroom." Retrieved from http://www.ihets.org/progserv/education/distance/faculty_papers/1998/indiana 2.html

Daloz, L. A. 1999. *Mentor: Guiding the Journey of Adult Learners.* San Francisco: Jossey-Bass.

Dante, E. 2010. "The Shadow Scholar: The Man Who Writes Your Students' Papers Tells His Story." *The Chronicle of Higher Education,* (November 12). Retrieved from http://chronicle.com/article/The-Shadow-Scholar/125329/

de Bono, E. 1986. *De Bono's Thinking Course.* New York: Facts on File Publications.

Dewey, J. (1938) 1963. *Experience and Education.* Reprint, New York: Collier Macmillan Publishers.

———. (1910) 1991. "What Is Thought?" Chapter 1 in *How We Think.* New York: Prometheus Books, pp. 1–13.

Digital Nation: Growing Up Online. 2010. PBS Frontline Documentary. http://www.pbs.org/wgbh/pages/frontline/digitalnation/ (February).

Eastmond, D. 1992. "Effective Facilitation of Computer Conferencing." *Continuing Higher Education Review* 56, pp. 15–20.

Ehrmann, S. C. 1995. "Asking the Right Question: What Does Research Tell Us About Technology and Higher Learning?" *Change: The Magazine of Higher Learning,* XXVII (2, March/April): pp. 20–27.

———. 2000. "On the Necessity of Grassroots Evaluation of Educational Technology—Recommendations for Higher Education." *The Technology Source, Michigan Virtual University* (November/December).

———. 2002a. "Improving the Outcome of Higher Education." *Educause* (January/February).

———. 2002b, June. Posting to the AAHEGSIT listserv on stages of faculty development.

Fall, J. 2002. "Teaching with Fun and Humor." *Teacher Help: Article Archive* (January 7). Albuquerque, NM: Wright Group Publishing. Retrieved from http://www.teacherhelp.com/article_archive/classroom_3.html

Fardouly, N. 2001. *Principles of Instructional Design and Adult Learning: How Students Learn.* University of New South Wales, Sydney, Australia.

Fisher, B. M. 2001. *No Angel in the Classroom: Teaching through Feminist Discourse.* Lanham, MD: Rowman & Littlefield Publishers, Inc.

Foresman, C. 2010. "iPad Gets the University Treatment This Fall." *Wired Magazine,* (July 24).

Forni, P. M. 2008. "Encouraging the Civil Classroom in the Age of the Net." *Thought and Action* (Fall). Retrieved from http://krieger.jhu.edu/civility/civil_classroom.pdf

Galinsky, E. 1999. *Ask the Children: What America's Children Really Think about Working Parents.* New York: William Morrow and Company, Inc.

Gardner, H. 2000. *Intelligence Reframed: Multiple Intelligences for the 21st Century.* New York: Basic Books Publishers.

———. 2011. *Truth, Beauty, and Goodness Reframed: Educating for the Virtues in the Twenty-First Century.* New York. Basic Books: A Member of the Perseus Books Group.

Glenn, D. 2011. "New Book Lays Failure to Learn on Colleges' Doorsteps." *The Chronicle of Higher Education.* (January 18). Retrieved from http://chronicle.com/article/New-Book-Lays-Failure-to-Learn/125983

Gopnik, A. 2011. "The Information: How the Internet Gets Inside Us." *New Yorker Magazine* (February 14).

Graham, C., K. Cagiltay, B. R. Lim, J. Craner, and T. M. Duffy. 2001. "Seven Principles of Effective Teaching: A Practical Lens for Evaluating Online Courses." *Assessment: The Technology Source, Michigan Virtual University* (March/April). Retrieved from http://ts.mivu.org.default.asp?show = article&id = 839

Grassian, E. [1995] 2000. "Thinking Critically about World Wide Web Resources." *Regents of the University of California.* Retrieved from http://www.library.ucla.edu/libraries/college/help/critical/index/htm

Grodney, D. 2001. May 21. Personal e-mail.

Hani, S. 2010. Grammar Presentations in My Hybrid Expository Writing Class. Retrieved from http://www.youtube.com/watch?v=duhJM2qJbf4, http://www.youtube.com/watch?v=Bocv1CanS-8

Hara, N., and R. Kling. 1999. "Students' Frustrations with a Web-Based Distance Education Course." *First Monday, 4* (12, December). Retrieved from http://www.firstmonday.dk/issues/issue4_12/hara/index.html

Hmieleski, K., and M. V. Champagne. 2000. "Plugging in to Course Evaluation." *Assessment: The Technology Source, Michigan Virtual University* (September/October).

Hoover, D. 2002. Personal e-mail.

Hudson, D. 1999. August 18. "Prescription for Learning: Humor in the Classroom." *Athens State University, School of Education.* Retrieved from http://hiwaay.net/%7Ekenth/diane/column/p_081899.htm

Hull, K. 2002. Personal e-mail.

Jackson, R. M. 1999. "Developing a Group Grading Strategy Including Peer Assessment." *The Equal Professor, A Forum for Frank Discussion about Teaching at NYU V* (3, April).

"John Dewey (1859–1952)." *The Internet Encyclopedia of Philosophy.* Retrieved from http://www.iep.utm.edu/dewey/

Johnson, S. 2006. *Everything Bad Is Good for You: How Today's Popular Culture Is Actually Making Us Smarter.* New York: Riverhead Books.

Kahn, A. 2000. Quoted in Finch, J., and E. Montambeau, "Beyond Bells and Whistles: Affecting Student Learning through Technology." Retrieved from http://www.cofc.edu/bellsandwhistles/index.html

Kakutani, M. 2010. "Texts without Context." *New York Times* (March 17).

Keller, J. 2009. "Studies Explore Whether the Internet Makes Students Better Writers." *The Chronicle of Higher Education* (June 11). Retrieved from http://chronicle.com/article/Studies-Explore-Whether-the/44476/

Kempster, J. 2002. Interviewed for a colloquy "One Year Later." *The Chronicle of Higher Education* (September 6).

Kolb, D. A. 1984. *Experiential Learning: Experience as the Source of Learning and Development.* Englewood Cliffs, N.J.: Prentice Hall.

Kramarae, C. 2001. *The Third Shift: Women Learning Online.* Washington, D.C.: American Association of University Women (AAUW), Educational Foundation Research. Retrieved from http://www.aauw.org/2000/3rdshift.html. See also Mayfield, K. 2001. "Women Face Third Shift Online." In *Wired Magazine* (September 17). http://www.wired.com/culture/education/news/2001/09/46689

Lanier, J. 2010. *You Are Not a Gadget.* "Missing Persons" (chapter 1). New York: Alfred A. Knopf.

Levine, M. 2002. *A Mind at a Time.* New York: Simon and Schuster.

Liu, Y., and D. Ginther. 1999. "Cognitive Styles and Distance Education Online." *Journal of Distance Learning Administration,* 2(3).

Lynch, D. 2002. "Professors Should Embrace Technology in Courses." *The Chronicle of Higher Education,* (January 18). Retrieved from http://chronicle.com/article/Professors-Should-Embrace/34437

MacManus, R. 2005. "What Is Web 2.0" Retrieved from http://www.zdnet.com/blog/web2explorer/what-is-web-20/5

Marcus, B. 2001. "Graded by My Students." *Time Magazine* (January 8).

McKeachie, W. J. 1978. "Doing and Evaluating Research on Teaching." Chapter 25 in *Teaching Tips: A Guide for the Beginning College Teacher,* 7th ed. Lexington, MA: Heath and Company, pp. 257–263.

———. "Six Roles of Teachers." Chapter 6 in *Teaching Tips,* pp. 68–82.

———. "Personalizing Education." Chapter 24 in *Teaching Tips,* pp. 244–256.

McNaught, C. 2002. "Quality Assurance for Online Courses: Implementing Policy at RMIT." *Assessment: The Technology Source,* Michigan Virtual University (January/February).

Menzies, H. 2005. *No Time: Stress and the Crisis of Modern Life* (Chapter 8). Vancouver: Douglas & McIntyre Ltd.

Moore, M. G. 1984. "The Individual Adult Learner." In *Adult Learning and Education,* ed. M. Tight. London: Croom Helm, p. 155.

National Research Council. 2001. *Knowing What Students Know: The Science and Design of Educational Assessment.* Washington, D.C.: National Academy Press.

Navarro, P. 2000. "The Promise—and Potential Pitfalls—of Cyberlearning." In *Issues in Web-Based Pedagogy,* ed. R. Cole. Westport, Conn.: Greenwood Press.

Nielsen Wire. (2010). "U.S. teen mobile report: Calling yesterday, texting today, using apps tomorrow" [blog post]. Retrieved from http://blog.nielsen.com/nielsenwire/online_mobile/u-s-teen-mobile-report-calling-yesterday-texting-today-using-apps-tomorrow (October 14).

Noble, D. 1997–2001. David Noble's articles on Digital Diploma Mills, Part I–V. Retrieved from http://www.communication.ucsd.edu/dl/

O'Reilly, T. 2005. "What Is Web 2.0: Design Patterns and Business Models for the Next Generation of Software." Retrieved from http://oreilly.com/web2/archive/what-is-web-20.html

Ouellette, R. P. 1999. "The Challenge of Distributed Learning as a New Paradigm for Teaching and Learning." University of Maryland University College. Retrieved from http://polaris.umuc.edu/~rouellet/dechallenge.html

Packer, S. 2002. "The Colorblind Cyberclass: Myth and Fact." In *Race in the College Class,* ed. M. Reddy and B. Tusmith. New Brunswick, N.J.: Rutgers University Press.

Parry, D. 2008. "So You Want to Microblog (Twitter) with Your Students?" *Academhack.* May 21.

Parsons, T. S., W. A. Ketcham, and L. R. Beach. 1958. "Effects of varying degrees of student interaction and student-teacher contact in college courses." Read at American Sociological Society, August, at Seattle, Washington (quoted in Mc-Keachie, 1978, p. 260).

Pascarella, E. T., and P. T. Terenzini. 1991. *How College Affects Students. Findings and Insights from Twenty Years of Research.* San Francisco: Jossey-Bass (quoted in Ehrmann, 1995).

Patenaude, M. 1999. "Keeping Them Awake or How I Learned to Relinquish the Spotlight." *CCV Handbook for Basic Writing Instructors.*

Pensky, M. 2001. "Digital Natives, Digital Immigrants." *On the Horizon,* MCB University Press, *9*(5) (October).

Powers, W. 2010. *Hamlet's Blackberry: A Practical Philosophy for Building a Good Life in the Digital Age.* New York. HarperCollins Publishers.

Princeton University. 2002. "Academic Integrity at Princeton." Retrieved from http://www.princeton.edu/pr/pub/integrity/pages/plagiarism

Richardson, J., and A. Turner. 2001. "Collaborative Learning in a Virtual Classroom." *National Teaching and Learning Forum Newsletter, 10* (2, February). Retrieved from http://ntlf.com

Richtel, M. 2010a. "Attached to Technology and Paying a Price." *New York Times: Business Day Technology,* (June 6).

———. 2010b. "Growing Up Digital: Wired for Distraction." *New York Times: Business Day Technology,* (November 21).

Rideout, V., U. G. Foehr, and D. F. Roberts. 2010. "Generation M2: Media in the Lives of 8–18 year olds." *A Kaiser Family Foundation Study* (January).

Robinson, P. 2000. "Where Is Every-Body?" In *Issues in Web-Based Pedagogy,* ed. R. Cole. Westport, Conn.: Greenwood Press.

Rohfeld, R. W., and R. Hiemstra. 1995. "Moderating Discussions in the Electronic Classroom." Berge Collins Associates. Retrieved from http://www.emoderators.com/moderators/rohfeld.html (Originally in *Computer-Mediated Communication and the On-line Classroom in Distance Education.* Creskill, N.J.: Hampton Press.

Rosen, L. D. 2011. "Teaching the iGeneration." *Teaching Screenagers 68*(5): 10–15.

Ruhleder, K., and M. Twidale. 2000. "Reflective Collaborative Learning on the Web: Drawing on the Masterclass." *First Monday, 5*(5, May). Retrieved from http://www.firstmonday.dk/issues/issue5_5/ruhleder/

Runyon, L. 2009. "Facebook in the Classroom: New Application Acts to Aid in Education." *The Journal: University of Illinois Springfield.* (March 4). Retrieved from http://www.uis.edu/journal/studentlife/2009/20090304facebook.html

Russell, B. Quoted from http://www.quotationpage.com/quotes/Bertrand_Russell/11

Saba, F., and R. L. Shearer. 1994. "Verifying Key Theoretical Concepts in a Dynamic Model of Distance Education." *The American Journal of Distance Education, 8*(1): pp. 36–59.

Salley, R., E. C. Wadsworth, R. Terry, and N. Richardson. 2002. "Tips for Teachers: Encouraging Students in a Racially Diverse Classroom." Derek Bok Center for Teaching and Learning, Harvard. Available at www.fvtc.edu/public/itemattach .aspx?type = page&id = 736

Salmon, G. 2000. *E-Moderating: The Key to Teaching and Learning Online.* London: Kogan Page.

Sample, M. 2010. "Practical Advice for Teaching with Twitter." *Chronicle of Higher Education.* (August 25). Retrieved from http://chronicle.com/blogs/profhacker/ practical-advice-for-teaching-with-twitter/26416

Schneider, A. 1998. "Insubordination and Intimidation Signal the End of Decorum in Many Classrooms." *The Chronicle of Higher Education.* Retrieved from http:// chronicle.com/colloquy/98/rude/background.htm

Schneps, M. H. (producer, director). 1987. *A Private Universe* [film]. Washington, D.C.: The Annenberg/CPB Project. (Quoted in Ehrmann, 1995).

Schonfeld, E. 2010 "Costolo: Twitter Now Has 190 Million Users Tweeting 6 Million Times a Day." (June). Retrieved from http://techcrunch.com/2010/06/08/ twitter-190-million-users/

Shakespeare, W. Reprinted 1991. *Complete Sonnets* (Sonnet 16). New York: Dover Publishers.

Shaw, G. B. 1983. *Man and Superman (The Revolutionist's Handbook).* Harmondsworth, Middlesex: Penguin, p. 260.

Sloan Consortium Practices. 2002. Retrieved from http://www.sloan-c.org/effective/ index.asp

Smiley, J. [1987] 1989. *The Age of Grief: A novella and stories of love, marriage and friendship.* New York: Ballantine Books, p. 151.

Smith, G. G., D. Ferguson, and M. Caris. 2001. "Teaching College Courses Online vs Face-to-Face." *T.H.E. Journal* (April).

Sonwalker, N. 2002. "A New Methodology for Evaluation: The Pedagogical Rating of Online Courses." *Syllabus Magazine* (January). Retrieved from http://www .syllabus.com/syllabusmagazine/article.asp?id = 5914

Sorrell, P. 2010. "Teaching with Twitter." Presented to the Language Institute, Rutgers University, New Brunswick, New Jersey (October).

———. 2012. Personal e-mail. (January).

Teachers' Views on Technology in the Classroom. 2010. *New York Times. Business Day Technology.* (November 20).

Teaching and Educational Development Institute (TEDI). 2002. March. "Tertiary Toolbox: Dealing with Teaching Anxiety." The University of Queensland, Australia. Retrieved from http://www.tedi.uq.edu.au/teaching/TertiaryToolbox/ TeachingAnxiet y.html

Thompson, C. 2007. "How Twitter Creates a Social Sixth Sense." *Wired Magazine,* *15*(7). (June 26). Retrieved from http://www.wired.com/techbiz/media/magazine/ 15-07/st_thompson

————. 2008. "Brave New World of Digital Intimacy." *New York Times Magazine* (September 5).

————. 2009. "Clive Thompson on the New Literacy." *Wired Magazine* (August 24). Retrieved from http://www.wired.com/techbiz/people/magazine/17-09/st_thompson

Turkle, S. 1995. *Life on the Screen: Identity in the Age of the Internet.* New York: Simon and Schuster.

————. 2010. Interviewed on *Digital Nation: Growing Up Online.* PBS *Frontline* Documentary. Retrieved from http://www.pbs.org/wgbh/pages/frontline/digital nation

————. 2011. *Alone Together: Why We Expect More from Technology and Less from Each Other.* New York: Basic Books, A Member of the Perseus Books Group.

Twenge, J. M. 2006. *Generation Me: Why Today's Young Americans Are More Confident, Assertive, Entitled—And More Miserable Than Ever Before.* New York: Free Press.

Vella, J. 1997. *Learning to Listen, Learning to Teach.* San Francisco: Jossey-Bass.

Walsh, K. 2010. "100 Ways to Teach with Twitter." *Emerging Educational Technology.* (February 7). Retrieved from http://www.emergingedtech.com/2010/02/100-ways-toteach-with-twitter

Webster's New World Dictionary. 1990. New York: Warner Books.

Wegerif, R. 1998. "The Social Dimension of Asynchronous Learning Networks." *The Journal of Asynchronous Learning Networks,* 2(1, March). Retrieved from http://www.aln.org/alnweb/journal/vol2_issue1/wegerif.htm

Wieder, B. 2011a. "Online Game Teaches Citation Skills." *The Chronicle of Higher Education* (January 7). Retrieved from http://chronicle.com/blogs/wiredcampus/online-game-teaches-citation-skills/28837

————. 2011b. "iPads Could Hinder Teaching, Professors Say." *The Chronicle of Higher Education* (March 13). Retrieved from http://chronicle.com/article/iPads-for-College-Classrooms-/126681

Wilson, R. 2002. "Faculty Members Care More about Students, Less about Prestige, Study Finds." *Chronicle of Higher Education* (November). Retrieved from http://chronicle.com/article/Faculty-Members-Care-More/115094

WNYC. 2011. "Marshall McLuhan at 100." Retrieved from http://www.wnyc.org/articles/arts/2011/jul/21/to-the-best-of-our-knowledge-marshall-mcluhan-100

Wolf, M. 2008. *Proust and the Squid: The Story and the Science of the Reading Brain,* Chapter 9. New York: Harper. An Imprint of Harper Collins Publishers. Reprint Edition. (August 26).

Wright, F. L. 1932. Quoted from http://www.geocities.com/sotto/1469/flwquote.html

Young, J. R. 2002a. "Hybrid Teaching Seeks to End the Divide between Traditional and Online Instruction." *The Chronicle of Higher Education* (March 22). Retrieved from http://chronicle.com/article/Hybrid-Teaching-Seeks-to-End/18487

————. 2002b. "Logging in with Charles Kerns: Designer of Free Course-Management Software Asks, What Makes a Good Web Site?" *The Chronicle of Higher Education,* (January 21). Retrieved from http://chronicle.com/article/Designer-of-Free/116189

————. 2008. "Forget E-Mail: New Messaging Service Has Students and Professors Atwitter." *The Chronicle of Higher Education.* (February 29). Retrieved from http://chronicle.com/article/Forget-E-Mail-New-Messaging/17813

————. 2009. "Professor Encourages Students to Pass Notes During Class via Twitter." *The Chronicle of Higher Education: Wired Campus.* (April 8). Retrieved from http://chronicle.com/blogs/wiredcampus/professor-encourages-students-to-pass-notes-during-class-via-twitter/4619